KAMIAKIN COUNTRY

Washington Territory
in Turmoil 1855 - 1858

KAMIAKIN COUNTRY

WASHINGTON TERRITORY
IN TURMOIL 1855 - 1858

JO N. MILES

CAXTON PRESS
Caldwell, Idaho
2016

ISBN: 978-087004-595-0

Library of Congress Cataloging-in-Publication Data

Names: Miles, Jo N.
Title: Kamiakin Country : Washington Territory in Turmoil, 1855-1858 / Jo
   N. Miles.
Description: Caldwell, Idaho : Caxton Press, 2016. | Includes bibliographi-
   cal references and index. | Description based on print version record and
   CIP data provided by publisher; resource not viewed.
Identifiers: LCCN 2015049178 (print) | LCCN 2015048100 (ebook) | ISBN
   9780870045967 () | ISBN 9780870045950 (alkaline paper)
Subjects: LCSH: Kamiakin, Yakama chief, approximately 1800-approxi-
   mately 1877--Military leadership. | Yakama Indians--Wars, 1855-1859.
   | Yakama Indians--Kings and rulers--Biography. | Yakama Indians--His-
   tory--19th century. | Wright, George, 1803-1865--Military leadership. |
   Washington (State)--History, Military--19th century. | Yakima River Val-
   ley (Wash.)--History, Military--19th century.
Classification: LCC E99.Y2 (print) | LCC E99.Y2 M55 2016 (ebook) |
   DDC 979.7004/974127--dc23
LC record available at http://lccn.loc.gov/2015049178

Cover
Sunrise in Central Cascade Mountains - Author's photo
Map of the Territories of Washington and Oregon
New York: J.H. Colton and Co., (1857)

CAXTON PRESS
Caldwell, Idaho
192697

TABLE OF CONTENTS

MAPS, PHOTOS AND ILLUSTRATIONS

PREFACE

When spelling the name "Yakima" with an "i" the word describes geographic places, like the river, valley, city and county. The alternate spelling, "Yakama" with an "a" describes the tribe and all its activities and documents following the original spelling used in the treaty of 1855.

Many Native tribes mentioned in the book maintain modern headquarters featuring websites and public educational resources open to all. It is recommended to learn directly from the descendants of the first people about Native culture, values and traditions.

Newspapers during the years 1855 – 58 deserve recognition for their editors publishing letters written directly from the field by eyewitnesses participating in important events. Official military reports sometimes were published in newspapers word for word. Editors also published plenty of anonymous correspondence, hearsay, and not so helpful speculation, but a few educated and thoughtful writers, usually soldiers and volunteer officers, signed their names to first-hand accounts that became useful references. Other thoughtful men such as L. V. McWhorter and A. J. Splawn collected and wrote down Native versions from eyewitness participants.

Excellent libraries, repositories and special collections across the country have provided rare journals, letters, books and records available for research. The author is grateful for the highly qualified and helpful archivists, librarians and devoted staff assistants who have contributed to productive, meaningful, and rewarding study. Research centers used by the author in the state of Washington include the University of Washington Libraries-Special Collections; Washington State University-Manuscripts, Archives and Special Collections; Gonzaga University-Cowles Rare Book Library Special Collections; Central Washington University-Brooks Library; Whitman College-Penrose Library; Washington State History Research Center; Washington State Archives; Washington State Library; Spokane Public Library-Downtown Northwest Room; Joel E. Ferris Library-Northwest Museum of Arts & Culture; Yakama Nation Cultural Center Library and Museum; Yakima Valley Libraries-Relander Collection; Yakima Valley Museum; Yakima Valley Genealogical Society; National Archives and Records Administration-Pacific Alaska Region; and Archives of the Archdiocese of Seattle. Oregon research centers visited include the Oregon Historical Society-Research Library; Multnomah County Library – Portland; University of Oregon-Special Collections; Pendleton Public Library; and Tamastslikt Cultural Institute of the Confederated Tribes of the Umatilla Indian Reservation. Additional Washington and Oregon history documents have been located outside of the Pacific Northwest at the Bancroft Collection of Western Americana, University of California Berkeley; Huntington Library - H. Russell Smith Foundation Library for Western History in San Marino, CA; and Yale Collection of Western Americana, Beinecke Rare Book and Manuscript Library, New Haven, CT. The Library of Congress and National Archives and Records Administration in Washington D.C. have provided extraordinary documents that have benefitted this research.

Special gratitude goes to the late Martin N. Chamberlain (1914-2010) for his permission to use the Granville O. Haller papers at University of Washington Libraries, during the early stages of my research, and to Washingtonian authors Teresa Knudsen and Steve Plucker for generously sharing records from their personal research files. I am also grateful to Pacific Northwest History instructor Dr. Ken Zontek at Yakima Valley Community College for his inspiration and instruction.

INTRODUCTION

Nineteenth century travelers who happened to meet Yakama Chief Kamiakin in person realized the man was something special. Commander Charles Wilkes' expedition in 1841 described Kamiakin as, "One of the most handsome and perfectly formed Indians they had met with."[1] Captain George B. McClellan declared after meeting Kamiakin in 1853, "He is by far the richest & most influential chief in this part of the territory."[2] Hudson's Bay Company trader Angus McDonald at Fort Colvile knew Kamiakin for many years. "He was a fine well-formed and powerful Indian, standing five feet eleven in his moccasins; his weight was about two hundred pounds, muscular and sinewy."[3] And Catholic missionaries, who knew Kamiakin better than anyone else, wrote about the chief. The priests lived with the Yakama people for eight years, and baptized all of Kamiakin's children. The missionaries saw the chief's stormy moods and strong determination balanced by prayer and affection for his family.

Kamiakin accumulated wealth by raising herds of horses and cattle, and growing irrigated crops of corn and potatoes that he began in the 1840's prior to the arrival of the missionaries. In war, Kamiakin was compared to the legendary Tecumseh for his ability to unite fighters from numerous tribes across a wide region.[4]

The war between tribal combatants and Euro-American soldiers in Washington Territory began and ended in the Yakima Valley. During the fall of 1855 a band of warriors attacked and killed seven miners followed by Chief Kamiakin's victory over U.S. Army troops at Toppenish Creek. For three years fighting persisted throughout the territory until the last resistors either surrendered, fled the region, or were executed, with the last of the hangings taking place at Fort Simcoe.

War's impact spread beyond the Yakima Valley. According to Arthur A. Denny (1822-1899), co-founder of Seattle and a first lieutenant in the Washington Territory Volunteers, "ruin and desolation" spread across Puget Sound caused by Indian uprisings and war.[5] Captain Urban E. Hicks (1828-1905), later assessor and county clerk of Thurston County, declared, "Terror and confusion prevailed generally."[6] War created dread among settlers sending some fleeing from the region never to return. The remaining white population faced years of business stagnation that lasted until 1865. Rural homes that had not been protected by armed defenders in settlements, blockhouses and at military posts were burned or destroyed.

At least 370 victims died violently in Washington Territory between September of 1855 and November of 1858 including soldiers, chiefs, warriors, volunteers, civilians, non-combatants, women and children. Witnesses and survivors on all sides called the period war. No other description sufficed.

During war's turmoil, many Native peace chiefs, scouts and warriors cooperated with the territorial government that had been established by Congress and approved by the President of the United States. Not all volunteers behaved ruthlessly, and at least one high ranking military officer compared tribal resistance to that of the founding fathers of the American Revolution.

Trouble began after treaties had been signed by many of the region's tribes that extinguished title to vast areas of traditional lands in exchange for cash payments, useful goods, schools, medical services, and limited tracts of land defined as reservations. Drastic changes resulted from tribes having to give up long-standing homes and ancient burial grounds. Conflicts escalated after encroachment from settlers and miners caused many Natives to forcibly resist. In pastoral Puget Sound the outbreak came as a surprise to many white residents that had co-existed peaceably with indigenous neighbors. Only an estimated one in five settlers owned a gun because most farmers did not need to hunt for food.

The conflict became more complicated than just one culture pitted against another. At least five culture groups were affected, and most were split amongst themselves for and against critical issues. Tribes divided into branches following war chiefs or peace chiefs while other Natives served the U.S. Army as scouts, guides and couriers. Some Native people stayed employed at settlers' commercial establishments such as Yesler's mill in Seattle. Still more tried to disappear into the landscape and avoid the conflict altogether. Snoqualmie Chief Patkanim's warriors fought and died on the side of the Americans. So did Nez Perce Chief Spotted Eagle's mounted scouts attached to the

1st and 2nd Regiments of Washington Territory Volunteers and the Ninth U.S. Infantry. Peaceful Native good Samaritans often warned settlers of impending dangers, some saved soldiers from disaster, and others rescued pioneer children from peril.

Members of the most predominant culture group at the time, Euro-American Protestants, were not the most numerous. They competed with more populous Native tribes, and other well established groups such as the British owned Hudson's Bay Company, and French-speaking settlers including Catholic missionaries. All claimed the frontier as their home and vied for land. A fifth group, the U.S. Army labored to keep peace between others. Civilian Euro-Americans often found themselves at odds with competitors. For example, Chief Kamiakin and the Hudson's Bay Company, together with many Frenchmen and U.S. Army Colonel George Wright, all agreed it would be fairer for Americans to be allowed a smaller portion of ground within a greater Native region rather than the other way around. The treaties ratified by Congress, however, gave smaller tracts to tribes as reservations leaving the larger portion for the United States.

Americans were not united about how to respond to tribal uprisings. Civilian territorial officials clashed politically with U.S. Army commanders rarely agreeing upon paths of operation. Territorial Governor Isaac I. Stevens objected vigorously to the policies of General John E. Wool in charge of the Department of the Pacific. Stevens appealed directly to Secretary of War, Jefferson Davis, recommending that Wool be removed for objecting to volunteers' participation in the war. Wool ordered his field commanders to disarm and arrest Stevens' volunteers if they interfered with U.S. troops. Territorial officials turned on each other during a period of martial law when the governor's armed volunteer officers arrested the territory's chief justice during court in Steilacoom and again in Olympia. A U.S. marshal countered the acts by jailing a volunteer commander.

U.S. Army officers' attitudes varied from Major Granville O. Haller's recognition of Indian courage and loyalty, to Major Gabriel J. Rains' threats and insults. Colonel George Wright, often overlooked as a supporter of Native rights, counseled more chiefs than he punished, and he advocated that tribes be granted more territory than the treaties provided.

The territorial governors of Washington and Oregon formed citizen volunteer armies of their own that were sometimes characterized by dissention, near-mutiny and insubordination. At other times volunteers demonstrated acts of fairness, compassion and kindness.

A number of pioneers accused the Hudson's Bay Company of intentionally starving and driving Americans out of the region. But timely rescues and generosity shown by Dr. John McLoughlin, Peter Skene Ogden and Governor James Douglas of the British owned corporation helped silence many critics.

French fur men and Catholic missionaries brought foreign language and a different religion near suspicious American Protestant pioneers. Some French men were accused of conspiracy and providing aid to the enemy. Others served the territorial government bravely and bridged communication gaps between Americans and Natives.

Colonel Wright spoke poignantly to tribal chiefs at councils he held during the middle of the war in 1856. "The 'bloody cloth' should be washed; not a spot should be left upon it. That the Great Spirit had created both the white and red man, and commanded us to 'love one another.' That all past differences must be thrown behind us."[7] Peace talks worked for some, but despite negotiation efforts, a number of hostile factions refused to end violence until defeated by a superior military force.

Pioneers migrated to Washington Territory despite dangers, hardships, risks and loneliness. As Winfield Scott Ebey proceeded by wagon train through the Yakima Valley and approached the Cascade Mountains in 1854, he wrote in his diary, "Here Nature triumphs I have never Seen a more Grand & Sublime display of the works of Natur(e)'s God."[8] And so, they came.

Introduction notes

1. Charles Wilkes, U.S.N., Narrative of the United States Exploring Expedition during the years 1838, 1839, 1840, 1841, 1842, 5 vols., (Philadelphia: Lea & Blanchard, 1845), 4:428.
2. George B. McClellan to I.I. Stevens, August 22, 1853, RBIA (RG 75) WS, LR, August 22, 1853-April 9, 1861, NARA microfilm M-5, Roll 23.
3. Angus McDonald, "A Few Items of the West", *The Washington Historical Quarterly* 8, (July, 1917), 228.
4. Lawrence Kip, *Indian War in the Pacific Northwest The Journal of Lieutenant Lawrence Kip*, (Lincoln, Nebraska: University of Nebraska Press, 1999), 91.
5. Arthur Armstrong Denny, *Pioneer Days on Puget Sound*, (1890; reprint-Fairfield, WA: Ye Galleon Press, 1979), 26, 77.
6. Capt. Urban E. Hicks, *Yakima and Clickitat Indian Wars 1855 and 1856*, (Portland, OR: Himes the Printer, 1886), 4.
7. Colonel George Wright to Major W.W. Mackall, October 31, 1856, U.S. House of Representatives, 34th Congress, 3rd session 1856-'57, Ex. Doc. No. 76 Indian Affairs on the Pacific, in thirteen volumes, vol. 9, 232.
8. Winfield Scott Ebey, *The 1854 Diary of Winfield Scott Ebey*, ed. Susan Badger Doyle and Fred W. Dykes, (Independence, MO: Oregon-California Trails Association, 1997), 193.

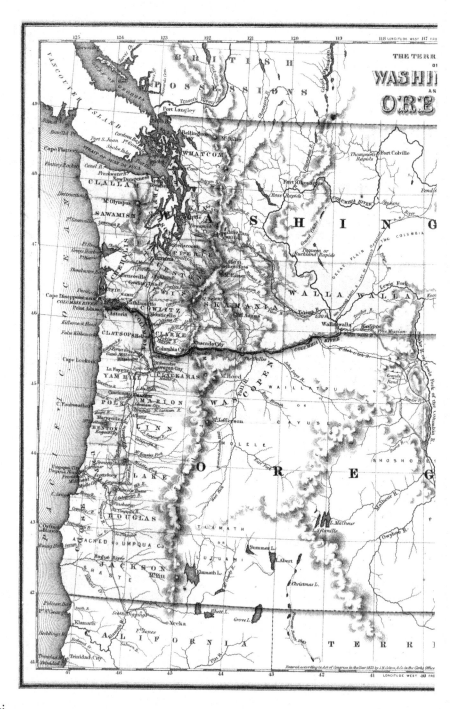

New York: J. H. Colton & Co., (1857), c1853

Washington Ter

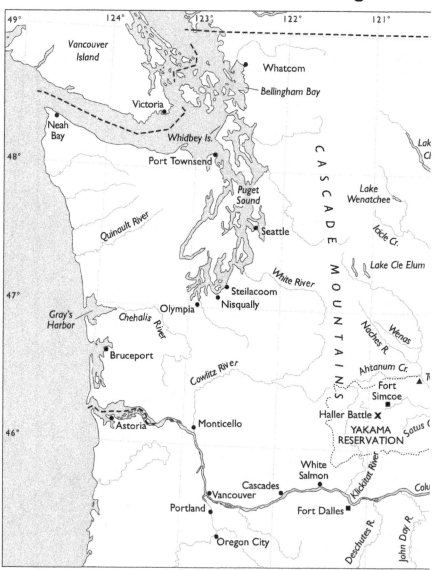

49°   124°   123°   122°   121°

Vancouver
Island

Whatcom

Bellingham Bay

Victoria

Neah
Bay

Whidbey Is.

48°   Port Townsend

Puget
Sound

Quinault River

Seattle

CASCADE MOUNTAINS

Lak
Cl

Lake
Wenatchee

Icicle Cr.

Lake Cle Elum

White River

47°   Gray's
Harbor

Chehalis River

Olympia   Steilacoom
Nisqually

Naches R.   Wenas

Bruceport

Cowlitz River

Ahtanum Cr.

T

Fort
Simcoe

Haller Battle ✗

YAKAMA
RESERVATION

Satus C

46°   Astoria

Monticello

White
Salmon

Cascades   Klickitat River

Colu

Vancouver

Portland

Fort Dalles ■

Deschutes R.

John Day R.

Oregon City

ritory Key Sites 1855–58

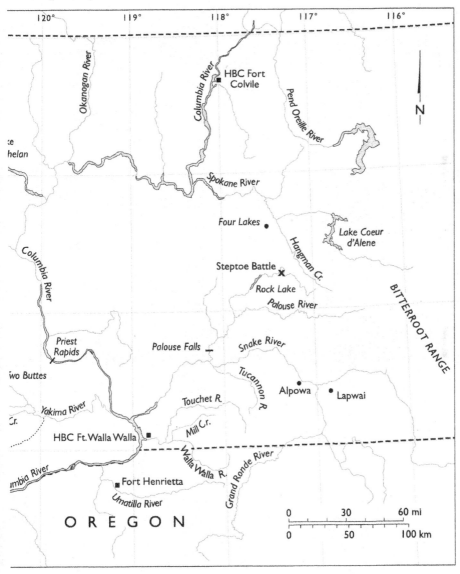

Author's photo

"Here Nature triumphs", the beauty of Mt. Rainier and the Cascade Mountains helped lure pioneer emigrants to Washington Territory in the 1850s.

BATTLE AT TOPPENISH CREEK 1855

KAMIAKIN'S OPENING VICTORY OVER THE U.S. ARMY

On June 9, 1855, after ten long days negotiating at the Walla Walla Council grounds, Yakama chiefs Kamiakin, Owhi and Skloom joined eleven other tribal leaders and inked their x-marks on treaty papers prepared by Washington Territorial Governor Isaac I. Stevens, who also served as Superintendent of Indian Affairs. Fourteen tribes and bands comprising the Yakama Nation consisted of horsemen, hunters, fishermen, warriors and resourceful women producing food, clothing, shelter, tools and medicine from a vibrant natural environment. Their ancestors had occupied the land for thousands of years. Influenced by Hudson's Bay Company traders, the families of Kamiakin, Owhi, and Skloom also took up raising potatoes, corn and beef cattle to supplement traditional food supplies.

Most of the tribesmen attending the council wore their hair straight, long and loose, characteristic of the Plateau tribes residing east of the Cascade Range and west of the Bitterroot Mountains. Absent were braids, bonnets or plains style adornments. Some men wore one or two feathers pointed downward, others donned a white man's hat.

The historic treaty formed the basis for legal policies affecting Native and non-Native residents in Washington for the next century and more. Two other treaties emerged from the same council, one with the Nez Perce tribe, and another with the Walla Walla, Cayuse and Umatilla. Not every chief residing in the region attended The Grand Talk but many did and acquiesced to Governor Stevens' terms after realizing the great white father in the east held the power to overwhelm the tribes if they refused. Still the governor obtained the signatures willingly by utilizing his persuasiveness and persistence while offering benefits and concessions in exchange for the tribes' extinguishing title to the greater part of their traditional lands.

The chiefs signed the papers and waited to see how good or bad the future might become. Perhaps Stevens' Indian agents would help Native people survive on a fraction of their original lands. Maybe the right to hunt and fish at traditional sites unclaimed by settlers would be enough. If not, there would later come a time to fight.

Before the ink dried at the council, reports of gold discoveries near Colville set off a frenzied reaction throughout Washington Territory. The lure of gold tempted residents envious of California's bonanza just six years earlier. A mad rush soon disrupted a sensitive landscape quickly becoming ripe for war. Hundreds of white, French and Metis residents dropped what they were doing and headed for mine fields along the Columbia River and Pend Oreille River near Colville. Prospectors came from Puget Sound, Oregon and California, some responding to newspaper ads selling outfits and offering pack train services. The migration depopulated much of Oregon's Willamette Valley causing farmers to face labor shortages during harvest.[1] A popular route used by many gold seekers led straight through the Yakima Valley.

Some unruly behavior from miners brought retaliation from Native men who did not want to give up their wives to armed strangers. A chief's physically disabled daughter was violated.[2] Add to that a flood of intruders treading across not yet ceded territory (Congress had yet to ratify the treaty or make promised payments), and young warriors could not be restrained. Gunfire cut down seven miners. Mattice, Jamison, Walker, Eaton, Cummings, Huffman, and Fanjoy lay dead east of Snoqualmie Pass.[3]

For all the trouble, little gold came out. Most claims turned out to be a bust. But the damage had been done. Indian Agent A. J. Bolon received word of the miners' killings from a concerned Chief Spokane Garry. Bolon took the incidents personally because he had assured travelers through newspaper reports that miners could safely travel the route along the Yakima River.[4] The tall, red-haired agent, age 29 set off alone from The Dalles on September 18 to investigate. Bolon sought Chief Owhi because the chief's son, Qualchan had been suspected of leading the ambushes. After several days with no results, the agent stopped at St. Joseph Mission on Ahtanum Creek on September 23, and asked Father Paul Durieu to notify Bolon at The Dalles when Owhi returned.[5] The mission's other priest, Father Charles Pandosy, was away on business in Olympia. Bolon turned south riding horseback 40 miles to Wahk-Shum Springs where he met a group of Yakamas including Mosheel, son of Kamiakin's brother, Showaway. Bolon admonished the men for the miners' murders and threatened to send soldiers to hunt down and punish their guilty brethren. Mosheel and his companions took exception. Bolon was an employee of Governor Stevens, who represented the great white father and caused local chiefs to sign away their homeland. The agent had also been sheriff at Vancouver the year lawmen hanged Mosheel's Cayuse uncles in nearby Oregon City in 1850 after having been found guilty of the Whitman massacre. Many Indians believed the Whitmans had purposely poisoned the Cayuse with a deadly measles disease. A white man employed by Marcus Whitman, Joe Lewis, had told them so.[6] Mosheel sought revenge for the Cayuse and others he believed had been wronged. For him, the miners received the punishment they deserved and Bolon's insults to the contrary would not be tolerated. The agent was silenced with a knife to the throat.[7]

The news came as a surprise to Kamiakin and his brother, Showaway, whose son had committed the crime.[8] But Kamiakin had contemplated the possibility of war for at least two years. The Yakama chief's allies in Cayuse and Nez Perce country shared alarm about thousands of pioneers arriving annually by wagon train on their way to Oregon.[9] Chiefs knew that Kalapuya survivors in the Willamette Valley had been decimated by diseases seemingly to clear the way for settlers and their homesteads. Early treaty efforts in Oregon had failed in 1851. Agreements with those tribes were not ratified and expected payments never arrived.[10] Captain George McClellan had told Kamiakin in August of 1853 to expect newly appointed Governor Stevens to arrive and hold councils about purchasing tribal land. McClellan also advised Kamiakin that pioneer wagon trains would soon be passing through Yakama country on their way to Puget Sound, and tribes should treat the emigrants peaceably.[11] Kamiakin responded politely to McClellan, but resisted the idea of giving up Indian land to white settlers. The 55-year-old chief had co-existed with French Catholic missionaries for years, but kept his distance from government officials who were intent on wresting control of Yakama country from

3

its traditional occupants. Once the miners and agent Bolon had been killed, a military response from the Americans seemed eminent, and Kamiakin prepared to take up arms and meet the adversaries face to face.

At Fort Dalles, Oregon, Brevet Major Granville O. Haller learned that Agent Bolon had been slain in Washington Territory. News came from a courier sent by Indian Agent Nathan Olney who had been told of the act by a Des Chutes woman who had been temporarily held by a group of Yakamas close to the scene.[12] By September 29, Major Haller had learned from Wasco Chief Kaskala and interpreter Billy Chinook the names of Bolon's killers, "Mish-shele, Wah-pi-wap-pight-tla, Now-ne-au-niuy, Soo-kyque and Stock-un."[13] Still another report came in from a Des Chutes chief sent from The Dalles. The chief had spoken directly with Kamiakin and brought a letter written by Father Durieu confirming that Bolon had last been seen alive on September 23 at the St. Joseph Mission.[14]

Such alarming events in the Yakima Valley triggered action on both sides of the Cascade Mountains. In Olympia, 25-year-old acting Governor Charles Mason called for a company of troops from Fort Steilacoom to cross over Naches Pass and apprehend those who had killed miners. Mason was filling in for Governor Stevens away negotiating treaties in Blackfeet country. The governor's extended territorial boundaries in 1855 included the panhandle of modern Idaho and the western part of Montana. Lieutenant William A. Slaughter and 40 soldiers left Steilacoom for the Yakima Valley on September 28th.[15] Meanwhile, Haller sent an express to his commanders at Fort Vancouver as soon as he learned of Bolon's demise. Haller began preparing troops while waiting for anticipated orders that arrived on October 1st. Acting Assistant Adjutant General Lieutenant John Withers directed Haller to send one company into the field and seize the miners' murderers. Haller immediately wrote back stating he intended to send two companies of 50 men each after learning of Bolon's death and hearing reports that Kamiakin had raised a large force to do battle.[16] Haller was no stranger to hunting down fugitives. He and his men had recently returned from Boise country where they had captured and executed a number of Snake tribesmen accused of massacring 19 members of the Ward wagon train. Haller's written order to his troops stated, "It is expected that the utmost decorum will prevail at the execution of these unfortunate warriors who (although their people have shown the utmost barbarity towards their victims deserve death) are executed as an example in hopes it will prevent other murders and not from the instinct of revenge."[17]

Granville O. Haller was born in 1819, raised and educated in York, Pennsylvania. Rather than attend West Point, he received a direct commission to the rank of 2nd lieutenant by a military board under Secretary of War Joel R. Poinsett in 1839.[18] One of Haller's first duties placed him in charge of a large group of Creek Indians growing corn crops that would allow the tribe to become self-sufficient. Haller participated in the Invasion of Mexico during 1845-7 when he was brevetted major. (A brevet promotion was an honorary recognition for meritorious service later replaced by military medals.) In 1852, the 4th Infantry Regiment received orders for deployment to the Pacific Coast. Major Haller sailed around Cape Horn during a seven-month voyage accompanied by his wife, Henrietta, two small children, and two companies of soldiers. They arrived at the remote post of Fort Dalles, Oregon Territory in June 1853.

On October 2, 1855, Haller prepared an aggregate of 106 officers and men at Fort Dalles to cross the Columbia River north into Yakama country. One company of 44 men remained to defend the fort and provide reinforcements if necessary. Half the soldiers rode horse-back while the others marched on foot. Each man carried a great coat, blanket, a change of underclothes, a smooth bore musket, canteen and 40 rounds of ammunition. The expedition's supplies included 2,000 rations of sugar, coffee, rice and soap plus 1,000 rations flour, hard bread and pork. They also took more than 500 extra rounds of ammunition and a portable artillery piece known as a mountain howitzer mounted on a two wheeled carriage pulled by a mule.[19] Civilian employees included a white guide, Douglas, Native guide Cutmouth John, and a number of mule packers including 19-year-old Donald McKay, a half Cayuse, who understood the Native language.[20] McKay was the younger half-brother of William, co-secretary at the treaty council held at Walla Walla earlier that year.[21]

On October 3, the military procession started slowly up the arid hills above the banks of the Columbia River headed toward the forested slopes of the Simcoe Mountains. On Saturday October 6, the column emerged from the mountains and zigzagged down the Eel (Assum)

Trail to where Toppenish Creek (also named Pisco on early maps) flowed onto the plains. Haller's scouts noticed signs of a recent track made by a party of Klickitats on their way to join Kamiakin. As the army approached Toppenish Creek they heard a sentry call out from a nearby bluff. A number of warriors hidden in the brush answered with rousing war whoops. The soldiers unhitched the howitzer and placed it into firing position. A single brave, possibly a medicine man, stepped into view and began gesturing antagonistically. A shot rang out, and at 3:00 p.m. the fight began. Warriors kept up a steady fire with deadly accuracy. Two soldiers died from the initial exchange, and six more sustained wounds. Soldiers eventually managed to free themselves from the stream bottom by charging forward with fixed bayonets. Haller took his troops across the stream to higher ground where they fortified themselves behind small knolls at the top of a hill. At dusk the warriors withdrew.

The soldiers arose at dawn on Sunday, October 7 with little or no sleep to find a field full of warriors advancing toward them. Haller's men beheld a sweeping view of the valley full of Indians with more horsemen riding in from the north. The previous evening troops had to separate themselves from wood, water and grass in order to obtain higher ground for defense purposes. An excavated base of a former Indian lodge shielded the wounded. The major sent armed pickets forming an outside perimeter to protect animals and supplies in the center.

As the day wore on the number of warriors grew from about 300 when the fight began to more than 1,000. The tribes possessed a limited number of rifles, but by handing off firearms in relays they kept constant pressure on the troops. Some of the braves crept dangerously close behind piles of rocks and brush. Soldiers charged again with bayonets to drive back the attackers. The mountain howitzer proved effective in the beginning, but the Indians soon learned to disperse whenever the 200-pound barrel was pointed in their direction. Off in the distance, Haller observed dust rising from a band of cattle being driven down Eel Trail by two drovers from Fort Dalles bringing fresh beef to the troops. The pitched battle in progress forced the drovers to turn and flee for their lives. A group of warriors took chase. One of the men, James Ferguson, threw himself from his mule pretending to be shot, while Mr. Ives escaped riding a swift horse. Ives reported

Ferguson killed when he arrived at The Dalles, and newspapers published reports of Ferguson's death. However, the missing man arrived safely days later after walking and crawling through brush avoiding capture.[22]

Haller believed his supplies of ammunition and food would last but the command could not survive without water or feed for the animals. Also, the number of wounded had grown dangerously large, and soon there would be too many to retreat. At night the attackers again withdrew. The major brought his men together, led them down to water where they filled their canteens, re-crossed the stream, and began the long march into the night back toward Fort Dalles. A group of 40 riflemen stayed at the rear to guard the main party slowed by wounded men and weakened pack mules. In the darkness, the two columns became separated. The guide, Cutmouth John kept the lead party on the trail by crawling on his hands and knees feeling for worn tracks.

The rear guard lost sight of the forward group. Haller stopped at 2:00 a.m. and built fires as beacons trying to draw the attention of the rear guard. The lost soldiers, however, upon seeing the fires, believed the gathering to be an Indian camp, and avoided the area by carefully slipping past under cover of night. Haller ordered several packs of supplies removed from the mules and burned to lighten loads. At daylight Monday October 8, the commander looked through his field glass, and viewed a valley still filled with hostile Indians. A number of loaded mules had escaped the night before and grazed leisurely in the distance. Nearly half of Haller's soldiers had vanished.

A large band of Indians began firing at the rear of the column, wounding one sergeant. The major pulled out a letter written earlier to Lieutenant E. H. Day at Fort Dalles requesting more soldiers be dispatched as reinforcements. Haller gave the message and his own horse, "named Selim, a Siskiyou, half-Cayuse, of remarkable endurance and speed", to Cutmouth John to make the important ride.[23] The dependable guide departed at 10:00 a.m. and made it safely to The Dalles that evening. The other guide, Douglas, was unable to locate the lost detachment. A running battle continued with attackers dogging the retreating soldiers up the trail.

A carriage holding the mountain howitzer broke, and the mule weak from lack of food could no longer manage its load. Haller ordered the howitzer abandoned, and buried it in a dry gravel streambed among some cottonwoods. He made sure no ammunition was left behind to render the weapon useable.

The soldiers approached a wooded grove surrounded by meadows where they stopped to rest and make a stand against the relentless attackers. As the men set up a defense perimeter and cleaned their fouled weapons, the pursuing warriors set fire to surrounding fields of dry grass. The soldiers set back fires, countering the assault. More Indians approached at about 4:00 p.m. while creeping through the cover of smoke. Another bayonet charge by the troops dispersed the attackers but three more soldiers died, Private Charles Dreyer, Private William Miller, and Sergeant James Mulholland.

Additional supplies, mostly sacks of pork, were abandoned in order that weary infantrymen could ride. Horses and men had lost strength. Animals were fed flour directly from storage bags.[24] Wounded men were in such pain that a companion had to ride behind in the saddle to hold each stricken soldier upright. By Tuesday October 9 the beleaguered party advanced beyond their pursuers to a small lake where they met up with a lost comrade from the rear guard that had made camp ahead of them. That evening the troops resumed their march, and met the rescue party responding from Fort Dalles.

The entire force returned to the post on October 10 after having suffered 5 men killed, 17 wounded, and a number of mules and supplies missing or abandoned. Haller's diary stated "several" Indians had been killed, and his men had done "some execution". He also gave credit to post doctor George W. Hammond for shooting four warriors with his personal sporting rifle, when the doctor was not caring for the wounded. A final number of enemy casualties could not be determined.

The company of soldiers sent earlier from Fort Steilacoom led by Lieutenant Slaughter did not make it to the battlefield. They were warned by scouts while crossing the Cascade Mountains that overwhelming forces lay ahead, and were compelled to turn back.

Indian eyewitness testimonies matched the military's with a few exceptions. Both sides verified a three day running fight, captured mules, abandoned supplies, loose beef cattle, increasing numbers of warriors, and a buried howitzer. Only questions remained about the number of casualties. To-ki-aken Twi-wash named two warriors,

Pah-chese and Kah-sah-le-mah, who had been killed at the battle.[25] However, Twiwash's brother, Snah-tupsh Ka-lula, claimed only one died.[26] But the latter also believed that no soldiers were killed during the fight in the woods on the third day when three of Haller's men died. For a time it seemed as though half of the major's men had been killed during the first two days of fighting. Or so it appeared to those who pursued about sixty soldiers up Eel trail. The bodies of just two men had been left behind, buried at the battle at Toppenish Creek, adding to the mystery of what became of the others. Reports reached Father Pandosy that just ten soldiers had survived and returned to The Dalles.[27] Word began to spread across the territory that Kamiakin's victory was larger than it actually was.

A Klickitat witness, Tumwater, later described frightening wounds inflicted by blasts from the mountain howitzer. Tumwater carried long jagged scars on his chest, and told of others who died months after receiving injuries.[28] Each spherical case fired by the army's artillery piece contained 78 musket balls packed with four and a half ounces of gunpowder that traveled 800 yards before exploding after a fuse lasting three or four seconds expired.[29] On the battlefield, the howitzer became known as the gun that fired twice.

One of Chief Owhi's sons, Lishhaiahit, told how his brother, Qualchan, received revolvers and race horses from Kamiakin, and used them to kill miners and others during the war.[30] A Nez Perce, Te-pe-al-an-at-he-kek, rode to the Toppenish Creek battlefield, "to learn if Kamaiaken could break the soldiers' guns and keep the bullets from hitting him."[31] Special powers held by Kamiakin, Qualchan, Owhi and others were legendary among tribal members. Elders once said, "There were about thirty warriors, all told who could not be harmed by a bullet."[32]

Another participant, 26-year-old Quetalican, a Columbia Sinkiuse later known as Chief Moses, gained fame as a prominent tribal leader and advocate for peace during the early development of Washington Territory. In 1895, Moses gave a revealing interview about his participation at the battle at Toppenish Creek in 1855. "I fought the white people for Ka-mi-akin. I was very sharp when I was a young fellow: I was shot pretty nearly all over but they never killed me. When my father died Ka-mi-akin was the big chief and then the Indians started a war and they all got nearly beat. Ka-mi-akin got scared, so he came to me and hired me to be a warrior for him; he gave me a whole lot of horses and I said all right. Then we started a war here and we whipped most of the soldiers; we kept fighting the soldiers right here at Toppenish on the little river that runs into the big river. We kept fighting the soldiers and drove them to The Dalles and then we quit and came back. After that I was good and peaceable."[33]

The large force of warriors that routed Haller's troops included an alliance of Yakama, Klickitat, Columbia Sinkiuse, Walla Walla, Palouse, a few disaffected Nez Perce, Cayuse and some Columbia River bands. Many arrived on the second and third days after hearing from couriers about the attack. The casualties, captured mules, cattle, and packs of supplies seized while driving the soldiers out of Yakama country caused Toppenish Creek to become an inspiring, albeit temporary victory for the tribes.

Private Regan and Private Herman were buried near Toppenish Creek at the scene of battle on October 6 and 7. Most likely it was one of their scalps reported brandished just days afterward during a war dance held by the Walla Walla tribe at the mouth of the Yakima River.[34] Private Charles Dryer and Private William Miller were buried with ceremonial military honors in the field above Eel trail on October 8. Sergeant James Mulholland's body was strapped to the back of a mule and accompanied to Fort Dalles for burial.[35]

One explanation for part of Kamiakin's early success came from a type of military draft the chief implemented to obtain fighters. Many warriors served voluntarily. However, there were a number of instances when Kamiakin sent runners, also referred to as spies, to forcefully induce men to join his cause. One of Major Haller's informants, Yice, who lived on the John Day River, had been pressed to join Kamiakin under the threat of losing all of his property and being made a slave if he refused.[36] Chief Kaskala of the Wascopams received a similar threat, and sought protection from Major Haller by moving his village and livestock closer to Fort Dalles.[37] Indian Agent Nathan Olney captured one of Kamiakin's spies after attempting to infiltrate Native groups residing near The Dalles. A Klickitat band of 80 people forced to join Kamiakin in 1855, appealed to Colonel George Wright the following year, asking to be released from the chief's influence, and allowed to return to their homeland.[38]

News of Kamiakin's triumph shocked populations residing in Washington and Oregon. Some tribes west of the Cascades responded by attacking white settlements and soldiers. Territorial officials reacted by calling for volunteers to retaliate against the hostiles. Two more battles would be fought in the Yakima Valley, and many more throughout the territory before it would be over.

Chapter 1 notes

1. (Olympia, WA) *Pioneer and Democrat*, July 27, "Pend 'Oreille Gold Mines", and August 31, 1855, "The Fort Colville Gold Mines"; (Steilacoom, WA) *Puget Sound Courier*, July 5, 1855, "GOLD! GOLD! GOLD!", and September 7, 1855, "Nachess Express for Fort Colville Gold Mines".
2. Granville O. Haller, "Kamiarkin in History: Memoir of the War in the Yakima Valley 1855-1856", manuscript, ND., 7, MSS P-A128, Bancroft Collection of Western Americana, University of California, Berkeley.
3. Elwood Evans, ed., *History of the Pacific Northwest: Oregon and Washington*, 2 vols. (Portland, OR: North Pacific History Company, 1889), 1:493.
4. Weekly (Portland) *Oregonian*, August 4, 1855, "Colville Gold Mines–Gratuitous Advice".
5. Pierre-Paul Durieu to Pascal Ricard, September 30 1855, ACAS.
6. Spokane Garry in James Doty, *Journal of Operations of Governor Isaac Ingalls Stevens of Washington Territory in 1855*, ed. Edward J. Kowrach, (Fairfield, WA: Ye Galleon Press, 1978), 49; J.B.A. Brouillet, *Authentic Account of the Murder of Dr. Whitman and Other Missionaries*, (Portland, OR: S.J. McCormick,1869), 33-6.
7. Lucullus Virgil McWhorter, *Tragedy of the Wahk-Shum: The Death of Andrew J. Bolon Indian Agent to the Yakima Nation, in Mid-September, 1855*, (Fairfield, WA: Ye Galleon Press, 1968), 25-32; Jo N. Miles, "The Life and Death of A.J. Bolon 1826-1855", *Pacific Northwest Quarterly* 97, (Winter 2005/2006), 31-7.
8. A.J. Splawn, *Ka-mi-akin, Last Hero of the Yakimas*, (1917; reprint Caldwell, Idaho: The Caxton Printers, 1980), 42-4.
9. Charles Pandosy to Toussaint Mesplie, April 1853, ACAS; Joseph Ellison, "The Covered Wagon Centennial: March of the Empire Builders Over the Oregon Trail", *The Washington Historical Quarterly* 21 (July 1930), 175-6.
10. C.F. Coan, "The First Stage of the Federal Indian Policy in the Pacific Northwest, 1849-1852", *The Quarterly of the Oregon Historical Society* 22, (March 1921), 55-8.
11. George B. McClellan, diary, August 18-23, 1853, George Brinton McClellan Papers, Manuscript Division, Library of Congress, Washington, D.C.
12. R.R. Thompson to Joel Palmer, September 28, 1855, RBIA (RG 75), OS 1848-1873, LS, LR by Superintendent Joel Palmer 1854-55, NARA microfilm M2 Roll 5.
13. Granville O. Haller, Diary September 29, 1855, microfilm, acc. 3437-001, Granville O. Haller Papers, UW Libraries Special Collections, Seattle, WA.
14. Durieu to Ricard, Sept. 30, 1855; Joel Palmer to George Manypenny, October 9, 1855, NARA microfilm, M2 Roll 5; Joel Palmer to I.I. Stevens, October 6, 1855, RBIA (RG 75), WS, Misc. LR August 22, 1853-April 9, 1861, NARA microfilm M2 Roll 23.
15. C.H. Mason to "My Dear Major", (Rains), October 3, 1855, RBIA (RG 75), WS, Misc. LR August 22, 1853-April 9, 1861, NARA microfilm M5 Roll 23.
16. Haller, "Kamiarkin in History", 10.
17. Granville O. Haller, "Order No. 6, Winnass Expedition, Camp at Massacre Ground, Boise River", July 18, 1855, typescript, box 55-14, Relander Collection, YVL.

18. Granville O. Haller, "Indian Fighting in Oregon and Washington", typescript, January 1, 1885, Pac MS B-60, Bancroft Collection of Western Americana, Bancroft Library, University of California, Berkeley.

19. Post Order 78, Records of United States Army Continental Commands 1821-1920, (RG 393), Misc. Correspondence of Posts, Districts, and Military Organizations, 1847-1856, Orders & Circulars, Box 1 & 2 Relating to Miners Murders, Bolon's Murder - NARA Washington D.C. as published in T.G. Boyden (Knudsen), *Warrior of the Mist*, (Fairfield, WA: Ye Galleon Press, 1996), 164-5.

20. Granville O. Haller, "The Indian War of 1855-6 in Washington and Oregon", typescript ca. 1894, part 4, 4-5, box 2 acc. 3437-001, Granville O. Haller Papers, UW Libraries Special Collections, Seattle, WA.

21. Jo N. Miles, "Kamiakin's Influence on Early Washington Territory", *Pacific Northwest Quarterly* 99 (Fall 2008), 166-7.

22. Robert A. Bennett – ed., *We'll All Go Home in the Spring Personal Accounts and Adventures as Told by the Pioneers of the West*, (Walla Walla, WA: Pioneer Press Books, 1984), 107-10; Weekly (Portland) Oregonian, October 20, 1855, "Mr. James Ferguson".

23. Theodore N. Haller, "Life and Public Services of Colonel Granville O. Haller", *The Washington Historian* 1, (April, 1900), 103.

24. G.O. Haller to Lieut. Henry C. Hodges, 4th Inf. AG to Head Qrs. of Dist. Fort Dalles, O.T., "Report of the Operations of the Troops of the Yakima Expedition Oct. 16, 1855", typescript, box 42-11, Relander Collection, YVL.

25. "Smat-Lowit's Story of the Yakima War: 1855", January, 1912, Louis Mann, interpreter, L.V. McWhorter Papers, cage 55, box 45, folder 434, MASC, WSU, Pullman, WA.

26. "Narrative of: Snah-tupsh Ku-lala Battle of Thappanish", McWhorter Papers, Box 16, folder 124, MASC, WSU, Pullman.

27. Haller, "Kamiarkin in History", 22.

28. Robert Ballou, Early Klickitat Valley Days, (Goldendale, WA: *Goldendale Sentinel*, 1938), 334.

29. Alfred Mordecai, ed., *The Ordinance Manual for the Use of the Officers of the United States Army* (Washington: Gideon & Co., Printers, 1850), 137,148.

30. "Narrative of: Too-Skas Pot-Thah-Nook: Seven Mountains also known as Lesh-hi-hit, October 29, 1911", McWhorter Papers, box 44, folder 428, MASC WSU, Pullman.

31. Peter M. Lafontain quoted in "Proceedings of a court martial held at Camp Cornelius, Whitman's Valley, Washington Territory", February 16th,1856, House of Representatives 34th Congress 3rd session 1856-'57, Ex. Doc. No. 76, Indian Affairs on the Pacific, in thirteen volumes, vol. 9, 210.

32. "Yakima Indian History-Smith Luc-ie: November 24, 1908", McWhorter Papers, box 16 folder 122, MASC WSU Pullman.

33. *The Spokesman* (WA) *Review*, October 5, 1895, "Moses Gets a Yakima Attorney"; Yakima (WA) *Daily Republic*, May 13, 1935, "Chief Moses Recalls Early Day When He Fought Whites".

34. Antoine Placie in "Proceedings of a court martial held at Camp Cornelius", HED No. 76, 208.

35. Haller, "Indian War of 1855-6", 4:20.

36. Haller, "Indian War of 1855-6", 4:6.

37. Haller, "Kamiarkin in History", 18.

38. George Wright to R.R. Thompson, June 8, 1856, NARA M5 Roll 23.

Chapter Two

RETALIATION AT TWO BUTTES 1855

RESPONSE IN THE YAKIMA VALLEY BY THE MILITARY

Washington and Oregon territorial officials wasted little time reacting to Kamiakin's triumph over army troops at Toppenish Creek. The day after Haller returned to Fort Dalles, Oregon governor George L. Curry issued a proclamation calling for volunteers to respond to the Indian uprising.[1] Oregon residents feared there would be an attack on settlements in the Willamette Valley if they didn't suppress the rebellion immediately.[2] Three days later, Washington's acting governor Mason issued a similar call for volunteers.[3]

A sense of terror prevailed among many settlers because the army had been beaten and Governor Stevens was cut off somewhere near the Rocky Mountains. Washington's volunteers set up defenses around Puget Sound while Oregon produced a mobile militia from its population much larger than Washington's estimated 4,000 non-Native inhabitants at the time. Oregon rapidly organized ten companies totaling more than 800 armed citizens mustered into service at Portland, and transported by boat, barge and horseback to The Dalles where they prepared for an assault into Washington. The two governors collaborated with Major Gabriel J. Rains, U.S. Army commander at Fort Vancouver, to combine forces and invade the Yakima Valley in retaliation for the damage that warriors had done to U.S. troops. Governor Mason bestowed a temporary rank of brigadier general upon Rains, 52, giving him authority over two companies of Washington volunteers from Vancouver mustered into U.S. service, and Oregon Mounted Volunteer (OMV) commander Colonel James W. Nesmith, 35.[4] Five of the Oregon companies prepared to accompany Rains' troops. They included Company C of Clackamas County under

Captain Samuel B. Stafford, 93 men, Company D of Washington County under Captain Thomas Cornelius, 100 men, Company E of Yamhill County under Captain A. J. Hembree, 99 men, Company F of Marion County under Captain Charles Bennett, 81 men, and Company G of Polk County under Captain Benjamin Hayden, 104 men.[5] Company A, of Multnomah County, under Captain A. V. Wilson with 97 men, stayed at The Dalles to procure additional supplies to be transported to the other units after they reached the Yakima Valley. Three more companies, Company B of Wasco County under Captain Orlando Humason, 65 men, Company H of Linn County under Captain Davis Layton, 74 men, and Company I of Benton County under Captain Lyman Munson, 71 men prepared for a separate expedition into the Walla Walla Valley. A final company, K of Marion County under Captain Narcisse Cornoyer, stood by to provide scouting, guiding and interpreting services from its 31 mostly French Canadians and Metis, some of them former trappers and mountain men.[6]

Making matters worse was a simultaneous Indian outbreak near Rogue River in southern Oregon Territory requiring mobilization of additional U.S. troops at Fort Hall. Major Rains left Fort Dalles for the Yakima Valley on October 31, 1855 with 365 officers and men ahead of the volunteers. Among the regulars were Major Haller's survivors plus reinforcements from Fort Vancouver and California including 24-year-old Lieutenant Philip H. Sheridan who led a detachment of 18 dragoons, a group of mounted soldiers similar to army cavalry.

The command traveled just four miles each of the first two days slowed by a long line of heavily loaded mules, civilian packers, two mountain howitzers, and the infantry's foot soldiers ascending steep slopes above the Columbia River. Yakama warriors had no trouble tracking the procession. At the fourth camp made on November 3 raiders ran off 25 horses and five mules just east of the Little Klickitat River near Chief Skloom's abandoned log cabin.[7] The theft answered acts the day before by soldiers who had unearthed and destroyed large caches of dried salmon, roots and berries that had been stored for winter.[8]

Major Rains chose a route over the Simcoe Mountains that followed Satus Creek (known as Canyon Creek in 1855) into the Yakima Valley a few miles east of the trail Major Haller had taken three and a half weeks earlier.[9] By November 5, the 470 or so Oregon Mounted

Volunteers that had left The Dalles three days behind Rains caught up and camped just beyond the regulars. At 7:00 a.m. the following morning OMV members assembled in formation to salute the troops, "Volunteers gave Major Haller and his company three hearty cheers as they passed, which was returned with a will by Major Haller and his company."[10]

By November 7, volunteers and regulars had crossed the Simcoe Mountains and marched into the Yakima Valley where they camped on lower Toppenish Creek (also called Simcoe Creek in some reports). On Thursday November 8, the main body of soldiers marched to the Yakima River between the future town of Toppenish and the winter mission known as Alachikas at present day Sawyer. Colonel Nesmith detailed a reconnaissance party led by 28-year-old Captain Thomas Cornelius and 25 men from Company D plus ten men from each of the other companies to ride up Toppenish Creek to search for "the enemy" and capture any cattle and horses they may find.[11] Cornelius' men traveled about 15 miles west, and then circled back north easterly toward Two Buttes, also known as Payh-oy-ti-koot, a gap where the Yakima River divides Ahtanum Ridge and Rattlesnake Hills.

Most of the Yakama population had congregated at winter villages just north of the gap. When Cornelius' 69 volunteers approached within five miles of Two Buttes, some 100 mounted warriors galloped out firing as they came. Shots were exchanged as warriors kept volunteers away from the entrance to the gap. Private Robert Moore Painter of Company D recorded in his journal "several Indians" falling from their horses.[12] Volunteers retreated battling downriver to within two miles of the soldiers' camp before the braves withdrew. Cornelius' party suffered three men wounded, Sergeant Bridges of Marion County, Corporal Holmes of Clackamas County, and Stephen Waymire of Polk County.[13]

During the same afternoon U.S. troops on the south bank of the Yakima River discovered approximately 40 painted warriors gathered across the river. Lieutenant Sheridan and his 18 mounted dragoons splashed across the river to an island and exchanged fire without inflicting or receiving casualties. Major Rains ordered his infantry soldiers to cross but the swift current swept two men off their feet causing Private Joseph Moxeimer and Private Edward Crogan to drown.[14] Rains immediately sent a dispatch to Colonel Nesmith some two miles away requesting additional mounted troops. Nesmith responded with Captain Bennett and 40 men of Company F and 24 men with Lieutenant Conner of Company C. The mounted volunteers crossed the river to join the dragoons. A few shots were exchanged but the soldiers could not catch the fleet warriors who dashed away astride fresh horses disappearing beyond the hills.[15]

The next day, volunteers and regulars marched upstream toward Two Buttes intent upon forcing a fight with the Yakamas. The soldiers' progress was impeded along the way by harassing shots from snipers. As the combined force of more than 800 approached the buttes, some 300 warriors assembled atop the west hill challenging entry through the gap. The Yakima River and a steep adjacent butte prevented access from the east. The soldiers decided they would make camp at the bottom of the west butte and attempt to extricate the warriors from the top. The army fired two howitzer shots uphill but the distance was too great to do damage. Likewise, bullets fired from above by the warriors fell harmlessly below. Major Haller and Captain Christopher Auger decided to narrow the distance by charging uphill on foot with two companies of regulars followed by a detachment of volunteers. The rush drove off the defenders, and at dusk soldiers built fires at the top of the hill.[16] When nightfall arrived, troops descended to their camp for supper, and before long, the Indians re-claimed the top and warmed themselves around the army's fire. The same night, Yakama raiders ran off twenty more army horses and four mules despite being guarded by the highly regarded young packer, Donald McKay.[17]

On the morning of Saturday November 10, the whole military force marched through the gap and found the Yakamas had packed their baggage, women, children and elderly, and evacuated except for a straggler, Tow-tow-nah-hee who was overtaken, shot and killed by one of the army's Indian scouts. A second Yakama was also reported shot at the base of the butte by Captain Bennett's volunteer Company F.[18] OMV Company D Private William Charles Painter reported in his journal, "2 scalps" taken.[19] Soldiers made a sweep through the next few miles of the Yakima River Valley rounding up 40 head of horses and 15 cattle. No further signs of warriors could be found. The troops circled back toward Two Buttes and began to advance west along the banks of Ahtanum Creek toward St. Joseph Mission.

Temporary General Rains ordered Colonel Nesmith to take 250 volunteers and Lieutenant Sheridan's dragoons on Sunday, November 11, to look for soldiers expected to arrive from Fort Steilacoom via Naches Pass. Captain Maurice Maloney had been ordered by Rains to take 75 infantrymen from Steilacoom on October 21 and join Lieutenant Slaughter's 40 regulars camped at White River Prairie and proceed across the mountains to meet Rains at the Ahtanum Mission. Maloney's regulars had been joined by Washington Territory Volunteer Company A led by Captain Gilmore Hays. Together, regulars and volunteers marched to camp on the Naches River arriving October 27. Maloney had received a dispatch from Fort Steilacoom's courier advising that Major Rains was several days late getting his troops out of Fort Dalles. Because Maloney didn't have enough supplies to wait for Rains, and due to snow falling in the mountains plus reports of new Indian attacks around Puget Sound, the captain decided to turn back.[20]

Rains did not receive Maloney's letter explaining the change of plans for several days. Therefore, the major believed soldiers should still be at the Naches River. Rains feared the Yakamas had fled from Two Buttes for the purpose of attacking Maloney's troops when in fact they had taken their families to Priest Rapids, crossed the Columbia River in canoes, and secured dugouts on the far bank to prevent soldiers from coming after them.[21]

Nesmith and Sheridan's men plodded up the Naches River on horseback through a snowstorm for two days and nights until bad weather forced them to halt. Finding no sign of Maloney or Indians, the soldiers turned back and re-joined Rains at St. Joseph Mission. Priests had recently abandoned the mission leaving behind caches of potatoes, wheat, oats, peas, turnips, cabbages and a herd of pigs feasted upon by hungry soldiers. Also found was a half keg of gunpowder buried in the priests' garden. Volunteers alleged that the buried powder proved that missionaries had provided Indians with ammunition for war. Lieutenant Sheridan took the opposite view contending that burying the keg showed that Father Pandosy had kept gunpowder out of the hands of hostiles.[22] Vengeful volunteers, however, set fire to the mission buildings before any responsible officer could intercede. OMV's Colonel Nesmith later reported to Governor Curry that the mission had burned by accident.

Father Pandosy left behind a revealing letter he wrote to the soldiers at the request of Chief Kamiakin. It was dated October 6, 1855, the day Major Haller met the warriors at Toppenish Creek.[23]

Write to the soldiers tell them that we are quiet, friend to Americans, that we were not thinking of war at all; but the way in which the governor has talked to us at the Cayuses has irritated us and made us determine to general war which will end with complete destruction of all the savages or all Americans.

If the governor had told us my children, I am asking you a piece of land in each tribe for the Americans, but the land and your country is still yours, we would have given willingly what he would have asked us and we would have lived with all others as brothers. But he has taken us in number and thrown us out of our native country in a strange land among a people who is our enemy, for between us we are enemy, in a place where its people do not even have enough to eat for themselves.

Then we have said, now we know perfectly the heart of the Americans; since a long time. They hanged us without knowing if we are right or wrong; but they have never killed or hanged one American, though there is no place where an American has not killed savages. We are therefore dogs. They tell us that our ancestors had no horses nor cattle, nor crops nor instruments to garden, that we have received everything of these riches from the Americans that the country was already full of us and at the same time they chase us from our native land, as if they were telling us: I have sent you all these things so that you increase them until my people arrive, as soon as they will be on the place they will find what to eat. You want, therefore you Americans, make us die of famine little by little. It is better for us to die at once. It is you, governor, who has wanted war, by these words: the country will be for us from all tribes, all nations you will go to such place and leave here your land. Our heart has been torn when you have said these words. You have shot the first gun. Our heart has been broken. There is only one breath left; we did not have the strength to answer. Then we took common cause with our enemy to defend all together our nationality and our country.

However the war was not going to start so soon, but the Americans who were going to the mines having shot some savages because they did not want to give them their wives, we have taken the care of defending ourselves. Then came Mr. Bolon who has strongly insulted us, threatened us of war, death when announcing us that he was going back to the Dalles from where he would send soldiers to destroy us. Nevertheless we have let him pass quietly, after having thought of what he had just told us, we went to join him. We were without arms and without any idea to kill him but as he went on talking to us with too much harshness and threatened us with soldiers we have seized him and have killed him so that we can say it is not we who have started war, but we have only defended ourselves.

If the soldiers and the Americans after having read the letter and taken knowledge of the motives which bring us to fight, want to retire or treat friendly, we will consent to put arms down and to grant them a piece of land in different tribe, and that they do not force us to be exiled from our native country, otherwise we are decided to be cut to pieces and if we lose the men who keep the camp in which are the wives and our children will kill them rather than see them fall into the hands of the Americans to make them their toys. For we have heart and respect ourselves. Write this to the soldiers and the Americans and they give you an answer to know what they think. If they do not answer it is because they want war; we will then, 1050 men assembled. Some only will go to battle, but as soon as the war is started the news will spread among all our nations and in a few days we will be more than 10,000. If peace is wanted, we will consent to it, but it must be written to us so we may know about it.[24]

Pandosy struggled with language when writing in English. He usually wrote letters in French. For example, the word "savage" in French represented a respectful term for Native or Indian. The other meanings were clear enough to Major Rains. The army officer took

19

exception to the letter and wrote a bitter response of his own penned on oilcloth, and then hoisted on a pole in front of the mission:

Letter to Kam-i-ah-kanHead Quarters Yackima Expedition
Roman Catholic Mission
November 13th 1855
Kam-i-ah-kan
Highass Tyhee of the Yackima Indians

Your talk by Padre Pandosy is just received.

You know me and I know you, you came among the white people, and to my house at the Dalles with Padre Pandosy, and gave me a horse, which I did not take, as Pau-awok had given Lieut. Wood another horse for him. You came in peace, we come in war, and why, because your land has drank the blood of the white man and the great spirit requires it at your hand.

You make the sign of the cross and pray to the God of truth for mercy, and yet you lie when you say you "were very quiet, the Americans were our friends, our heart was not for the war", until Governor Stevens changed your feelings; for long before the treaty, which you agreed to, you proposed to the Walla Walla Chief Pe-pe-o-mox-i-mox to go to war, and kill off all the whites, he told us so, you had been preparing for this purpose a very long time, and your people agreed with the Cayuse at the Walla Walla Council before the treaty was made to murder all the whites there, which was only prevented by the Nez Perces disagreeing.

You know that you murdered white men going to the mines who had done you no injury, and you murder all Americans though no white man had trespassed upon your lands. You sent me a delegation to stop Hamilton and Pierce settling in your country. I wrote them a letter, and they left. You murdered your agent Bolon for telling you the truth, that the troops would come upon you for these murders. Has his death prevented their coming? I sent a handful of soldiers into your country to inquire into facts, it was not expected that they should fight you, and they did right to return back.

Your foul deeds were seen by the eye of the Great Spirit who saw Cain when he killed his brother Abel and cursed him for it. Fugitives and vagabonds shall you also be, all that remain of you upon the face of the earth, as well as all who aid and assist you, until you are gone.

You say now, "if we will be quiet and make friendship, you will not war, but give a piece of land to all the tribes" - we will not be quiet but war forever until not a Yackima breathes in the land he calls his own,- the river only will we let retain this name, to show to all people that here, the Yackimas once lived.

You say that you will fight us with thousands, and if vanquished, those of you that remain will kill all your women and children, and then the country will be ours. The country is ours already, as you must see from our assembled Army, for we intend to occupy it, and make it too hot to hold you. We are braves and no brave man makes war with women and children,- you may kill them as you say, but we will not, yet we are thirsting for your blood, and want your Warriors to meet us, and the Warriors of all tribes wishing to help you at once to come- the snow is on the ground, and the crows are hungry for food – your men we have killed your horses and your cattle do not afford them enough to eat.

Your people shall not catch Salmon hereafter for you, for I will send Soldiers to occupy your fisheries and fire upon you. Your cattle and your horses, which you got from the white man, we will hunt up, kill and take from you. The Earth which drank the blood of the white man shed by your hands, shall grow no more wheat nor roots for you for we will destroy it. When the cloth that makes your clothing your guns and your powder are gone, the white man will make you no more, we looked upon you as our children, and tried to do you good, we would not have cheated you. The treaty which you complain of, tho' signed by you gave you too much for your lands, which are most all worthless to the white man, but we were not sorry, for we are able to give and it would have benefitted you. After you signed the treaty with Governor Stevens and Genl. Palmer, had you have told us that you did not wish to abide by it, it would have been listened to. We wanted to instruct you in all our learning, to make axes, plows and hoes to cultivate the ground- blankets to keep you from cold, Steam Boats, & Steam Wagons which fly along swifter than the birds fly, and to use the lightning which makes the thunder in the Heavens to carry talk and serve as a servant. William Chinook at the Dalles, Lawyer Chief of the Nez perces, Stickus and We-atti-tuminee Highass Tyhee of the Cayuse and many others of their people can tell you what I say is true. You, a few people we can see with our glasses a long way off which the whites are as the stars in the Heavens, or leaves of the trees in the summer time. Our warriors in the field are many as you must see, but if not enough, a thousand for every one man will be sent to hunt you out, to kill you, and my kind advice to you, as you will see, is to scatter yourselves among the Indian tribes more peaceable and then forget you were ever Yackimas.

G.J. Rains

Major U.S.A. Brig Gen'l Wash. Tery[25]

Rains drew plenty of criticism from other military officers. Lieutenant Sheridan and Captain Edward Ord questioned the major's capabilities, and the commander of the Department of the Pacific, Brevet Major General John E. Wool advised Rains to expect an investigation by court martial concerning his command of the Yakima Expedition.[26]

In contrast, Major Granville Haller (later Colonel) penned a much different attitude regarding actions by the tribes in his memoirs.

And if we are candid, we must admit that the Indians of Washington and Oregon are entitled to some commendation for their patriotic spirit in resisting the tyranny of civilization as our Revolutionary fathers were in resisting the tyranny of Royalty-for we find that they were loyal to their Indian customs, and rights, fought for them-were individually brave-but lacking the cohesion of discipline and material for war, they...had to yield to the iron hand of destiny.[27]

On November 15, 1855 volunteers found and burned Kamiakin's house about four miles west of the mission. The following day troops turned south toward the Simcoe Mountains and marched 15 miles to the Haller battlefield. Skulls and bone fragments from privates Herman and Regan lay on the ground scattered by predators. Soldiers re-buried the men's remains and conducted a military funeral with honors. From there, troops ascended the Eel Trail into miserable mountain weather. Snow drifts between two and four feet deep slowed progress for foot soldiers carrying litters with sick and wounded. From The Dalles, OMV Captain Wilson and Company A attempted to bring 45 pack animals carrying 200 pounds each with supplies to last the volunteers ten more days. But heavy snow obliterated the trail forcing Captain Wilson to halt and wait for assistance from Captain Cornoyer's French Canadians who found their way under the worst conditions. Wilson lost 16 pack animals, 1600 pounds of flour, 350 pounds of peas, two boxes of soap and two sacks of salt in the storm.[28]

On Sunday November 18 the whole procession crossed the mountains and set up camp in the Klickitat Valley where they found ample grass, firewood, water and shelter. The army remained and built a blockhouse approximately 25 miles northeast of Fort Dalles.[29] The Yakamas returned home after the soldiers left, and Captain Edward Ord wrote a summary of the expedition published in the *New York Herald*, February 17, 1856. "Our expedition went into the Yakima country some 800 strong about 500 volunteers and 300 regulars. A big fight was expected but the commanding officer of the regulars was by nature adapted for any thing but a partisan chief. He marched about over plains and mountains, got into rivers, drowned some men, lost a lot of horses and mules, got into snows, marshes and every type of scrape except a battle (tho' there was some chance of it) lost some of his party, burned a Catholic mission and then came in with about the most disgusted set of young army officers and volunteers that we have seen lately."[30]

Major Rains attempted to prefer charges against Captain Ord for conduct unbecoming an officer and Major Haller for neglect of duty, but counter charges aimed at Rains and a shortage of ranking officers to conduct hearings prevented formal proceedings from going forward. General Wool focused his attention on bringing additional soldiers from the east coast and an experienced commanding officer, Colonel George Wright, to restore order in the Yakima Valley and throughout eastern Washington.

Chapter 2 Notes

1. Weekly (Portland) *Oregonian*, October 13, 1855, "A Proclamation".
2. E.M. Barnum to J.W. Nesmith, October 16, 1855, U.S. House of Representatives, 34th Congress, 3rd session 1856-'57, Ex. Doc. No. 76 Indian Affairs on the Pacific, in thirteen volumes, vol. 9, 158.
3. (Steilacoom, WA) *Puget Sound Courier*, October 19, 1855, "Call for Volunteers".
4. Cpt. T.J. Cram, "Topographical Memoir of Dept. of Pacific", U.S. House of Representatives, 35th Congress, 2nd session 1858-'59, Exec. Doc. No. 114, 91; *Puget Sound Courier,* December 14, 1855.
5. "Claims Growing Out of Indian Hostilities in Oregon and Washington", U.S. House of Representatives, 35th Congress, 2nd session 1858-'59, Exec Doc. No. 51 ss. 1046, 79.
6. Elwood Evans, ed., *History of the Pacific Northwest: Oregon and Washington*, 2 vols. (Portland, OR: North Pacific History Company, 1889), 1:538; William Bischoff, ed., We Were Not Summer Soldiers the Indian War Diary of Plympton J. Kelly 1855-1856, (Tacoma, WA: Washington State Historical Society, 1976), 28-30.
7. Lt. R. Macfeely to John E. Wool, January 6, 1856, Records of U.S. Army Commands 1784-1821 (RG 98) Dept. of The Pacific selected LR 1856-58, NARA microfilm 1953, Relander Collection, box 63-11, YVL.
8. Philip H. Sheridan, *Personal Memoirs of P.H. Sheridan*, 2 vols. (New York: Charles L. Webster & Company, 1888), 1:54.
9. "Yakama Indian Country Reconnaissance - in part by Lt. Mendell Topographical Engineers in the command of Maj. Rains against the Yakamas, Nov. 1855," Records of the Office of the Chief of Engineers (RG 77), NARA Quarters Map file Drawer 144, sheet 23, plate 1.
10. Weekly (Portland) *Oregonian,* November 24, 1855, Lieut. A.J. Price, "A Journal of Col. Nesmith's Expedition."
11. J.W. Nesmith to Gov. George G. Curry, November 19, 1855, Records of the Adjutant General's Office (RG 94), LR 1854-58, NARA microfilm 1954, Relander Collection, box 63-5, YVL.
12. J. Orin Oliphant, ed., "Journals of the Indian War of 1855-1856", *The Washington Historical Quarterly* XV (January, 1924), 14.
13. *Weekly Oregonian*, November 25, 1855.
14. "Register of Deceased Soldiers, 1848-1861" (entry 97), Records of the Adjutant General's Office (RG 94), NARA; Waman C. Hembree, "Yakima War Diary", The Washington Historical Quarterly XVI, (October, 1925), 276, n 4.
15. Nesmith to Curry, November 19, 1855.
16. Granville O. Haller, "Kamiarkin in History: Memoir of the War in the Yakima Valley 1855-1856", manuscript, ND, 20, MSS P-A128, Bancroft Collection of Western Americana, University of California, Berkeley.
17. Macfeely to Wool, January 6, 1856.
18. Weekly *Oregonian*, November 25, 1855; Nesmith to Curry, November 19, 1855.
19. Oliphant, 29.
20. M. Maloney to Major G.J. Rains, October 29, 1855, in W.P. Bonney, *History of Pierce County Washington* 2 vols. (Chicago: Pioneer Historical Publishing Company, 1927), 1:177-8.
21. "War of 1855", McWhorter Papers, box 16, folder 128, MASC, WSU, Pullman.
22. Sheridan, 63.
23. Haller, "Kamiarkin in History", 21.
24. Typescript by Click Relander (ca. 1955) box 55, folder 19 YVL; a similar version can be found in Edward J. Kowrach, Mie. *Charles Pandosy O.M.I. A Missionary of the Northwest* (Fairfield, WA: Ye Galleon Press, 1992), 95-7.
25. G.J. Rains to Kam-i-ah-kan, November 13, 1855, RBIA, (RG 75) WS, misc. LR

August 22, 1853-April 9, 1861, NARA microfilm M5 Roll 23.

26. W.W. Mackall to Major G.J. Rains, August 30, 1856, War Dept. Letters Rec'd, 1854-58, Relander Collection, typescript, box 42-12, YVL.

27. Granville O. Haller, "The Indian War of 1855-6 in Washington and Oregon" typescript ca. 1894, ND, part 1, 6, box 2, acc. 3437-001, Granville O. Haller Papers, UW Libraries, Special Collections, Seattle, WA.

28. Weekly *Oregonian*, November 24, 1855, A.V. Wilson to Col. J.W. Nesmith.

29. Cpt. T.J. Cram, HED No. 114, 95.

30. G.J. Rains to Lieut. R. Arnold, April 27, 1856, (RG 98), NARA microfilm 1953, Relander Collection 63-11, typescript 43-3, YVL.

CHAPTER THREE

SHOCKWAVES WEST OF THE CASCADES 1855-56

ATTACKS AND COUNTER-ATTACKS AROUND PUGET SOUND

V iolence erupted west of the Cascade Mountains at the same time Major Rains prepared troops at Fort Dalles getting ready to invade the Yakima Valley more than 100 miles from Puget Sound.

Captain Maloney's soldiers had left Puget Sound's Fort Steilacoom expecting to cross the mountains and meet Rains in the Yakima Valley. Maloney arrived at the Naches River on October 27, 1855 several days ahead of Major Rains. That same afternoon near western Washington's White River, gunfire cut down militia lieutenant James McAllister and settler Michael Connell. They had been part of a detachment of civilian Puget Sound Rangers under the command of volunteer captain Charles H. Eaton trying to find and meet with Nisqually leader, Leschi, said to have "been preparing his band for active hostilities against the settlements."[1] Leschi's half- brother, Sehi, guided the rangers.

McAllister and Connell separated from the main party believing they could discuss matters peacefully with Leschi who they had known as neighbor, acquaintance and friend for years. But the two men were attacked and killed before they had a chance to meet with Leschi, and the surviving 11 rangers took cover inside an abandoned cabin barely managing to hold off an estimated 150 hostile warriors. The rangers reported seven of the attackers killed, but the militia's horses all were stolen. The following morning settlers' families were surprised and slain in their homes on White River approximately 30 miles south of Seattle. The dead included William H. Brannan, his wife Elizabeth and their infant child, Harvey H. Jones and his wife Eliza Jane, hired man Enos Cooper, and George E. King, his wife Mary and their infant child.[2] The incident became known thereafter as the White River

THEATRE OF WAR ON PUGET SOUND

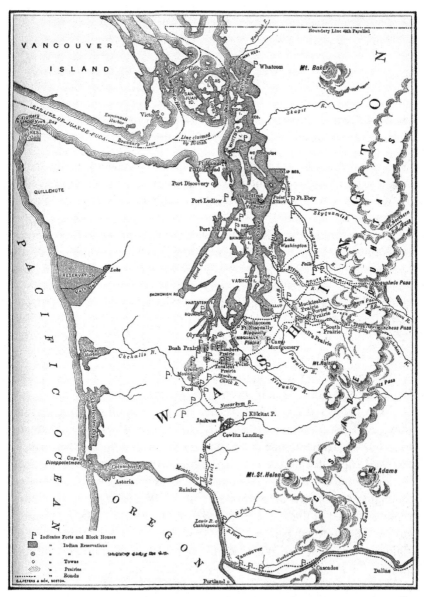

Hazard Stevens, The Life of Isaacc Ingalls Stevens, vol II, *(Boston: Houghton, Mifflin and Company, 172);*
Clinton A Snowden, History of Washington, vol. IV, *(New York: The Century History Company, 1909).*

Massacre. A six-year-old step-son of victim Harvey Jones along with a four-year-old and a two-year-old half sibling, managed to survive after being rescued by a Native friend, Tom Wiletchtid and another Native man, Dave, who delivered the children safely to Seattle.[3]

When Captain Maloney decided to turn back from the Naches River, he sent five militia guards and two express messengers ahead to advise Fort Steilacoom's acting commander, Lieutenant John Nugen that troops were on the way. The party included Colonel A. Benton Moses, Lieutenant Colonel Joseph Miles, Dr. Matthew Burns, former Lewis County Sheriff Antonio B. Rabbeson, George R. Bright, and express riders, Major William Tidd and Andrew J. Bradley.

Toward the evening of October 31, the men approached Connell's prairie near White River where they met a party of 150 warriors – possibly the same group that had attacked McAllister and Connell and the settlers on White River just three days earlier. Noting that Connell's cabin had recently burned the militia asked the warriors if they knew anything about it. None claimed knowledge, and the two groups went their separate ways.

A few minutes later, shots rang out in a muddy swamp about a mile and half from where the recent talk had taken place. Bullets hit Moses in the torso and Miles in the neck. William Tidd took three slugs to the head, but none penetrated his skull, and Tidd escaped with minor injuries. Miles died in the swamp while the others fled on horseback for a mile and a half until Moses became too weak from loss of blood to continue. The men concealed Moses in the brush before continuing on toward Steilacoom, except for Doctor Burns who charged off into the woods on his own to pursue a small band of Indians nearby.[4] Burns arrived safely at the settlements three or four days later without his horse, instruments and medicine bag all lost during his escape through the forest and underbrush.[5]

Captain Maloney's troops arrived at Connell's Prairie and recovered the bodies of McAllister, Miles and Moses. Connell was buried near his home place while the other victims were taken to the settlements. On November 3, Lieutenant Slaughter mounted 50 regular troops joined by 50 Puget Sound volunteers under Captain Gilmore Hays, and met approximately 200 warriors at White River. An eight-hour battle ensued with the army reporting 30 Indian fatalities documented by two of Slaughter's men observing from a hilltop. One soldier, Private

Arthur Kay, died during the fighting and another was wounded. Three days later Slaughter's men crossed the Puyallup River and came under fire again. The army's guide, John Edgar, a retired Hudson's Bay Company shepherd, died after being shot through the lungs.[6]

Eighty-four regular army soldiers arrived from California on November 24 to reinforce the troops at Fort Steilacoom. Lieutenant Slaughter went afield once again to the White River and Puyallup valleys accompanied by Company D of the Pierce County Volunteers under Captain W. H. Wallace. The soldiers found three more settler's homes burned, but this time the occupants escaped. While camped at night, the command lost 32 head of horses and mules stolen by warriors creeping through cover of fog and cutting picket ropes. On the morning of November 26, volunteer Elijah G. Price died after being shot while kneeling at the edge of a stream.

On the evening of December 4, Lieutenant William Slaughter, age 29 fell dead from a snipers bullet striking him in the heart while soldiers camped on Brannan's Prairie near the forks of the White and Green Rivers.[7] Also killed during the ambush were Corporal Ganett L. Barry of the 4th Infantry, Corporal Julian Clarendon of the volunteers, and U.S. Army private, John Cullum.[8] Slaughter had graduated from West Point in 1848, receiving an assignment to Washington Territory in 1852. His wife Mary had accompanied her husband from Michigan to Fort Steilacoom.

As winter set in, Qualchan joined the Puget Sound conflict leading 47 Yakamas and three Klickitat warriors over the Cascade Mountains on snowshoes to join his Nisqually relative, Leschi.[9] Leschi's Yakama mother was related to Chief Owhi, Qualchan's father.[10] The east side warriors participated in several fights around Puget Sound, and after a period of weeks returned over the mountains again on snowshoes, bringing with them a group of Nisqually people. At least one Yakama, Chief Kopt-chin-kin, died during the west side battles.

Most western Washington tribes had agreed to treaties with Governor Stevens before the war began. Only the Chehalis, Cowlitz and Chinook remained unsigned.[11] Indian Agent Wesley Gosnell identified the hostile factions living around Puget Sound. "Nisquallys and a portion of the Lower Puyallups, under Leschi and Quiemuth 65 warriors: The Green and White River Indians together with the disaffected of the Upper Duwamish, under Nelson and Kitsap, 35 warriors: The Klickitats and their relatives, west of the mountains, living on and near the head of Green and White rivers, under Kenaskut 55 warriors: and the Upper Puyallups, under Quilquilton, 20 warriors."[12] Gosnell also observed that some tribesmen participated in the war out of fear that powerful east side tribes would kill or make slaves of those who refused. Many on the west side stayed peaceful, including Chief Seattle representing Duwamish and Suquamish tribes. Pacific Coast tribes from the Quinault River to Neah Bay, along with tribes near Bellingham Bay, remained far enough away from Puget Sound disturbances to avoid the conflict.

A state of alarm prevailed through most of the territory. White residents near Fort Steilacoom abandoned their homes and sought refuge at the military post. Others fled from the territory never to return. For those who remained, settlers and militia constructed dozens of blockhouses for protection throughout the region. Regular army troops built four temporary forts near trouble spots along the Puyallup River and Green River.[13] Farmers served in the militia while their families sought safety in and around the blockhouses. Fires set by renegades destroyed most of the houses abandoned by pioneer families. Some help arrived from James Douglas, governor of nearby Vancouver Island (a British possession), who dispatched Hudson's Bay Company steamer *Otter* to cruise Puget Sound's coastline and help defend American neighbors. Douglas also provided a large supply of arms, powder and ammunition for use by Washington Territory Volunteers.

On January 25, 1856, friendly Indians brought word to 120 or so settlers residing around the fledgling town of Seattle that a large number of hostile Indians had crossed Lake Washington in canoes preparing to attack. In the town's favor, a United States ship, *Decatur*, with 14 cannons and 145 sailors and marines, happened to be anchored near Yesler's landing.[14] Thick forest along the east edge of town hid an unknown number of warriors when the battle broke out at 7:30 a.m. on January 26. Fighting lasted throughout most of the day ending about 3:30 in the afternoon. The attackers did not charge the settlement due to heavy fire coming from the ship's cannons and a howitzer placed near the town's entrance, but Indians kept up steady rifle fire from the woods, killing two civilians, Milton Holgate and Christian White.[15] Despite the ship's heavy bombardment, there were no apparent

Indian fatalities according to eyewitness, Henry Yesler, and Yakama participant, To-ki-aken Twi-wash. Others guessed about additional fatalities, but no bodies other than the two civilians were confirmed.

The first week of February, 1856, territorial officials recruited Snoqualmie Chief Patkanim (Pat Kanim) to join the territory's militia, assigning him the title of captain.[16] Muster rolls identified Patkanim's regiment consisting of a chief, 11 sub-chiefs and 68 privates who earned up to $116 each for two months service.[17] Patkanim was said to have thrown his support behind the government after taking a voyage by ship to San Francisco in 1852. The site of thousands of white people and great numbers of ships and houses in California caused the chief to realize that Americans were too numerous to oppose.[18]

Indian Agent Michael T. Simmons accompanied Patkanim as far as Snoqualmie Falls before the chief took his warriors to hunt down and attack Leschi and his accomplices. On February 8, Patkanim captured three Klickitats on the Snoqualmie River. He executed two of them and kept the third as an informant. On February 16, the Snoqualmies found and attacked Leschi's camp on the White River.[19] Nine of Leschi's men were killed, and Patkanim lost five by the end of the day.[20] Elwood Evans, a historian, editor and lawyer who lived in Olympia during the 1850s, reported, "During the war he (Patkanim) brought to Olympia the heads of two alleged hostile chiefs as an evidence of his loyalty."[21] Money, blankets and other goods rewarded the chief for his efforts. Other less active Indian auxiliaries also assisted the territorial militia even though some of them had not signed a treaty. They were the Chehalis under Captain Ford, Cowlitz under Pierre Charles, and Squaxon under agent, Lieutenant Wesley Gosnell.[22]

A teamster, William Northcraft, who worked for the territory's quartermaster, was shot and killed on February 24, near Steilacoom. Two days later, an army sentinel struck a severe blow against the warring tribes when he fatally shot Klickitat Chief Kanasket near the Puyallup River.[23] The loss of Kanasket's fierce presence and the departure of Qualchan's braves significantly dampened the spirit and resolve of tribal resistance in the Puget Sound area.

Army Private David Reitman died March 1 during a fight near the Puyallup River and Muckleshoot Prairie while serving under Captain Erasmus Keyes. William White was attacked and killed on March 2 while returning home from church on Chambers Prairie. The tide turned further against the tribes on March 10 when Major Gilmore Hays' 100 volunteers routed some 150 warriors during a seven-hour fight at Connell's Prairie. The militia confirmed two enemy bodies found and evidence of many more wounded and carried away.[24] One of the participants, then-lieutenant Urban E. Hicks, admitted in his memoirs that Thurston County Volunteers had shot at women near the scene who were described as "beating drums, dancing and yelling and otherwise encouraging their men."[25] The March 10 fight would be the last significant battle from warriors west of the Cascade Mountains. Puget Sound chiefs Leschi, Nelson and Kitsap left the region and joined Qulachan in the Yakima Valley taking refuge away from military pressure that persisted west of the Cascades.

Action against the tribes around Puget Sound increased when Captain Hamilton J. G. Maxon's company of mounted rifles from Clark County scouted the Nisqually River Valley looking for hostiles and any Native people that had not yet reported to a reservation. Maxon's roster included three paid Indians, Wallas, Frank and Andy. Those not yet under the supervision of an Indian agent were considered hostile. Also, some settlers with Native wives had been suspected of providing aid to hostile warriors. Territorial officials worried about loyalty of former Hudson's Bay Company employees who seemed to enjoy relative safety while other settlers became victims of hostilities. Between March 30 and April 1 near Ollala Lake and the Mashel River, Maxon's men attacked and killed eight Nisqually men and took two other men, two women and some children captive.[26]

Volunteers had orders from Governor Stevens to bring as many Indians as they could gather to the reservation opposite Fort Steilacoom. On April 3, 1856, Maxon's men also took prisoner a group of former Hudson's Bay Company employees that Governor Stevens suspected of furnishing supplies and harboring hostiles. The prisoners were taken to Olympia, and then transferred and locked up in the Fort Steilacoom guardhouse.[27] Regular army troops also captured several Nisqually families. On April 13, Lieutenant August V. Kautz brought in seven males and eleven women and children. They joined 17 other men and more than 20 women and children that had been taken to the reservation by army personnel earlier the same week.[28] Lieutenant Colonel Silas Casey held eight additional prisoners at Fort Steilacoom identified by Nisqually informants as the killers of William White and Northcraft. Casey asked for Governor Stevens' assistance as Superintendent of Indian Affairs to provide clothing for the captives who had arrived in poor condition[29]

About a year later, Lieutenant Kautz wrote that a band of Nisqually had informed him that women and children had been killed during Maxon's attack at the Mashel River in March. Only two women had been captured according to Andrew J. Kane's eyewitness report, leaving open the possibility that more women may have accompanied the eight slain men and may have been killed but not documented by the volunteers.[30] A credible eyewitness description of a massacre came from another unit, that of Urban E. Hicks who had been promoted to captain of the Pioneer Company from Thurston County. Hicks' company was in the field around the base of Mt. Rainier at approximately the same time Maxon was at Mashel River. Hicks wrote in his memoirs that his men approached a Native encampment and "shot down, big and little, squaws and all."[31]

One of the most destructive episodes of the war began March 26, 1856 when an estimated 100 to 200 warriors swooped down on the Cascades settlement along the Columbia River killing 14 civilians and 3 soldiers. Some Native and white residents claimed that Yakama and Klickitat made up the majority of assailants, but unlike other incidents between 1855 and 1858, sources left out names of participants and leaders involved. At one point military officers and a group of Klickitats blamed Kamiakin for orchestrating the raid.[32] But Kamiakin typically directed his aggression toward military targets not civilians. The chief often received credit and blame for incidents whether he participated in them or not. Perhaps the death of unarmed civilians discouraged revealing actual identities, or maybe no prominent chiefs participated. The Cascades attack became known as a massacre because it took the lives of a woman, a boy, and several non-combatants including laborers, carpenters and deckhands. Nearly all settlers' homes were burned. Of the 50 or so Cascade village men living near the settlement, approximately 15 were suspected to have joined the assault. Nine, including Chief Chenowith, were charged as accomplices and hanged by the U.S. Army. One was taken prisoner, and five more ran off with the unnamed perpetrators. Other Cascade Indians had lived peacefully among white neighbors for years performing useful labor hauling and portaging supplies around the Cascades rapids.

Yet another atrocity against non-combatants occurred when members of an innocent family belonging to peaceful Klickitat Chief William Spencer were found slain by strangulation shortly after the Cascades attack. Members of the group had obtained passes from Colonel Wright to take a steamship from Cascades to Vancouver but were accosted while walking to the steamboat landing. The victims included Spencer's wife, father and child, a man –Scow-ites– and a daughter of "Umtux".[33] The father of one of the victims, Chief Umtuch of the Taitnapam band (Upper Cowlitz/Klickitat), had earlier been accidently shot and killed by his own men in late October north of Fort Vancouver.[34] No one was charged or convicted of killing the Native non-combatants although it was suspected that vengeful white relatives of victims from the Cascades Massacre had been responsible.

The Cascades surprise attack began at 8 a.m. Wednesday March 26 at Upper landing, one of three stations known as Upper, Middle and Lower Cascades along a four-mile stretch of rapids on the Columbia River. A line of warriors concealed in dense woods north of the settlement opened fire on civilians as they began their day of work. The first shots killed operators at a sawmill at the mouth of nearby Mill Creek, B. W. Brown, his wife Mrs. Brown, sawyer Jacob White and a man named Calderwood. Two men driving a team, Jimmy Watkins and Norman Palmer, also died. Two other wounded men ran to the steamship, *Mary*, docked at the mouth of Mill Creek. One of them, Montoui Bourbon, died of his wounds. The other, John Chance, survived being shot in the leg and fought back by killing an attacker with a pistol. Engineer Buckminster shot another attacker with a revolver on the ship's gangplank. The cook, Dick Turpin, jumped into the water after being shot and drowned.

The ship's fireman, Hardin Chenowith, succeeded in building up enough steam to sail the boat away. Chenowith climbed up from the engine room to the pilot house and steered the *Mary* toward The Dalles where he expected to find help from soldiers stationed there. The ship's captain, Dan Baughman, and its first officer, Thompson, both unarmed, had been on shore hauling lines when they came under fire. The two men took cover in the woods and remained away from the boat to avoid being shot.[35]

Residents fled from their homes seeking refuge at Bradford's Store, a two-story building where there were a few rifles, some ammunition and enough room to hold 40 defenders. Mr. Bush shot one attacker while women and children ran toward the building. Several men working on two bridges nearby also made a dash for the store. Three other men, George Watkins, M. Bailey, and a Mr. Finley were finishing a new warehouse on an island directly across from Bradford's. The men became trapped after warriors paddled across in canoes from the mainland. All three workers ran toward the water in front of the store. Bailey, shot in the arm and leg, plunged into the river and swam across safely. Finley also swam across untouched through a hail of bullets. Watkins had been shot in the wrist with a bullet that exited his elbow. The wounded man hid behind a large rock while defenders inside the store tried to keep attackers away. But he could not be rescued for two more days and eventually died from his injuries. At the store, James Sinclair peered out the back door. A single bullet struck him in the head killing him instantly. Sinclair had recently arrived at the Cascades to escape hostilities around Fort Walla Walla where he had been employed by the Hudson's Bay Company.

Assailants threw firebrands on the roof attempting to burn the store down. People inside removed embers by sweeping them away, cutting away part of the roof, and pouring pork brine on the flames. Survivors watched in horror as their homes, sawmill and new warehouse in the distance burned to the ground. Henry Hagar, who had been shot in the Watkins house, burned to death inside the building. Lack of water for those trapped in the store became a problem when it was discovered that only a few bottles of ale and whiskey remained inside. At night, teenager John McBean, who had been traveling with Sinclair, volunteered to slip down to the river under cover of darkness and bring back a pail of water.[36] Next morning the attack resumed with shots exchanged throughout the day. The second night, young McBean managed to bring back enough water to fill two barrels.

When Upper Cascades first came under attack, gunfire broke out simultaneously at Middle Cascades approximately one and a half miles downstream. A blockhouse there had been guarded by a small detachment of nine U.S. soldiers. All were outdoors doing various tasks when the shooting began. Private O. McManus immediately received a mortal wound to the groin. Seven other soldiers retreated to the blockhouse joined by members of three families running for their lives. George Griswold, disbelieving that his former Native friends had turned hostile, received a mortal wound while waving at nearby warriors attempting to get them to cease fire. Young Jake Kyle, a German boy, was shot from his horse about 100 yards from the blockhouse. He lay wounded on the ground until attackers finished him off with arrows. The ninth soldier, Private Laurence Rooney, had been separated some distance from the blockhouse while cutting firewood. He died after being captured, stripped, and tortured. His fellow soldiers had to listen to Rooney's cries of agony outside while the others stayed inside the blockhouse defending it with rifles and six pounder cannon.

At Lower Cascades, two and a half miles farther downstream, residents heard reports from the cannon at the blockhouse, but because of routine blasting taking place during road building the previous week, the explosions did not cause alarm.[37] A friendly Indian, Jack, warned the settlers that an attack was underway at Middle Cascades. A group made up mostly of women and children then boarded a bateau schooner fixed with a sail and set off down river. A few men stayed behind temporarily to ward off attackers but soon left in a second craft after realizing the crisis was beyond their control. Refugees on the first boat were met by steamers *Belle* and *Fashion* navigating upriver from Fort Vancouver. Upon learning of the urgency ahead, the crew on the steamers took the bateau in tow and turned back down river to pick up soldiers at the fort nearly 40 miles away.

The first help arrived the next morning, March 27, when Lieutenant Philip Sheridan and 40 soldiers from Vancouver reached the lower landing aboard the steamship *Belle*. But troops found themselves outnumbered. Sheridan's men spent the day skirmishing with hostiles, losing one man killed, and unable to rescue those trapped at the blockhouse and Bradford's store. On the morning of March 28, Sheridan began transporting his soldiers by bateau from the Oregon side to the north bank about a mile below the blockhouse.[38] While hostiles watched Sheridan's men crossing the river, steamships *Mary* and *Wasco* loaded with U.S. soldiers arrived unseen from The Dalles at upper Cascades. Lieutenant Colonel Edward Steptoe's troops, numbering more than 200 men, rushed from the boat to free the settlers trapped at Bradford's Store. The army may have completed a rout of the hostiles had not Sheridan's men spotted reinforcements on the ground and shouted out a hearty cheer. Steptoe's men answered with a bugle call, and the warriors quickly disappeared into the woods.[39]

The local Cascade band found itself abandoned and left to face military justice alone. Colonel George Wright conducted a military commission examining evidence and hearing testimony from cooperative local Indians. Nine Cascade men, including their chief, Chenowith, were found guilty of murdering civilians and hanged for the crimes.

Weary citizens in the territory had been terrorized since October and expressed impatience at the seemingly slow response by the U.S. Army and its regional commander, General John E. Wool. A newspaper column from the *Pioneer and Democrat* in Olympia reflected a common editorial attitude of the day. "Gen. Kamiakin versus Gen. Wool – The attack of the Indians upon the Cascades shows that Kamiakin is a better general than Wool. After Wool has been preparing five months to move into the Indian country, he loses his first depot-has to stop his advance, and make a retrograde movement of half his force to recapture it and re-open his line of communication. Why was the Cascades left so unprotected? Is there now an Indian war in Oregon?"[40]

The Cascades attack came unexpectedly for the military. General Wool had spent the winter raising hundreds of troops brought in from the east coast and California to address the crisis and had effectively shut down violence in Puget Sound. The general was in the process of moving troops to the Walla Walla Valley where he intended to displace Oregon Mounted Volunteers who had been active there since December. The Cascades attack, however, made it necessary to change plans and focus military attention directly on the Yakima Valley.

Chapter 3 notes

1. (Olympia, WA) *Pioneer and Democrat*, November 9, 1855, J.W. Wiley to George B. Goudy October 30, 1855.

2. *Pioneer and Democrat*, November 16, 1855, Christopher C. Hewitt, letter November 5, 1855; Werner Lenggenhager, *Historical Markers and Monuments of the State of Washington,* vol. 1, (Seattle, WA: Seattle Public Library, 1965), 18.

3. Emily Inez Denny, *Blazing the Way True Stories, Songs and Sketches of Puget Sound and other Pioneers,* (Seattle, WA: Rainier Printing Company, 1909), 91-5; Stan Flewelling, "One Pioneer Family's Story of War in the White River Valley", *White River Journal* – A Newsletter of the White River Valley Museum (April 1998).

4. *Pioneer and Democrat*, November 9, 1855, Letter from A.B. Rabbeson.

5. *Pioneer and Democrat*, November 9, 1855, Letter from Dr. Burns.

6. Cpt. M. Maloney to Hon. C.H. Mason, November 6, 1855 in William P. Bonney, *History of Pierce County Washington*, 2 vols., (Chicago, IL: Pioneer Historical Publishing Company, 1927), 1:183-7; "Register of Deceased Soldiers, 1848-1861" (entry 97) RG 94, Records of the Adjutant General's Office, NARA.

7. Elwood Evans, *History of the Pacific Northwest Oregon and Washington*, 2 vols., (Portland, OR: North Pacific History Company, 1889), 1:547

8. John A. Hemphill, *West Pointers and Early Washington*, (Seattle, WA: West Point Society of Puget Sound, 1992),129.

9. "Smat-lowits"s Story of Yakima War", L.V McWhorter Papers, Cage 55, B 45 F 434, MASC, WSU Libraries, Pullman, WA.

10. G. Wright to Capt. D.R. Jones, June 11, 1856 in William N. Bischoff, "The Yakima Campaign of 1856", *Mid-America*, 31, reprint 20 (1949), 188; *Pioneer and Democrat*, March 27, 1857, "Evidence and Proceedings in the Case of Leschi", Dr. Wm F. Tolmie.

11. Kent D. Richards, *Isaac I. Stevens Young Man in a Hurry*, (Pullman, WA: WSU Press, 1993), 197-208.

12. Wesley B. Gosnell, "Documents-Indian War in Washington Territory-Special Agent W.B. Gosnell's Report in 1856", *The Washington Historical Quarterly* 17 (October, 1926): 294-7.

13. J.S. Whiting, *Forts of the State of Washington*, (Seattle, WA: J.S. Whiting, 1951), 4-6.

14. Bernard C. Nalty and Truman R. Strobridge, "The Defense of Seattle, 1856", *Pacific Northwest Quarterly* 55 (July, 1964): 105-10.

15. *Pioneer and Democrat,* February 1, 1856, "The Indian War!!"

16. Edmond S. Meany, "Chief Patkanim", *The Washington Historical Quarterly* 15 (July 1924): 196.

17. "Muster Roll of Friendly Indians of Snohomish and Scanamish Tribes, under the chiefs, Pat Kanim and John Taylor, regiment of Washington Territory Volunteers", Biennial Report of the Adjutant General of the State of Washington for the Years 1891 and 1892, appendix, schedule B, Olympia, Wash., 1893, 173-4, WSL.

18. James Gilchrist Swan, *The Northwest Coast Or, Three Years' Residence in Washington Territory,* (New York: Harper & Brothers, 1857) reprint (Seattle, WA: UW Press, 1992), 396.

19. Evans, 1:576-7.

20. Swan, 396.

21. Evans, 2:513.

22. Bonney, 1:208.

23. Erasmus D. Keyes, *Fifty Years Observation of Men and Events*, (New York: Scribner, 1884) reprinted as, *Fighting Indians in Washington Territory*, (Fairfield, WA: Ye Galleon Press, 1988), 10-14.

24. Bonney, 1:201-5.
25. Capt. Urban E. Hicks, *Yakima and Clickitat Indian Wars 1855 and 1856*, (Portland, OR: Himes the Printer, 1886), 11.
26. *Pioneer and Democrat*, April 11, 1856, A.J. Kane; Evans, 1:579-80.
27. Evans, 1:579-81.
28. Lt. Col. Silas Casey to Gov. I.I. Stevens, April 13, 1856, William Winlock Miller Collection, Yale Collection of Western Americana, Beinecke Rare Book and Manuscript Library, New Haven: CT, in William N. Bischoff S.J. Microfilm Collection, Special Collections, Foley Center, Gonzaga University, Spokane, WA.
29. Casey to Stevens, April 28, 1856, Miller Collection.
30. "Mashel (sometimes Maxon) Massacre", Washington Department of Archaeology and Historic Preservation, www.historylink.org.
31. Hicks, 16.
32. G. Wright to W.W. Mackall, July 27, 1856, in Bischoff (1949), 204-5.
33. H. Field, Local Indian Agent, Vancouver W.T. May 12, 1856, RBIA (RG 75), WS, Letters from employees assigned to the Columbia River or southern district and Yakima Agency 1854-1861, NARA microfilm M5 Roll 17.
34. Chief Stwire Waters in Charles Miles and O.B. Sperlin, eds. *Building A State: Washington 1889-1939*, (Tacoma, WA: Washington State Historical Society, 1940), 512-14; Lieut. Jno Withers to Colonel S. Cooper, November 12, 1855, HED No. 93, 14.
35. J.H. Herman, Lawrence W. Coe, Robert Williams, "The Cascade Massacre Told by Three Different Eye-Witnesses", *Oregon Native Son* (February, 1900): 495-505.
36. D. Geneva Lent, *West of the Mountains-James Sinclair and the Hudson's Bay Company*, (Seattle, WA: UW Press, 1963), 286.
37. F.M. Sebring, "The Indian Raid on the Cascades in March, 1856", *The Washington Historical Quarterly* 19 (April, 1928): 99-107.
38. Philip H. Sheridan, *Personal Memoirs of P.H. Sheridan*, 2 vols. (New York: Jenkins & McCowan, 1888), 1:74-80.
39. James J. Archer Letters, March 30, 1856, Relander Collection, typescript 40-2, microfilm 62-1, YVL.
40. *Pioneer and Democrat,* April 4, 1856, "Gen. Kamiakin versus Gen. Wool".

CHAPTER FOUR

Battles of Walla Walla and Satus Creek
1855 - 56

OREGON VOLUNTEERS' INVASION OF EASTERN WASHINGTON

Oregon Mounted Volunteers and their U.S. Army companions emerged less than victorious after the episode at Two Buttes in mid-November 1855. No decisive battle occurred; however, soldiers did succeed in driving Yakama families temporarily from their homes and destroying winter food supplies. After the soldiers left, the Yakamas returned somewhat damaged, but not beaten.

Most of the regular army wintered in barracks at Fort Dalles and Fort Vancouver waiting for reinforcements to arrive from the Atlantic states and California, along with badly needed boots, clothing and fresh horses. The citizen volunteers waited for no one. Territorial governors kept volunteers in the field planning to strike warring tribes and demand surrender regardless of season or weather. Oregon volunteers set off for Walla Walla on November 12 with Captain Orlando Humason's Company B, and Captain Davis Layton's Company H under command of Major Mark A. Chinn at the same time other companies were operating against the Yakamas. Volunteers targeted Walla Walla because of alarm expressed by Indian Agent Nathan Olney and others who saw signs that neighboring tribes had gathered there to join the war. Antoine Placie, a "half breed" settler who had been married to Peo Peo Mox Mox's late daughter Angelique, witnessed a hundred warriors dancing around an American scalp believed to have come from the Haller battle, and brought to the chief's lodge near the mouth of the Yakima River.[1] Peo Peo Mox Mox had told Placie he intended to go to war against the whites and the chief refused to meet with Nathan Olney despite the agent's requests. Olney wrote that he feared a major outbreak was about to happen and he would throw all ammunition at

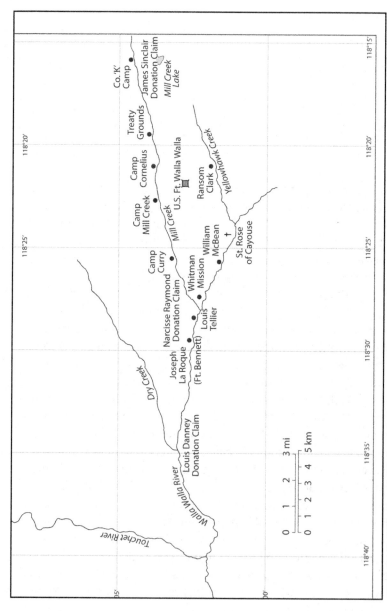

Walla Walla Valley and Mill Creek became areas of war activity beginning with the invasion by Oregon Mounted Volunteers in December of 1855.

Hudson's Bay Fort Walla Walla into the Columbia River to keep it out of hostile hands.[2]

As Chinn's 150 men approached the Umatilla River in mid-November they received a letter sent by messenger from Narcisse Raymond, a French settler married to a Walla Walla woman, warning that local tribes had seized Fort Walla Walla, burned neighboring buildings and awaited OMV's arrival with 1,000 warriors.[3]

The major decided to halt at the Umatilla River and construct a temporary fort of cottonwood logs, naming it Henrietta in honor of Major Haller's wife, who had donated a wagon to the cause. The volunteers waited for reinforcements expected to arrive after other companies returned from Two Buttes. But severe weather crossing the Simcoe Mountains delayed the soldiers' return and diminished the number of troops and horses fit to proceed to Walla Walla. One-hundred twenty-five of the men returning from the Yakima Valley received discharges and went home. Others expected to recover were assigned scouting duties around The Dalles. Volunteer Lieutenant Colonel James K. Kelly, a 36-year-old lawyer from Pennsylvania who had moved to Oregon City in 1851, managed to prepare four companies, A, F, I and K to join Chinn and companies B and H at Fort Henrietta.

On a cold, rainy night, December 2, 1855, Kelly and 339 men rode from Fort Henrietta through the darkness expecting to slip unseen upon 1,000 warriors at Fort Walla Walla. But the volunteers arrived to find the post ransacked and deserted. No strong force contested the soldiers. Only about 40 warriors dashed away after skirmishing for a while with the new arrivals.

Two days later, Kelly led 200 of his men up the Touchet River looking for hostiles, while the remaining volunteers guarded baggage and pack animals at the Touchet's junction with the Walla Walla River. After advancing approximately 12 miles, Kelly confronted a group of about 70 warriors. Seven of them approached under a white flag led by the renowned Walla Walla Chief, Peo Peo Mox Mox. A conversation took place with the help of Nathan Olney's Des Chutes interpreter, Sababoo, and 17-year-old John McBean, a Walla Walla Valley resident and son of retired Hudson's Bay Company chief trader William McBean and his wife, Jane Boucher.[4] The chief announced that he did not wish to fight and claimed that he had done nothing wrong. Kelly reminded the chief that he had been seen by cooperative Cayuse Chief Howlish Wampoo and Walla Walla Chief Pierre Mowatit distributing looted items from Fort Walla Walla. The amount of goods stolen was substantial, including 534 blankets valued at $5,874, thousands of yards of cloth and fabric, more than two tons of flour, sugar, coffee, bacon and tobacco, along with hundreds of fur pelts, tools and utensils, 77 horses and 10 cattle.[5] Eyewitnesses also reported offenders setting fire to settlers' buildings.

The colonel announced that he was there to "chastise" wrongdoers.[6] Kelly gave the chief two options. Peo Peo Mox Mox could stay with the OMV troops until warriors surrendered their arms and ammunition, or he could return to his people and be promptly attacked. The chief chose reluctantly to stay with the troops and agreed to restore the value of stolen items and provide Kelly with horses and cattle to sustain volunteers while they fought against the tribes that continued to refuse to surrender. One hostage was sent as a messenger to announce the terms to nearby warriors.

No surrender occurred the following day, nor had the chief's messenger returned as promised. A Walla Walla village nearby was found to have been hastily abandoned. Kelly decided on December 6 to march with Peo Peo Mox Mox back to camp at the mouth of the Touchet and re-join the volunteers left there guarding the baggage. They planned to move the entire command up the Walla Walla River to a fresh camp site near the abandoned Whitman's Station. At night, one of the hostages attempted to escape, but was run down by guards and recaptured after a 100 yard foot chase. Kelly ordered all hostages tied for the evening, with instructions to be unbound at daylight. He warned the chief that the next man attempting to escape would be shot.

On the morning of December 7 the hills in the distance were seen filled with "a considerable force" of armed and mounted Indians.[7] Warriors that had gathered in the area came from more than the Walla Walla tribe. Also present were Stock Whitley's band of Des Chutes from Oregon, several Cayuse, Umatilla and a number of Palouse.[8] Those tribes also had chiefs who did not participate and were considered peaceful.[9] Kelly sent envoys under a white flag offering to release the Walla Walla chief in exchange for surrender. The other chiefs refused, and Stock Whitley warned the volunteers not to move camp. Kelly insisted upon moving upriver where his troops and stock could access fresh forage, wood, water and more time to negotiate with the reluctant chiefs.

The pace began leisurely at first because the volunteers did not expect to be attacked while holding hostages. Some disagreement took place over what happened next. Kelly and four of his officers later testified that two volunteers in advance of the main party came under fire while herding loose cattle.[10] Nathan Olney at first reported the volunteers were attacked, then later stated he thought the volunteers may have fired first because "it was evident the Indians did not meditate an attack, for they were at the same time preparing the morning meal."[11] In either event some 50 volunteers mounted on the command's swiftest horses charged and chased a sizeable group of warriors for nearly ten miles up the Walla Walla River. The braves halted near Joseph La Rocque's abandoned cabin where they received reinforcements from newly arriving warriors and made a stand behind cover of surrounding brush and low hills.

A spirited fight commenced that resulted in the death of Lieutenant J. M. Burrows of Company H and the wounding of three others. The remaining volunteers galloped up to the scene with hostages in tow. As more shots rang out, Kelly ordered the six prisoners tied and told guards to shoot any that tried to escape. Five of the captives, understandably agitated by the fighting going on around them, did resist. Peo Peo Mox Mox, known to be a strong and proud man, grabbed a rifle held by Samuel Warfield and attempted to wrest it from the guard's hands. Warfield managed to pull back and fired a shot that missed the chief. The guard next swung the empty gun, striking a fatal blow with the barrel against the chief's skull. Other hostages were immediately shot except for Nez Perce youth Billy who quickly offered to be tied.[12] A bayonet charge by volunteers scattered the warriors and the fight moved two miles upstream to Louis Tellier's farmhouse where tribesmen fortified themselves behind the buildings' walls. Here witnesses gave credit to bold warriors for "holding their ground well" and fighting "bravely face to face."[13]

Volunteers stormed the cabin but lost Captain Charles Bennett of Company F and Private Andrew Kelso of Company A, both killed during the battle. Fighting continued two more days taking the lives of Private Simon Van Hagerman, Private Henry Crow and Private Jesse

Fleming. Eventually reinforcement companies D and E arrived from The Dalles and Fort Henrietta bringing fresh troops and ammunition on December 10 causing the last of the opponents to withdraw. Kelly reported 39 enemy bodies found. Sam Warfield explained after hearing about the fate of William C. Andrews who had been shot and scalped while guarding horses a week earlier at Fort Henrietta, volunteers vowed to scalp their victims as well.[14] Sam did just that with Peo Peo Mox Mox, and to add to OMV's controversial reputation, Dr. R. W. Shaw reportedly pulled the chief from his shallow grave, and dismembered the body.[15] Some men were said to have taken body parts as souvenirs. Souvenir-taking from the dead was not necessarily new. When volunteers responded to the Whitman massacre in 1847 some of them collected specimens of Narcissa Whitman's attractive blonde hair that had been scattered across the ground by predators.[16] Once again tribes were driven from winter homes, but this time volunteers resolved to stay in the field until they could obtain total surrender.

Squads of volunteers spent the following week rounding up corn, wheat, potatoes, squash, hogs and other food from abandoned homesteads of retired fur company employees. They also gathered loose cattle found roaming the area. The encampment near La Rocque's house had been converted to a hospital and fortified with cottonwood logs as a temporary fort named for the late Captain Bennett. Trampling hooves and battle activity had beaten the ground into mud and fouled the area with dead bodies and cattle entrails.

Volunteers packed up December 15 and moved to a fresh camp site at Mill Creek about two miles above Whitman's station where there was ample wood and grass. They named the place Camp Curry in honor of Oregon's territorial governor.[17] Major Chinn issued an order on December 16 prohibiting volunteers from looting settlers' farms because over-zealous men had taken more than food. Lieutenant Colonel Kelly helped make up for some of the losses six months later by supplying displaced families with flour, coffee, sugar and salt from the OMV commissary.[18]

On December 19 the volunteers elected Thomas Cornelius, 28, to the position of colonel in place of James Nesmith who had earlier resigned. Kelly took a temporary leave of absence to participate in the territorial legislature at Salem. A party left for The Dalles taking with them sick and wounded men and the remains of Captain Bennett.

Governor Stevens arrived at the Oregon Volunteer's camp on December 20 after completing an arduous trip across the snow covered Bitterroot Mountains after treating with Blackfeet and conferencing but not making a treaty with the Spokane, Coeur d'Alene and Colville. He was greeted by rousing cheers and a series of rifle salutes. The governor gave a speech encouraging volunteers to carry on the fight against hostiles and persevere through the winter. After Stevens left, temperatures plunged below zero, and men shivered in tents under one or two wool blankets each. Captain Absalom J. Hembree wrote from a frozen camp on December 27, 1855, "We will never give up the ship till the last red-skin is whipped."[19]

The Walla Walla Valley held 150 or so friendly Indians who did not intend to go to war against Americans. The Oregon volunteers safeguarded those peaceful families in addition to about 90 French residents who had no place to go. Company K set up camp next to the refugees on Mill Creek three miles above the treaty grounds and approximately ten miles from the main party at Camp Curry. The unit consisted mostly of French and Metis volunteers under the leadership of Captain Narcisse Cornoyer, Lieutenant Antoine Rivais and Lieutenant Thomas Small. They provided protection and companionship for the settlers and Natives who resided with Cayuse Chiefs Howlish Wampoo, Stickus and Tintinmetzey, and Walla Walla Chief Pierre Mowatit.

Narcisse Raymond, who was married to a Walla Walla woman, provided Governor Stevens with a list of peaceful or "good" Indians.[20] Victor Trevitt, an Oregon resident selected by Nathan Olney to assist with Indian affairs, also kept Oregon superintendent Joel Palmer apprised of the friendly Indians' status at Walla Walla.[21] Raymond soon joined the Washington militia as a lieutenant from January 11 to February 10, 1856, along with his neighbors William McBean, Joseph LaRoque, Louis Tellier, Antoine Placie, John McBean and 23 other Walla Walla Valley residents. Their captain, Sidney S. Ford, was a Chehalis settler and Indian agent temporarily transferred to The Dalles, also a confidant of Governor Stevens.[22] Three local Cayuse chiefs assisted settlers by hiding cattle for them in the Blue Mountains and keeping livestock out of hostile hands. Lloyd Brooke later paid the chiefs $300 for returning 21 head of his cattle.[23]

Brooke and his partners, George Bomford and John Noble had formed a partnership in February 1853 just days before President Millard Fillmore signed a bill creating Washington Territory. The three men set up a trading company and cattle operation on the old Whitman Mission site after obtaining a license from then-Superintendent of Indian Affairs, Anson Dart.[24] At the time war broke out in 1855 the partnership had expanded northward and staked out three claims of 320 acres each next to the Touchet River about six miles west of the future town of Dayton. These three and Henry M. Chase also on the Touchet, plus cattleman J. C. Smith on Dry Creek and newly arrived Ransom Clark on Yellowhawk Creek were about the only residents in the Walla Walla Valley who were not associated with the Hudson's Bay Company or related to a tribal member.[25] Two white men, Frank Tolman and John Whitford, married to Cayuse women, contributed to the tribal unrest. Tolman helped others set fire to Brooke's buildings, and Whitford, who had been an interpreter at the 1855 treaty council, tried to convince others to shoot Narcisse Raymond in revenge for the five Cayuses hanged in 1850 convicted of conducting the Whitman massacre.[26]

On December 28, 1855, a pack train brought Oregon volunteers 800 pounds of flour and 100 pounds of tobacco. Another supply train followed on January 2, accompanied by Adjutant William Farrar, U.S. district attorney for Oregon, who assisted Colonel Cornelius with administrative duties. Journals and letters from some of the volunteers complained of dwindling supplies and delayed deliveries from a territorial commissary that never seemed to keep up with demand. Pack trains arrived every few days but did not seem to provide enough to satisfy expectations of those who served in the field. Challenges included supplies having to be transported by ox teams from Fort Henrietta and The Dalles after being shipped by boat from Portland.

Men spent most of the month of January scouting in small groups for loose cattle to supplement food supplies and wild horses to be broken for riding and packing. Twenty-five of the captured cattle were later determined to have belonged to Lloyd Brooke who was compensated $400 by OMV for the loss.[27] Thomas Cornelius reported to the governor that friendly Cayuse were also compensated for their confiscated cattle at prices, "The same as allowed to our own citizens."[28]

On January 6, 1856, the main camp moved farther east to a new location named Camp Mill Creek. A scouting trip led by Captain Absalom J. Hembree reported that a large winter encampment of Indians was located at the junction of Snake River and Columbia River. On January 31, another pack train arrived carrying clothing and provisions. At the beginning of February, messengers brought additional information that Kamiakin had joined forces with those at the mouth of the Snake River bringing the total number of Indians estimated to be there from 1,000 to 1,500. Colonel Cornelius ordered work parties on February 4 to cut timber and whip-saw logs to build corrals and construct six boats needed to transport soldiers across the Snake River in the spring. Officers stayed busy holding courts-martial and boards of inquiry regarding behavior of Indians and volunteers.

A board of investigation in January looked into the conduct of five Cayuses found at the friendly Indians' camp suspected of participating in the battle at the Walla Walla River. Three of them, Wat-astee-mee-nee, Tock-i-us-us and Tock (Potato Heap) were found guilty and sentenced to be transported to Governor Curry at Salem, Oregon, and detained there until the end of the war. Two others were found to have been present during the battle, but did not fire their weapons. They remained free, and were to be watched over in camp.[29] A board of investigation looked into the conduct of Yellow Hawk, also Cayuse, accused of fighting against whites. He was acquitted and released. Another Native man that had been found guilty received 33 lashes across the back and had his head shaved. Other court-martial trials took place involving soldiers. A corporal found guilty of neglect of duty and willful disobedience of orders was reduced in rank and lost ten days' pay. A private found guilty of the same charges lost ten days' pay.

On February 7, camp again moved two miles farther up Mill Creek to a new location named Camp Cornelius in honor of the regiment's young colonel. More supplies arrived February 15. The following day, a more serious court-martial took place that tried a Nez Perce man, Te-pe-al-an-at-ke-kek, accused of spying for Chief Kamiakin. Tribal chiefs and local residents testified under oath that the suspect had acted upon orders from Kamiakin to come to the Walla Walla Valley to recruit fighters and burn buildings and property that belonged to Lloyd Brooke. The suspect was found guilty and hanged.[30]

Tom Hubbard's pack train arrived at the volunteer camp on February 25 bringing ten wagons loaded with provisions and clothing. On the same day another pack train under B. F. Dowell was raided at Wild Horse Creek, losing 25 horses while managing to retain all of its equipment and provisions.[31]

Reports came from some local Cayuses complaining that unidentified volunteers had confiscated horses and cattle belonging to friendly Indians and that OMV did not discriminate between them and the hostiles. Agent Olney advised Superintendent Palmer that Nez Perce Chief Red Wolf had offered to take friendly Cayuses out of reach of unruly volunteers and keep them safe until the war was over.[32] Father Chirouse wrote to Father Mesplie at The Dalles asking if General Wool could help the Cayuse protect their property from the volunteers.[33] Wool sympathized with the complaints and planned to send regular army troops to the Walla Walla Valley in March so that volunteers could be sent home.

Cornelius needed more livestock, and sent Lieutenant W. H. Meyer of Company D and Lieutenant Wright from Company E on February 27 to Nez Perce country to purchase up to 300 horses for the upcoming spring campaign. The two men returned March 6 with a disappointing 42 head. Also needing ammunition, Cornelius sent another detachment toward The Dalles to intercept the Johnson wagon train in the process of hauling additional supplies to Walla Walla.

Lieutenant William Stillwell met the train and loaded 200 pounds lead, 200 pounds powder and 1,500 percussion caps into a wagon, and brought them as quickly as possible forward to the troops. Lieutenant Charles Pillow traveled to Fort Walla Walla to find and collect canoes that would supplement the recently constructed boats for crossing the Snake and Columbia Rivers. Lieutenant Pillow remained at the fort to receive supplies and transfer courier messages to and from the front lines. Cornelius did not wait for more supplies to arrive before getting started. He needed to take advantage of the recent arrival of five fresh recruiting companies sent by the governor to strike the tribes before leaving their winter camps. The colonel placed troops on half rations of flour and announced the order on March 7 to prepare to depart for Snake River.

It took four days for nine companies comprised of 500 men to travel up the Touchet Valley, make camp, and wait for the ammunition supplies to arrive. Only then could they cross the Snake River. After making the crossing approximately 25 miles above the junction with the Columbia, volunteers disrupted a Palouse village on the north bank and sent occupants fleeing. The advance guard galloped after them and killed four men out of about twenty who put up a brief resistance.[34] Villagers were forced to abandon more than 100 horses, some loaded with packs, and a boy five or six years of age left behind during the melee. Captain Hembree rescued the boy and delivered him to the care of Lieutenant Pillow at Fort Walla Walla where the men there described the young lad as "quite an interesting little chap."[33] Captain Alexander P. Ankeny, 33, a married father of four and successful businessman, was said to have brought the boy home to live with him in Portland, Oregon.[36]

After routing the Palouse village, Colonel Cornelius took 200 men mounted on the command's best horses and rode down to the mouth of the Snake River expecting to find Kamiakin and a large force of warriors. No Indians were found, and the volunteers continued another 12 miles up the Columbia to the mouth of the Yakima River where they found a small group of Indians crossing the river, killing two of them. Cornelius figured that the main party of warriors must be located on the Palouse River.[37] The command turned back to their camp on Snake River and prepared to march up the Palouse River. Along the way they found no signs of large encampments. The men did notice evidence of smaller family groups that had since departed. At one site, a feeble old man unable to move had been left behind in a lodge. Volunteers assisted the man by giving him a portion of their dwindling bread supply and fresh water.[38]

The command continued up Palouse River a mile above the falls where they established a camp and grazed their horses waiting for another supply train. Lieutenant Colonel Kelly, who had returned from the capitol, took eight detachments further up the Palouse River riding through the region looking for signs of hostiles. He found a well-worn trail in the direction of Columbia River leading west to Priest Rapids. Volunteers planned to follow the trail in the days to come.

All troops were present at the Palouse River camp on a rainy March 20 with nothing to eat but horse meat. Two of the recruiting companies that had recently arrived as reinforcements threatened to mutiny led by their popularly elected major, 58-year-old James Curl. Curl announced to Colonel Cornelius that he intended to take his troops back to The Dalles because he did not believe the governor wanted them to suffer and starve under such harsh conditions. In rebuttal, Cornelius, Kelly and future congressman George K. Shiel gave patriotic speeches that stirred the men's emotions and convinced them to stay and endure the hardships. The following day a pack train brought fresh supplies and new hope to the depleted soldiers.[39] Victory still was not assured. A large contingent of warriors was thought to be nearby and ready to strike at any moment. Some of the men contemplated their own deaths as did Colonel Cornelius who wrote home to his wife that if he did not make it back alive she should invest all they had into their children's education because "scooling (sic) is worth more than property or money."[40]

The colonel ordered the command to march west toward Priest Rapids on March 23. The first night's camp found good water at Sinking Springs. The second night after traveling through rugged coulees, only alkali ponds could be found to camp near. March 25 marked the beginning of two tortuous days without fresh water. Horses broke down from thirst and exhaustion, and many men walked on foot. On March 26 Lieutenant Colonel Kelly walked 14 miles beside his horse. His men reported lips blackened and tongues swollen from dehydration. They finally reached the Columbia River, and found it unapproachable, two hundred feet below. The men had to march three more miles upstream before reaching the river bank.

The next day, most of the troops rested near Priest Rapids while the indefatigable Captain Hembree led a scouting party a few miles above the campsite continuing to look for hostiles. Cornelius presumed that Kamiakin's forces had taken refuge somewhere in the Yakima Valley. The colonel spent the next three days marching troops west, and then south down the banks of the Columbia over difficult terrain until they reached the mouth of the Yakima River. Cornelius sent Lieutenant R. S. Coldwell of Company D downstream by boat to Walla Walla with orders to transport subsistence and extra coffee for 500 men for 15 days to the mouth of the Yakima River. Campsites on the Yakima provided ample grass and wood for several days while the men waited for Cornelius to organize the upcoming expedition in pursuit of Chief Kamiakin. The colonel assigned two potentially mutinous companies A and D from the second battalion to various duties around the Walla

Walla Valley and The Dalles. He retained companies B and C that had performed faithfully. He also sent for Lieutenant Pillow at Fort Walla Walla to join him with trusted members of companies A, D and E from the First Battalion. Cornelius hand-picked the skilled guide Antoine Rivais from Company K who had recently been elected captain.

Not long after Major Curl had been sent away to perform scouting duties, Cornelius received complaints that Curl had been harassing quartermaster employees at the Walla Walla River. The colonel gave orders to Lieutenant Colonel Kelly to go the scene and take control over the disruptive major.

Captain Hembree sent a letter to the editor of the *Weekly Oregonian* dated April 3. "The boys are very anxious to have a fray with the Indians though I have lost all hope of finding the red devils...You shall hear from me again."[41]

On April 7, 1856, Colonel Cornelius and 241 of his most resolute citizen soldiers rode into the Yakima Valley searching for Kamiakin and his warriors.[42] Volunteers proceeded upriver three days until turning south up the first tributary they called Canyon Creek (now Satus Creek) camping six miles from the confluence with the Yakima River. On the morning of April 10 at about 6:30 a.m. a party of ten scouts left camp to ascend the highest point on Toppenish Ridge and look over the valley for signs of hostiles. The group consisted of Captain Hembree, Captain Hiram Wilbur, Captain Alfred Wilson, Captain Ives (from the pack train), Lieutenant William Stillwell, Lieutenant Thomas Hutt and Privates A.K. Wright, Albert Gates, James Wooley and Andy Mulligan.[43]

As the men approached the top of the hill they entered a flat where approximately 50 warriors suddenly appeared on their right. Some 40 more warriors on horseback circled around behind to cut off the volunteers. Captain Hembree ordered his men to charge the first group that had fired and missed. Right away, Indians began yelling and waving blankets to panic the scouts' mounts. Hembree shouted out a command to turn back and the men began to retreat downhill.

Hembree took a shot that entered his right side and knocked him from his mule. The wounded man propped himself on one elbow while holding a pistol in the other hand. Quickly a warrior approached and fired a fatal shot to Hembree's chest. The remaining nine had stopped momentarily to see if they could help, but quickly resumed their retreat downhill after realizing that the captain was lost. Volunteers at camp below heard the shots and looked up to see riders on their mounts scrambling toward them. Narcisse Cornoyer, who had recently been elected battalion major, rushed across the creek with two detachments from companies D and E. Rescuers soon learned the fate of Hembree and they hastily proceeded to recover the body. They were not in time to save the captain's remains from being stripped and scalped. Cornoyer's troops charged the warriors and pursued them for several miles up Satus Canyon.

Just east of Hembree's location, Captain Alexander Ankeny from Company C of the recruiting battalion drove away another party. At the campsite along the creek, detachments from companies E and B kept attackers away from the pack animals. Still another group of warriors on a butte just south of camp was driven up the creek by Captain Benjamin Burch of Company B, recruiting battalion, and Lieutenants Stillwell and Hutt of Company C. Meanwhile, Captain Wilson and Lieutenant Pillow held the strategic south butte overseeing access to stored baggage and equipment.

By noon all the attackers had fled and the volunteers reassembled at camp. Scouts soon reported up to 300 warriors gathered and fortified among rock breastworks along steep cliffs six or seven miles up the creek near the trail that volunteers would soon follow on their way to The Dalles. While Cornelius and half the command waited for a squad of soldiers that had been sent back to the Yakima River to recover lost animals, Major Cornoyer went forward with approximately 100 men at 2:30 p.m. to dislodge the warriors from the canyon. Cornoyer, the former mountain man, and Captain Rivais inspired volunteers to storm the cliffs under fire as though they had no fear. Witnesses reported seeing and hearing Kamiakin directing the actions of his fighters with a commanding voice, flag-waving and sending couriers back and forth.[44] But volunteers overran the position, driving the braves away. Warriors carried off their wounded leaving, behind one fatality that was scalped by a volunteer even though the practice was generally disapproved of, according to Sergeant Major A. H. Sale.

On April 11 the full command marched 11 miles farther up the canyon without incident. On April 12 the volunteers surprised, killed and scalped two Klickitat men who may not have been involved in the earlier fight.[45] Volunteers reached the Klickitat Valley on April 13, where camp was made next to ample grass, water and timber. A pack train arrived next day bringing fresh provisions. The men remained at camp until April 17 when they moved to within six miles of Fort Dalles. Here they waited for news of anticipated discharges and authorization to return home.

Captain Hembree's body was transported to Yamhill County for burial. Hembree, 43, was survived by his wife Nancy and eight children. His scalp was reported recovered three months later at a battle near Grand Ronde River when Washington Territory volunteer surgeon Matthew Burns recovered a white man's scalp with short dark hair and gray in it that matched the captain's description.[46] The Yakamas lost at least three killed at Satus Creek, Pah-ow-re, Shu-win-ne and Waken-shear.[47] The warrior, Pon-mah-po, was said to have been the one who shot Hembree.[48]

Tribesmen continued to keep close watch on the volunteers. Early in the morning of Sunday April 20, the men of Company B were raided at Fort Henrietta by a hostile band that ran off horses and scalped the guard, Private Lot Hollinger. Company A, camped about a mile away, pursued the raiders for three days but was unable to overtake them.[49]

At 7:00 in the morning, Monday April 28th, another raiding party swept into camp across the Columbia River from The Dalles and drove off 500 horses, stranding the volunteers on foot. Kamiakin again was given credit and blame for the incident. Adjutant William H. Farrar wrote, "It is a devil of a lick to us; Kamiakin is playing a strong hand. The old fellow got about $100,000 worth of property out of us before breakfast."[50]

Due to the surprise attack at Cascades on March 26, regular army troops under Colonel George Wright changed their plans from going to the Walla Walla Valley and re-directed efforts to the Yakima Valley. Oregon volunteers decided to hold on to Fort Walla Walla until regular army troops could take over. Oregon volunteer Davis Layton received a promotion to major, and took command of a new battalion named the Oregon Rangers that included three companies led by Captains A. V. Wilson, Hiram Wilber and William G. Haley.[51] Lieutenant Colonel Kelly set Layton up with two more months of supplies consisting of three wagons loaded with flour, sugar, salt, coffee, tobacco, bacon, soap and saleratus (baking soda).[52]

Chapter 4 notes

1. Harriet D. and Adrian R. Munnick eds., *Catholic Church Records of the Pacific Northwest Missions of St. Ann and St. Rose of the Cayouse 1847-1888*, (Portland, OR: Binford & Mort, 1989), 39,44; "Proceedings of a court martial held at Camp Cornelius, Whitman's Valley, Washington Territory", Feb. 16, 1856, House of Representatives 34th Congress 3rd session 1856-'57, Ex. Doc. No. 76, Indian Affairs on the Pacific, in thirteen volumes, vol. 9, 208.
2. Nathan Olney to Gen. Joel Palmer, Supt. Ind. Affairs, Oct. 12 and 13, 1855, RBIA (RG 75), OS, LS and LR by Supt. Joel Palmer 1854-55, NARA microfilm M2 Roll 5.
3. Narcisse Raymond to "the Commander in Charge coming to Ft. Walla Walla", Nov. 14, 1855, HED No. 76, 195-6.
4. John McBean deposition, November 11, 1895, Records of the United States Court of Claims 1835-1966 (RG 123), Indian Depredation Case #2117, NARA; Olney to Palmer, Nov. 30, 1855, NARA M2 Roll 5.
5. "List of Goods Abandoned at (Fort) Walla Walla", 16 October, 1855, State Department of General Records, War Records Division, Misc. Letters, 1856-1859, microfilm G,I,13, Crosby Library, Gonzaga University, Spokane, WA (Courtesy of Steve C. Plucker).
6. The *Weekly* (Portland) *Oregonian*, January 5, 1856, James K. Kelly to Wm. H. Farrar.
7. James K. Kelly to George L. Curry, Jan. 15, 1856, HED No. 76, 198-201.
8. Olney to Palmer, Dece. 8, 1855, NARA M2 Roll 5.
9. Nathan Olney wrote on October 12 that Umatilla chiefs Win-im-snoot and Water-stuand "will not join the war." On the other hand, Indian Agent R.R. Thompson wrote on November 19, "The Umatilla as a tribe are against us." Thompson to Palmer, "Indian Hostilities in Oregon and Washington", House of Representatives, 34th Congress, 1st session, Ex. Doc. No. 93, 69, 70,124.
10. HED No. 76, 196-206; (Steilacoom, WA) *Puget Sound Courier*, Jan. 25, 1856, Lt. John Thomas Jeffries, "Particulars of the Fight at Walla Walla".
11. "Topographical Memoir of the Department of the Pacific and Report of Captain T. J. Cram", U.S. House of Representatives, 35th Congress 2nd session 1858-'59, Ex. Doc. No. 114,13 volumes, vol. 12, 98-9.
12. Clarence L. Andrew, "Warfield's Story of Peo Peo Mox Mox", *The Washington Historical Quarterly* 25, (July 1934): 182-4.
13. *Puget Sound Courier*, January 25, 1856.
14. J. W. Reese, "OMV's Fort Henrietta: On Winter Duty, 1855-56", *Oregon Historical Quarterly* 66 (Mar-Dec 1965): 148.
15. Plympton J. Kelly, William N. Bischoff ed., *We Were Not Summer Soldiers The Indian War Diary of Plympton J. Kelly 1855-1856*, (Tacoma, WA: Washington Historical Society, 1976), 70, 169; HED No. 93, 108.
16. Elwood Evans, ed., *History of the Pacific Northwest: Oregon and Washington*, 2 vols. (Portland, OR: North Pacific History Company, 1889), 2:339.
17. Orin Oliphant, ed., "Journals of the Indian War of 1855-1856", Robert Moore Painter, *The Washington Historical Quarterly* 15 (January 1924): 17-19; Plympton Kelly, n. 140,124.
18. James Kelly to George Curry, May 13, 1856, Davis Layton Papers, Oregon Historical Society, Portland, OR, microfilm, William Bischoff Collection, Gonzaga University Cowles Rare Book Library Special Collections, Foley Center, Spokane, WA.
19. *Oregon Weekly Times*, Jan. 26, 1856.
20. Narcisse Raymond to Gov. I.I. Stevens, Dec. 9, 1855, RBIA (RG 75), WS, Misc. LR 1853-1861, NARA, microfilm M5 Roll 23.
21. Victor Trevitt to Joel Palmer, Dec. 11, 1855, RBIA (RG 75), OS, NARA, microfilm M2 Roll 13, typescript Relander Collection Box 41-14, YVL.

22. State of Washington Office of the Adjutant General, *The Official History of the Washington National Guard* volume 2 Washington Territorial Militia in the Indian Wars of 1855-56, (Tacoma, WA: Camp Murray, 1961), 130; William S. Lewis, "First Eastern Washington Militia", *The Washington Historical Quarterly* 11 (October 1920): 247-8.

23. Lloyd Brooke deposition January 1, 1887, U.S. Court of Claims Case #2117, 5.

24. "Abstract of in the case of Brooke, Bomford & Co.", Nov. 6, 1888 Case #2117.

25. J. C. Smith - Deposition, November 11, 1895 U.S. Court of Claims Case #2117.

26. Narcisse Raymond to John Noble, November 14, 1855, Case #2117.

27. John McBean – Deposition, Nov. 11, 1895 U.S. Court of Claims Case #2117; John F. Noble deposition December 17, 1897, U.S. Court of Claims Case #2117.

28. Col. Thos. Cornelius to His Excellency Geo. L. Curry, June 13, 1856, RAGO (RG 94), LR 1854-58, NARA microfilm 1954, Relander Collection box 63-5, YVL.

29. Regimental Order Book, 1st Regiment OMV, Jan. 29, 1856, Thomas R. Cornelius Correspondence and Records 1856-1864, NWC-043, Spokane Public Library.

30. Proceedings of a court martial, Feb. 16, 1856, HED No 76, 215; Oliphant, 22.

31. *Pioneer and Democrat*, April 25, 1856, Cornelius to Curry, April 3, 1856; Oliphant, 21.

32. Olney to Palmer, Feb. 23, 1856, RBIA (RG 75) OS, NARA microfilm M2 Roll 14, typescript, Relander Collection box 41-4, YVL.

33. Robert H. Ruby and Jon A. Brown, *The Cayuse Indians*, (Norman: University of Oklahoma Press, 1972), 226.

34. Cornelius to Curry, April 2, 1856, NARA microfilm 1954, Relander 63-5.

35. Plympton Kelly, 90.

36. George Wright to Capt. A.J. Cain, March 12, 1857, RBIA (RG 75) WS LR from employees assigned to the Col. R. or So. Distr. and Yakima Agency 1854-1861, NARA microfilm M5 Roll 17.

37. Thomas Cornelius to Florentine Cornelius, April 3, 1856, Cornelius Correspondence.

38. James K. Kelly, "Memory Book", Friday March 12, 1856, MS 28, Oregon Historical Society, Portland.

39. A.H. Sale, "Indian War Recollections", *Oregon Native Son*, (December, 1889): 389-90.

40. Thomas Cornelius to Florentine, Walla Walla Valley, March (5th) 1856, Cornelius Correspondence.

41. *Weekly Oregonian*, April 19, 1856, A.J. Hembree to Mr. Dryer, April 3, 1856.

42. *Pioneer and Democrat*, April 25, 1856, Cornelius to Curry, April 13, 1856.

43. William D. Stillwell, "Account of April 10th, 1856", MSS 1514 Military Coll., Oregon Historical Society, Portland; (Portland) *Oregon Weekly Times*, April 26, 1856, A.V. Wilson, "Particulars of the Death of Capt. Hembree".

44. A.H. Sale, "Indian War Recollections", *Oregon Native Son*, (February, 1900): 492-3; A. J. Splawn, *Ka-Mi-Akin* (1917), reprint (Caldwell, ID: The Caxton Printers, 1980), 73; Cornelius to Curry, April 13, 1856.

45. Plympton Kelly, 97.

46. *Weekly Oregonian*, August 2, 1856, "Letter from Matthew P. Burns" July 28, 1856.

47. Splawn, 75.

48. L.V. McWhorter Collection, cage 55, box 16-24, MASC, Holland Library WSU Pullman, WA.

49. Reese, 154-5.

50. William H. Farrar to Lt. Col. Kelly, April 30, 1856, Layton Papers.

51. "Claims Growing Out of Indian Hostilities in Oregon and Washington", U.S. House of Representatives, 35th Congress 2nd session, 1859, Ex. Doc. No. 51, 69, 72.

52. Kelly to Davis Layton, May 20, 1856, Layton Papers.

Author's photo

The land around Puget Sound, an inlet from the Pacific Ocean beginning north at Port Townsend and extending south to Olympia, became the most frequent destination for pioneer settlers in Washington Territory during the 1850's. The Olympic Mountain Range is visible in the background.

CHAPTER ONE

Author's photo

Indian Agent A.J. Bolon died in Klickitat County in September 1855. Monument erected by Washington State Historical Society in 1918 .

58

Evans v. 1, op. 48

Dr. William Cameron McKay, 1824-1893, more than one half Native heritage, grew up at Fort Vancouver and served as secretary to Oregon superintendent Joel Palmer at the Walla Walla Treaty Council held in 1855.

Library and Archives Canada, Acc. No. 1981-55-28 Bushnell Collection, Copy neg. C-114447

"Cut Mouth John, a Cayuse Indian." The U.S. Army scout's frequently documented facial deformity (Kip, 32 and Howard, 265) is evident in Emile de Girardin's 1856 sketch.

U.S. Ordnance Department, "The Ordnance Manual for the Use of the Officers of the United States Army", Alfred Mordecai-ed., Washington, 1850, digitalized by Google.

The U.S. Army pulled the mountain howitzer along the trail with a mule hitched to a wheeled carriage. A second mule carried two full ammunition chests weighing 238 pounds. Each shell or spherical case contained 78 musket balls and 4.5 ounces of rifle powder that detonated after a fuse lasting three or four seconds expired, exploding its contents in all directions. The howitzer was known in Indian country as the gun that fired twice.

Gustav Sohon-Washington State Historical Society #1918.114.9.65

"Kamayakhen." Yakama Chief Kamiakin's name was spelled more than a dozen different ways by people who knew the chief during his lifetime.

Gustav Sohon - Washington State Historical Society, 1918.114.9.38

Tribesmen gathered at the Walla Walla Treaty Council in 1855 wore their hair straight, long and loose as seen in drawings by artist Sohon who attended the event.

University of Washington Libraries,
Special Collections, UW2961
Major Granville O. Haller (1819-1897) served as commander at Fort Dalles in 1855.

Courtesy of Yakima Valley Libraries,
Relander Collection, 2002-851-995
Columbia Sinkiuse Chief Moses (ca. 1829-1899). He was peaceable most of his life but fought for Chief Kamiakin in 1855 when he was a young man.

CHAPTER TWO

Author's photo
Two monuments erected in 1916 and 1917 on Hwy 97 near Union Gap, WA memorialize Pah-oy-ti-koot or Two Buttes, where Tow-tow-nah-hee died in November 1855.

Courtesy of the Yakima Valley
Museum 2008-800-291

Gabriel J. Rains (1803-1881). He served as a U.S. Army major in the 1850s and became a Confederate general during the Civil War.

Photo from Personal Memoirs of P. H.
Sheridan, *v. 1, New York. 1888*

Philip H. Sheridan (1831-1888). He participated in battles at Two Buttes and Cascades as a lieutenant in 1855 and 1856.

Courtesy Archives of the
Archdiocese of Seattle

Father Charles Pandosy (1826-1891) began the Yakama Mission in 1848 with Father Chirouse and helped bridge communication gaps between Yakama people and U.S. Army officers.

Lucullus Virgil McWhorter Photograph
Collection, Manuscripts, Archives, and
Special Collections, Washington State
University Libraries

Ko-ti-akun (To-ki-aken) Twi-wash/Tom Smartlowit (1833-1922) ca. 1918. As a young Yakama warrior in 1855-56 he fought at Toppenish Creek, Two Buttes and across the Cascades with Qualchan's braves at Puget Sound.

CHAPTER THREE

Author's photo

This marker, erected in 1924, commemorates the ambush in 1855 at Connell's Prairie- Pierce County.

Photo courtesy Michael J. Dobb

Monument to the victims of the White River Massacre in October 1855. It is located in present day Auburn, WA erected by Washington State Historical Society.

Evans, v. 1 op. p 76

Snoqualmie Chief Pat-kanim served with the Washington Territory Volunteers, commanding a regiment of 81 warriors in 1856.

Washington State Historical Society, 2010.0.357

William A. Slaughter (1827-1855), graduated from West Point in 1848 and was assigned to Washington Territory as a lieutenant. He was joined by his wife Mary at Fort Steilacoom in 1853. He died after being shot by a sniper on December 4, 1855.

CHAPTER FOUR

Author's photo

Hembre Mountain on Toppenish Ridge was the site of a battle near Satus Creek in April 1856 where Oregon Mounted Volunteer captain Absalom Hembree and four tribesmen died.

Evans, v. 1 op. 72

Narcisse A. Cornoyer (1820-1909), was a former mountain man and later sheriff and Indian Agent. He commanded Co. K, Oregon Mounted Volunteers, comprised primarily of French Canadians and Metis in 1855-56.

Author's photo

Peu Peu Mox Mox, Walla Walla chief, died in December 1855. The marker is on old Highway 12, 3.8 mi. east of Lowden, WA. Eerected by home economic clubs of Walla Walla.

Author's photo

Hembree Memorial, Battle at Satus Creek, April 10, 1856. The marker is located in Post Office Park in Toppenish, WA.

Gustav Sohon-Washington State Historical Society #198.114.9.63

"Pier Moo-a-tet" (Pierre Mowatit), a friendly Walla Walla chief, risked his personal safety attempting to prevent looters from ransacking Fort Walla Walla and burning Lloyd Brooke's buildings.

Gustav Sohon-Washington State Historical Society #1918.114.9.46

"Sti-hass" (Stickus) a Cayuse chief, along with Chiefs Howlish Wampoo and Tintinmetzey, stayed consistently peaceful in their relationships with American officials.

Evans, v. 1, op. 64

James K. Kelly (1819-1903), commanded Oregon Mounted Volunteers during the invasion of Walla Walla Valley in December 1855. Afterwards he helped provide provisions for displaced French settlers.

Gustav Sohon-Washington State Historical Society #1918.114.9.64

"Pew-pew max-max," the Walla Walla chief, resisted signing the 1855 treaty until offered inducements including the right to use the mouth of the Yakima River as a trading post for five years to sell cattle.

Gustav Sohon-Washington State
Historical Society #1918.114.9.50

"Stackotly" (Stock Whitley),
a Des Chutes chief in Oregon,
attended the Walla Walla
Treaty Council then fought
against the Oregon Mounted
Volunteers in December
1855.

*Courtesy Archives of the
Archdiocese of Seattle*

Father Casimir Chirouse (ca.
1820-1892), established the
Yakama Mission with Father Pandosy in 1848. He also ministered
to the Cayuse and Walla Walla
people during the war years.

*Gustav Sohon-Washington State
Historical Society #1918.114.9.45*

Cayuse chief Five Crows, identified as hostile by other chiefs, was
also the abductor of 21-year-old
Esther Bewley after the Whitman
massacre in 1847.

CHAPTER FIVE

Courtesy of the Yakima Valley Museum 2008-800-450

Isaac I. Stevens (1818-1862), served as governor and superintendent of Indian affairs simultaneously in Washington Territory.

Daguerreotype, Southworth & Hawes, Boston, Wikimedia commons

General John E. Wool (1784-1869), opposed many of Governor Isaac Stevens' war-time actions and policies.

CHAPTER SIX

Author's photo

A swollen Naches River in May of 1856 caused Colonel Wright and hundreds of his troops to wait for flood waters to subside. They established a camp on the north bank later called a "basket fort" due to the shaded bowers woven from willow branches that dominated the landscape.

Courtesy of Yakima Valley Libraries 2002-850-651

Colonel George Wright (1803-1865), commanded U.S. Army troops east of the Cascade Mountains during 1856-1858.

Gustav Sohon – Washington State Historical Society #1918.114.9.66

"Ou-hi" (Owhi), a Yakama chief, was one of the original signers of the 1855 treaty, brother of peace chief Teias, and father to warrior sons Qualchan, Lishhaiahit and Lo-kout.

CHAPTER SEVEN

Gustav Sohon-Washington State Historical Society #1918.114.9.59

Nez Perce chief Spotted Eagle led more than 100 warriors serving with the Washington Territory Volunteers, and led 30 warriors with Colonel Wright's U.S. Ninth Infantry.

Evans, v. 1, op. 464

Benjamin F. Shaw (1829-1908), was known as "Quatlitch." He interpreted Chinook jargon at the Medicine Creek Council in 1854. He also commanded the 2nd Regiment of Washington Territory Volunteers, and interpreted at Leschi's trials.

CHAPTER EIGHT

Author's photo

Fort Simcoe was established by the U.S. Army in 1856. It became the Yakama Agency in 1859, including a children's training school and eventually a state park.

Gustav Sohon-Washington State
Historical Society #1918.114.9.67

"Skeloon" (Skloom), was a Yakama chief, brother of Chief Kamiakin and one of the original signers of the 1855 treaty.

69

CHAPTER NINE

Evans, v. 1, op. 564

Antonio B. Rabbeson, born in New York in 1824, arrived at Puget Sound in 1846. He gave eye-witness testimony in court that helped convict Leschi of the murder of A. Benton Moses in 1855.

Library of Congress LC-B813-1710

Silas Casey (1807-1882), took command of Fort Steilacoom as lieutenant colonel in 1856, and tried unsuccessfully to prevent civilians from executing Nisqually leader Leschi in 1858.

CHAPTER TEN

Author's photo

Memorial to Qualchew (Qualchan), located near Fairfield, WA. It was erected by Spokane County Pioneers Association, 1935.

Yakima Valley Libraries 2002-850-940

James J. Arher (1817-1864). After serving as a U.S. Army captain in Washington Territory in the 1850s he became a Confederate general during the Civil War.

Author's photo

Lake Wenatchee – U.S. Army troops under Major Robert S. Garnett pursued Native fugitives near here after attacks on miners in 1858.

Author's photo

Monument to the Battle of Spokane Plains, 1858. It was erected near Fairchild AFB by the Washington State Historical Society.

Courtesy of Yakima Valley Libraries 2002-850-653

Lieutenant Colonel Edward J. Steptoe (1815-1865), served as commander at Fort Walla Walla 1856-58.

Author's photo

Memorial to the Steptoe Battle, 1858, near Rosalia, WA. Erected by the Daughters of the American Revolution in 1914.

Library of Congress LC-B814-1634

Erasmus Darwin Keyes (1810-1895), graduated from West Point in 1832 and served as a captain during Colonel George Wright's Spokane campaign in 1858. Keyes' admiration for Coeur d'Alene missionary Father Joset influenced the officer to become a Catholic.

Gustav Sohon-Washington State Historical Society #1918.114.9.57

Nez Perce chief "Te-ma-Tee" (Timothy), served with Spotted Eagle and the Washington Territory Volunteers. He also rescued Steptoe's army troops and led Protestant worship services at the Treaty Council of 1855.

Gustav Sohon-Washington State Historical Society, 1918.114.9.61

Chief Spokane Garry's formal education and English speaking skills helped him become an important liaison between Native people and American officials.

Drawn by Gustav Sohon, Bowen & Co. lith. Philada. in Capt. John Mullan, Report of the Construction of a Military Road from Fort Walla Walla to Fort Benton, Government Printing Office, 1863, op. 16

Coeur d'Alene Mission of the Sacred Heart at Cataldo was constructed prior to 1855. It was overseen by Jesuit priest Joseph Joset, dedicated to helping mend relationships between the Coeur d'Alene tribe and the U.S. Army.

Author's photo

Monument commemorating the Battle at Four Lakes in 1858 was erected by Spokane County Pioneer Society, Medical Lake Commercial Club and Four Lakes Grange in 1935.

Courtesy of Yakima Valley Libraries 2002-850-643

Major Robert S. Garnett (1819-1861), served as commander at Fort Simcoe 1856-58.

CHAPTER ELEVEN

*Northwest Museum of Arts and Culture/Eastern
Washington Historical Society, Spokane, Washington,
#L94-14.56, Earl E. Reisner Collection*

Indian Agent L. T. Erwin (center) with Chief Moses (left) and Chief White Swan (Joe Stwire) ca. 1895.

Evans, v. 1, op. 104

Elwood Evans (1828-1898), was a lawyer and chief clerk of the first Washington Territorial Legislature. He experienced the war first-hand and edited the book *History of the Pacific Northwest: Oregon and Washington*, published in 1889.

CHAPTER FIVE

Feuds and Martial Law 1856

STEVENS/WOOL CONTROVERSY AND USURPATION OF POWER

Governor Stevens dueled politically with military and civilian officials at the same time he fought against hostile chiefs and warriors. The governor's dispute with General John E. Wool flared up in November, 1855, when the general declined to outfit a company of Washington rangers under William McKay with U.S. Army equipment requested by acting Governor Mason. The rangers were to be sent to the Rocky Mountains to escort Stevens back to Olympia.[1]

Wool had arrived at Fort Dalles from California the same week Major Rains' troops straggled in from the snow-covered Simcoe Mountains with worn out shoes, tattered clothing, spent horses and equipment unfit for service. The soldiers had also delayed for a time in the Little Klickitat Valley constructing a blockhouse that Wool ordered abandoned. The general figured that Stevens could return safely down the Missouri River and take a ship to the west coast without the army's help if need be. The dauntless governor, however, surprised many people by returning overland via the Bitterroot Mountains despite early winter snowstorms. He got assistance from a company of Nez Perce auxiliaries and Spokane Valley volunteers.

Stevens never forgave General Wool's rebuff. The two men argued back and forth throughout the war, penning lengthy and critical correspondences about each other published in newspapers from Washington D.C. to Portland, Oregon. Wool opposed volunteers participating in the war because recently armed citizens in Southern Oregon's Rogue River Valley had killed innocent Indian women and children, inciting outrage, including from Oregon Volunteers' own adjutant general E. M Barnum, who ordered field commanders to disband any unauthorized armed citizens.[2] General Wool turned down Oregon Mounted Volunteer colonel James W. Nesmith's request for artillery to take to the Walla Walla Valley in November partly because tribes there had not yet killed a white man. That changed after Major Chinn's Oregon volunteers advanced to the Umatilla River and Lieutenant Colonel Kelly's men joined them to invade the Walla Walla Valley.

The killing of Peo Peo Mox Mox under a white flag, and the dismemberment of the chief's body, gave Wool and his supporters plenty to complain about. Stevens lashed back claiming that were it not for Oregon governor Curry's volunteers, "there would have been a hurricane of war between the Cascades and Bitter Root and three thousand warriors would now be in arms."[3] Stevens may have exaggerated when emphasizing a point (in this case enlarging what might be a realistic number). He appeared to have inflated statistics 20 to 40 percent during testimony he made to the U.S. Congress when describing the number of miners killed at the beginning of the war, and civilian victims killed at White River and Cascades.[4]

Cooperation between military and civilians occurred at first for just a month or so, beginning in October when Stevens was in Blackfeet country and Wool was in California. Two companies of Washington Territory Volunteers were mustered into U.S. service under Captains Newell and Strong during the Rains campaign and two others joined Captain Maloney's command at Fort Steilacoom. Wool arrived on the scene in November prior to Stevens' return and declared he had no authority to accept or sanction volunteers into U.S. service. After the governor arrived, Stevens forbade volunteers to serve under U.S. authority while cooperating with, but staying independent from, regular army officers in the field.[5] The governor accused Wool of being unfit for his position and called for the general to be replaced. Stevens sent progress reports directly to Secretary of War Jefferson Davis criticizing the general, and justifying the governor's own actions.[6] Stevens saw himself as "the highest federal officer in the territory", being commissioned by the president and under authority of Congress.[7]

General Wool remained unconvinced the two civilian governors' "private war" accomplished anything more than "unwise, unnecessary and extravagant expeditions...for no other reason than to plunder the

Treasury of the United States and make political capital for somebody."[8] Wool complained to the assistant adjutant general in New York, that Indians would not make war if "the authorities of Washington Territory would treat them with ordinary justice. Governor Stevens is crazy, and does not know what he is doing."[9]

Local newspapers helped fuel the controversy by publishing editorials backing Governor Stevens in Olympia's *Pioneer and Democrat*, while *The Puget Sound Courier* in Steilacoom sided with General Wool.

Stevens stirred up more opposition, this time with his own territorial officials, by declaring martial law in two counties. A group of local lawyers and citizens immediately protested by sending an urgent letter to Secretary of War Jefferson Davis asking the federal government to step in and put a stop to the governor's "usurpation of power."[10]

The difficulty began when Stevens became concerned about foreign born (Canadian/British) settlers living on Muck Prairie near the Nisqually River. Some were former employees of the Hudson's Bay Company and some were married to Indian women. Other residents at Yelm Prairie tended sheep for Puget Sound Agricultural Company, a Hudson's Bay subsidiary, or had retired from service and settled in the area. Stevens and others became concerned that Leschi and other tribesmen had received aid and comfort from the Hudson's Bay Company settlers because Indians known to be hostile had been seen visiting at least one home at Muck Prairie in December, 1855, while settlers elsewhere were being attacked and fired upon.

On March 2, 1856, the day William White was shot down, Stevens requested that Chief Factor William Tolmie detain settlers at HBC Fort Nisqually because their presence on the farms was "incompatible" with public safety.[11] Governor Stevens sent a force of 20 men to gather up all but half a dozen shepherds left to guard sheep at Yelm Prairie and took them to Fort Nisqually. Former treaty secretary James Doty, a lieutenant colonel and aid decamp in Stevens' volunteer army, was supposed to bring in the Muck Prairie residents. Doty, however, was not up to the task and instead spent March 4–7 "in a helpless state of intoxication."[12] Stevens dismissed Doty from public service for his failure, and 15 months later, 30-year-old James Doty shot himself to death in Olympia.[13]

On March 9, Washington volunteers ordered Charles Wren, Lyon Smith, John McLeod, Henry Murray, Francois Gravelle, Peter Wilson and John McField to move from Muck Prairie to Steilacoom and not return to their farms. After a week or two, most did return to look after their stores of wheat and potatoes that were vulnerable to thieves while absent. Volunteer captain Hamilton J. G. Maxon found the men and arrested them for breaking parole. Stevens' logic saw the region as a theater of war and suspicious circumstances were present when a residence went unmolested while hostile Indians were near. The Muck Prairie settlers were again removed to Steilacoom and told to remain there. By the end of the month, Wren, McLeod, Lyon Smith, Henry Smith and John McField were back on their farms where they were again arrested by Maxon. This time the men were considered treasonous and imprisoned.

At once two private attorneys applied to Judge F. A. Chenoweth for a writ of habeas corpus demanding the men stand before a judge and be shown legal cause for their arrest and imprisonment. Stevens took steps to block the move because he intended to have the suspects tried by a military commission rather than civil court. Consequently, the governor declared a state of martial law in Pierce County on April 3, 1856 that suspended the functions of civil officers. For more than a month the five detainees and their families awaited trial away from their homes while being fed from the volunteer commissary.

Earlier in November before Governor Stevens returned home from the Blackfeet Council, a joint military commission comprised of volunteers and regulars had been held at Camp Montgomery where eight Indians were tried on charges of spying against the military and being accessory to the murders of citizens at Connell's Prairie and White River. One defendant, Bistian, was found guilty and sentenced to hang. He was retained in custody by Acting Governor Mason. The other seven were found not guilty and released.[14] After Stevens returned, the governor empowered volunteer officers to conduct additional military commissions that were independent from the regular army to determine innocence, guilt and sentences for hostile Indians, volunteer soldiers and citizens charged with war crimes.

District court in Steilacoom opened on May 5 before Stevens had a chance to build a case strong enough to begin a military hearing. Chief Justice Edward Lander arrived to substitute for Judge Chenoweth who was absent due to illness. Two volunteer officers approached the judge and advised him that Governor Stevens had declared martial law and that civil court should be re-scheduled for approximately a month later. Lander refused and gave Stevens two days to rescind martial law. Lander opened court on May 7 preparing to get started on a busy docket. A U.S. marshall and sheriff's posse stood by in the courtroom to provide security when an armed company of volunteers strode in led by Lieutenant Colonel Benjamin F. Shaw and Captain Walter W. DeLacy.

Under instructions from Governor Stevens to stop the court, Shaw placed the judge under arrest and when the U.S. marshall and sheriff's posse rose to intercede, Lander waved them off to avoid a confrontation. Shaw's volunteers took the judge and court clerk J. M. Chapman to Governor Stevens in Olympia where they were released. Members of the bar from different political parties immediately joined together in protest. George Gibbs, Elwood Evans, C. C. Hewitt, B. F. Kendall and others called a meeting citing the "violation of every principle of constitutional privilege and liberty" and charged Governor Stevens with "a violent outrage upon law, and upon the rights of this people."[15] Their letter of protest was forwarded to the President of the United States and both houses of Congress. Stevens stood by his action believing the Muck Prairie residents to be treasonous spies during wartime and deserved territorial volunteer justice rather than constitutional civil rights. His opponents vehemently disagreed.

On May 12 Chief Justice Lander opened the Second District Court in Olympia, Thurston County, and the following day issued a writ of habeas corpus in behalf of Wren, McLeod, McField, Lyon Smith and Henry Smith. Governor Stevens countered by declaring martial law in Thurston County and sent a volunteer detachment that broke down the locked door to the courthouse and took Lander and deputy court clerk Elwood Evans into custody.

Finally a military commission met on May 23 consisting of five volunteer officers, a prosecutor and a recorder to consider charges against Lyon Smith. After hearing arguments from three defense attorneys, the commission decided it had no jurisdiction over a trial for the crime of treason.

On May 24 Judge Chenoweth opened district court in Steilacoom while protected by the Pierce County sheriff and approximately 60 armed citizens. U.S. Army lieutenant colonel Silas Casey had met with and convinced a volunteer detachment in the area to leave. Chenoweth issued a writ of habeas corpus upon Lieutenant Colonel Shaw to produce Lander, Wren, McLeod and Lyon Smith. Shaw refused and the judge charged Shaw with contempt of court. The same day Governor Stevens abrogated his proclamations of martial law in Pierce and Thurston counties.

On May 26 at Camp Montgomery a military commission convened for a trial of two volunteers, Joseph Brannan and James A. Lake, accused of murdering an Indian, Mowitch, suspected of participating in the White River attack that killed Brannan's brother's family. Both of the accused men were acquitted. Another military commission took place in Seattle that tried 15 Indians suspected of participating in the attack on Seattle. All 15 were found not guilty and released.[16]

On May 28 a United States marshal arrested Lieutenant Colonel Shaw and placed him in confinement for refusing to abide by Judge Chenoweth's court order. Shaw was released on his own recognizance and scheduled to re-appear in November.

Wren, McLeod, and Smith went to trial May 31 in the court of J. M. Batchelder, United States Commissioner. Eyewitness testimony stated that the suspicious meeting observed between the Indians and settlers at Muck Prairie in December was actually for the purpose of arranging peace negotiations with American authorities. On a motion by acting district attorney Elwood Evans, all defendants were released, and the contentious martial law episode came to a merciful end.

Ironically, the threat of attack from tribes in Puget Sound had all but ended prior to martial law. Leschi and other formerly hostile chiefs had fled east of the Cascades to escape violence and sue for peace with Colonel Wright. Volunteers and regulars kept the upper hand in western Washington by rounding up bands of Native people in remote valleys and transporting them to Indian agents at Puget Sound reservations. A few who tried to resist or outrun the volunteers, including non-combatants, sometimes were shot down.

Not everyone disagreed with martial law. The *Pioneer and Democrat* newspaper and some other citizens stayed loyal to Governor Stevens. In the end, Stevens received a letter of reprimand from the secretary of state written by order of President Franklin Pierce affirming that martial law was not excusable for the purpose of acting against the existing government or to interfere with the discharge of duties by civil authorities. The incident stained the reputation of Governor Stevens but did not prevent him from continuing to remain in office, perform his official duties, and win future elections.

Chapter 5 notes

1. Chas. H. Mason to Lieut. John Withers, November 3, 1855, State of Washington Office of the Adjutant General, *The Official History of the Washington National Guard*, volume 2 Washington Territorial Militia in the Indian Wars of 1855-56, (Tacoma, WA: Camp Murray, 1961), 51.
2. "Indian Hostilities in the Territories of Oregon and Washington", U.S. House of Representatives, 34th Congress, 1st session, Exec. Doc. No. 93, 6-7.
3. Weekly (Portland) *Oregonian*, April 12, 1856, Stevens to John E. Wool, March 20, 1856.
4. Isaac Ingalls Stevens, "Speech of the Hon. Isaac I. Stevens Delegate from Washington Territory on the Washington & Oregon Claims. Delivered in the House of Representatives of the United States May 31, 1858", (Fairfield, WA: Ye Galleon Press, 1970), 5, 6, 11.
5. I.I. Stevens to Major Gilmore Hays, February 27, 1856, WOAG, 64.
6. I.I. Stevens to Jefferson Davis, March 21, May 24 and June 8, 1856, WOAG, 74-6, 87-8, 95-7.
7. I.I. Stevens to Lt. Col. Silas Casey, March 16, 1856, WOAG, 72.
8. *Weekly Oregonian*, June 21, 1856, John E. Wool to the Editors of the (Washington D.C.) *National Intelligencer*, April 2, 1856.
9. Major General John E. Wool to Lieut. Colonel L. Thomas, August 4, 1856, RAGO (RG 94), LR 1822-1860, microfilm NARA M567 Roll 545.
10. George Gibbs to Hon. Jefferson Davis, May 10, 1856, NARA M567 Roll 545.
11. Roy N. Lokken, "The Martial Law Controversy in Washington Territory 1856", *Pacific Northwest Quarterly* 43 (Spring 1952): 93.
12. I.I. Stevens to Lieut. Col. James Doty, March 8, 1856, WOAG, 67.
13. Executive Clerk to J.W. Nesmith, June 27, 1857, RBIA (RG 75) WS, Misc. LR August 22, 1853-April 9, 1861, NARA, microfilm M5 Roll 23.
14. "Proceedings of a Military Commission Which Assembled at Camp Montgomery W.T.", November 16, 1855, WOAG, 54-5.
15. "Meeting of the Bar May 7, 1856", NARA M567 Roll 545.
16. WOAG, 93.

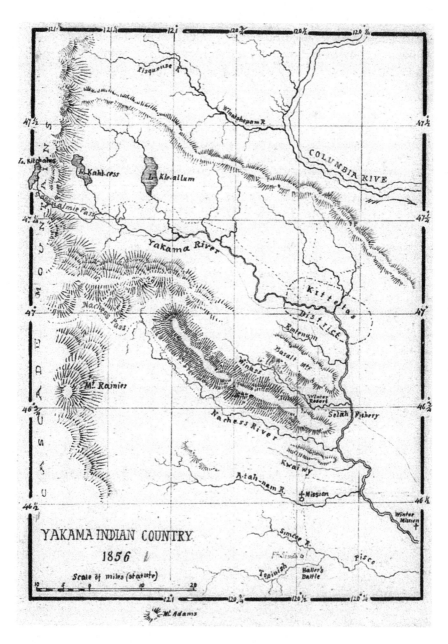

*Office of the Chief of Engineers RG77 fortifications map file, Department of the Pacific Booklet,
page xvii, National Archives and Records Administration, Washington, D.C.*

CHAPTER SIX

Colonel Wright's Yakama Campaign 1856

THE U.S. ARMY'S ATTEMPT AT PEACE BY INTIMIDATION

After the Cascades attack, Colonel George Wright kept newly-arrived U.S. Army reinforcements near the Columbia River at Fort Dalles and Fort Vancouver during the month of April 1856 to safeguard settlements in the region. He postponed an expedition to the Walla Walla Valley because it became more urgent to advance into Yakama country and give hostile factions there an option to either agree to peace or confront the force of the regular army.

At Fort Dalles, Major Haller hired five Columbia River Indians to ride into the Yakima Valley and report back concerning the status of the tribes there before Colonel Wright's troops departed at the end of the month. The scouts were each given a gun with 25 rounds of ammunition and a piece of white muslin tied around their heads as identification.[1]

On April 28 Wright left Fort Dalles and crossed the Columbia River with 300 soldiers plus several guides, interpreters, civilian packers and dozens of loaded mules. Shortly after landing on the Washington shore he received word that a raiding party had run off hundreds of horses belonging to the Oregon volunteers nearby. The colonel sent a company of dragoons to assist the volunteers but the raiders had gone too far to catch. After three more days of marching 25 miles up steep hills using ropes to keep four mountain howitzers upright on their wheels, Wright's troops reached a camping place in the Klickitat Valley.[2]

On May 2, the men advanced across the snow-covered Simcoe Mountains removing snow drifts by hand using spades while horses broke the trail to clear the way for foot soldiers. The troops camped about a mile from the Haller battle site and sent out scouts hoping to capture a local Indian to learn the whereabouts of others. At camp late at night on Ahtanum Creek on May 6 Wright's men came under fire from a raiding party that set fire to the surrounding prairie. The following morning dragoons chased a group of mounted braves but the army horses were unable to catch up to the swift Indian ponies. The army's friendly Indian scouts managed to contact a few local warriors who were told that Colonel Wright wished to hold peace talks. At the next camp on Cowiche Creek, envoys sent by Chief Kamiakin and his brother Skloom brought word that the chiefs would agree to hold talks as soon as Chief Owhi and others arrived. They apologized for the recent attack at Ahtanum Creek, blaming "some Indians living in the Mountains beyond their reach."[3]

Colonel Wright advanced to his next camp on the south bank of the swollen Naches River that had become too wide and deep from spring runoff for soldiers to cross. A Yakama messenger swam his horse over to the soldiers bringing communications from the chiefs that now included the son of the late Walla Walla Chief Peo Peo Mox Mox. The messenger advised that young Peo Peo Mox Mox was opposed to cooperating with the army due to the offensive circumstances surrounding the death of his father in December at the hands of Oregon volunteers. On the evening of May 9, Kamiakin sent two more couriers advising that the chiefs had decided to meet with the colonel the next day. Word from Kamiakin declared that the chief would send the more volatile young men back to their homes in order to ensure cooperation.

The next day, Wright observed many Indians leaving the area heading north toward the Wenas Valley, but none of the chiefs came across to hold the expected council. The colonel tried unsuccessfully to locate a ford upriver to intercept the Indians before they left. Wright had two India rubber boats with him, but they were not enough to carry his troops, and there were no logs or timber nearby to make rafts. The colonel sent for Lieutenant Colonel Edward Steptoe and Major Haller at Fort Dalles to join Wright and provide reinforcements to guard the pack train while other soldiers pursued and attempted to contact the Indians.[4]

The Naches River subsided on May 16 enough for Qualchan to swim his horse across and meet with Colonel Wright. The prominent warrior stated that his father and other chiefs would be able to talk on the following day. On May 17 Chief Owhi and his older brother, Chief Teias, swam their horses over to meet with Wright and professed a willingness to establish peace. The colonel returned the chiefs' gestures with courtesy and cordiality. But Wright became concerned that Kamiakin and his brothers had not come to council, and the colonel believed those chiefs needed to be contacted or "subdued" in order to gain stability in the region.[5]

Four companies under Lieutenant Colonel Steptoe and Major Haller arrived at Camp Naches on May 29 increasing the size of the colonel's command to 500 soldiers. They congregated on the south bank five miles above the Naches River's junction with the Yakima River. Troops worked building a fortress made of "earth and gabions" large enough to secure two companies of soldiers to guard stores of supplies while the main body of soldiers traveled throughout the countryside to contact as many Native people as possible.[6] The colonel also set crews to work constructing a series of bridges across the flooded Naches River by cutting through 600 yards of dense underbrush. Men used axes cutting green poplar saplings and laced them together with rope mule halters.[7]

Army officers enjoyed life as best they could at the remote outpost. Colonel Wright left camp from time to time to fish. Some dined on fresh grouse prepared at evening meals. Pack mules brought cases of canned oysters, chicken and lobster.[8] A few officers sipped from selections of brandy toddies, gin and whiskey at night while reading mail and newspapers brought from The Dalles by express riders. On rainy days officers relaxed in their tents reading books and novels or writing letters home. Major Haller enjoyed a bit of luxury over others by having his wife living nearby at Fort Dalles. She sent treats to the field including bottles of lemon syrup, cakes, preserves, pickles, and fresh butter that Haller shared with others. Additional amusements included riding down the Naches River to investigate Indian painted rocks and enjoying roast ox head prepared by guide Cutmouth John.

While the colonel waited for the bridge to be completed, several groups of Indians arrived to meet with Wright and profess their desire for peace. One group of 80 Klickitats "succeeded in escaping the powers of Kamiakin" and asked Wright to help them return safely to their homes in Oregon.[9] A party of 35 men with their chief from the mountains on the upper branches of the Naches River visited Wright to tell the colonel they were not associated with "any of the Great Chiefs" of the Yakama Nation.[10] Another group of 15, including a chief who had lived at the Ahtanum Mission presented Wright with a letter of recommendation written by Father Pandosy. Other small bands approached declaring they had nothing to do with the war and did not wish to be involved in it.

Nelson, a Puget Sound chief, requested that Colonel Wright compose a letter ordering all whites in western Washington to stop shooting Native men who had quit the war and wished to resume their lives in peace. Yakama chiefs Owhi, Teias, and their Nisqually relative Leschi, met with Wright on June 9, and held a long talk about the problems associated with the war. Interpreters William McKay and John McBean related a number of details from Owhi during conversations held in Major Haller's tent. The chief described losing six of his relations during the war. The army had killed three, Cutmouth John, one, and two were killed at Puget Sound. Owhi's son, Qualchan, also known as "Thunder", lost five warriors during his winter expedition to the Sound. Sergeant McGavery had killed one of Showaway's people.

Owhi told officers that when making peace with Blackfeet enemies in the past, all agreed to stop fighting and "let things stand just as they find them."[11] Wright and Haller explained that things could not remain the same with the army, and the chiefs would be required to return all horses, mules and equipment that had been stolen or captured. Wright gave the chiefs five days to return and comply with the terms. Owhi's family left shortly afterwards, and did not return. Kamiakin and his brothers Skloom and Showaway left the valley without ever meeting with Wright.

Major Robert Garnett arrived at Camp Naches with two additional companies on June 13, 1856. They came up the Columbia River from Fort Vancouver being unable to travel over Naches Pass from Fort Steilacoom due to snow. Wright had erected a large shaded bower anticipating a council, but when the chiefs didn't return, he decided to go after the tribes and demand unconditional surrender. The colonel prepared to lead a force of 450 troops including two battalions of three companies each under Major Haller and Major Garnett. They were to "pursue these Indians, and push them to the last extremity."[12] Colonel Steptoe and three companies stayed behind at Camp Naches.

The soldiers remaining at the Naches River did their best to live comfortably. Officers slept in two large wall tents while infantrymen occupied small common shelters. In front of the wall tents, overhead bowers woven from willow branches had leaves left on them to provide a cool shaded veranda used as a dining room and parlor. The ground was covered with long grasses making a carpet similar to straw matting. The men crafted benches formed by driving forked sticks into the ground and laying straight saplings fastened across with strips of bark. Captain James J. Archer described it as "quite a pretty little village of willow wyths (sic) thatched with the long grass."[13] Some of the soldiers and early settlers later described the compound as a "basket fort."

Wright's main force crossed the network of bridges to the north bank on June 18 and marched upstream about five miles before crossing over to Wenas Creek. They followed the Wenas upstream approximately four miles before making their next camp. Four Indians from the Columbia River that had been on the Naches a few days earlier brought in fresh salmon to the troops. Next day, soldiers marched over what later became Ellensburg Pass, and descended into the Kittitas Valley where they encountered wind, dust, ants and mosquitoes near the Yakima River while trying to find a suitable place to camp. The men rested for three days when they were contacted by William Pearson, express man for Governor Stevens, and N. B. Coffee, express man from Colonel Benjamin Shaw's Washington Territory Volunteers, bringing news and mail. Shaw's men had camped about 15 miles away on Wenas Creek during their expedition to the Walla Walla Valley after having recently crossed the Cascade Mountains via Naches Pass.

Reveille sounded at 3:00 a.m. Monday June 23, and at 5:00 a.m. Wright's troops began marching in the direction of Snoqualmie Pass. During the day they surprised and captured two Native men who were held as informants. At night the soldiers made camp on the upper Yakima River. Two days later Wright sent William McKay and Cutmouth John to inform local Indians who were fishing nearby that they should come to the colonel's camp for a council. One chief, Kitsap, from Puget Sound, had recently escaped to eastern Washington to avoid capture by Governor Stevens' volunteers. Soldiers remained at camp on the upper Yakima River for another week waiting for a pack train to arrive with provisions needed to sustain troops during a hundred miles or more into the Wenatchee Valley and back. While they waited, Major Garnett gave Major Haller a line and hook for fishing, and other officers exchanged books to pass the time. Scouts reported that many Indians avoided Colonel Wright because they had been told that soldiers had hanged the first prisoners who were taken. Actually none had been harmed.

Father Pandosy arrived with 50 Indians on June 30. The priest assured local Natives that soldiers had come in peace to talk and not to injure them. Pandosy and William McKay took supper with Wright and Haller, and sat up talking until 10:00 at night. The priest left on July 2 to meet with more Yakamas who had gathered along the Wenatchee River. Wright proposed to have all Yakama families travel with him back to the Yakima Valley and Fort Naches to fish and subsist themselves under supervision of the Army.

Reveille sounded at 2:30 a.m. Thursday July 3, but soldiers did not cross the Yakima River until 9:00 a.m.. They waited for six companies and pack animals to cross to the north bank before marching just four miles to the next camp on the Teanaway River. Next day the command followed Swauk Creek north approximately 12 miles and camped in an open area covered with lush grasses. Some of the officers celebrated the 4th of July by breaking out flasks of whiskey. Non-imbibers enjoyed mountain spring water sweetened with sugar. The next march on July 5 followed a steep and rocky path covered with fallen timbers some ten miles up into the Wenatchee Mountains. The stream where the soldiers camped beyond the summit yielded a few pans of gold flakes discovered by some of the packers.

The steep narrow path leading down to the Wenatchee Valley caused some problems for mules carrying heavy loads. On one of the steepest slopes, three pack animals lost their footing and tumbled 100 feet down a canyon. Remarkably, none were seriously injured. On the afternoon of Sunday July 6 the army reached the floor of the valley, and established a camp next to the Wenatchee River. Father Pandosy greeted the soldiers while accompanied by a friendly chief who returned 17 mules that had been captured the year before from Major Haller and the Oregon volunteers. Wright met again with peaceful Chief Teias, but Owhi's and Kamiakin's people stayed out of reach across the Columbia River. The colonel met again with Puget

Sound chiefs Leschi, Nelson and Kitsap who were "determined to be our friends", and Wright let them go concluding that "I can establish nothing against them worthy of death."[14]

The majority of Yakamas agreed to accompany Colonel Wright back to the Kittitas Valley and leave behind a few fishermen who would join the others later. The soldiers chose a return route that followed the Wenatchee River downstream to the Columbia River rather than re-cross the difficult Wenatchee Mountains. But there were problems with the river trail having only a few inches of width in places. The army's trail maintenance crew, known as pioneers, had to dig earth away with spades from the side of a steep bluff to widen the path.

The Natives, who had begun the journey by following the soldiers, detoured by taking a route over nearby hills. The soldiers followed the Columbia River for about three miles before striking a well-worn path leading into the eastern slope of the Wenatchee Mountains covered with timber and tall grass. Two days later troops caught up with the Indian party on Naneum Creek in the Kittitas Valley. Father Pandosy had traveled with the soldiers spending much of his time with Major Haller taking his meals and sleeping in the officer's tent.

Wright soon set up camp on the Yakima River where he received some 500 Yakama men, women and children with their horses and cattle. In order to keep the people under his supervision, he issued 250 pounds of flour daily for their subsistence.

The colonel had finished meeting with most of the Native people residing between the Cascade Mountains and Columbia River. He wrote a bold recommendation to his adjutant in California: "The whole country should be given to the Indians. They require it; they cannot live at any one point for the whole year. The Roots, the Berries, and the fish, make up their principal subsistence; these are all obtained at different places, and different seasons of the year:"[15] Wright re-stated his position a week later in no less direct terms. "It is out of the question to confine the Indians in this Country to a certain District unless the Government furnish their entire subsistence. The whole country between the Cascade Mountains and the Columbia River, should be given to the Indians, it is not necessary to the white people."[16]

By the end of July, Colonel Wright declared that he had established peace and understanding among the tribes inhabiting Yakima, Kittitas,

Wenatchee, and Klickitat valleys except for Chief Kamiakin, his brothers, and Chief Owhi who had departed for Big Bend and Palouse country. The army abandoned Camp Naches and left four companies at the Yakima River in the Kittitas Valley under Major Haller until mid-September. Local Native people gathered around Haller's camp receiving daily rations of flour and setting up shaded bowers where they sold milk, berries and meat to the soldiers. On the upper reaches of Toppenish Creek, two companies under Major Garnett began constructing new buildings at a site chosen for Fort Simcoe where there was a fresh natural spring known as Mool Mool. Other companies under the command of Colonel Steptoe at Fort Dalles left for the Walla Walla Valley to look for a suitable place to build a new post there. Father Pandosy reported that the howitzer Haller lost in October had been recovered by two Yakama men and packer Alex McKay who turned it over to Colonel Wright's men at Fort Simcoe. Wright personally returned the howitzer to Fort Dalles.

Work began in earnest to construct buildings at Fort Simcoe before the onset of winter. Captain Frederick T. Dent led a crew improving the road from Fort Dalles to make it suitable for wagons hauling supplies to the new fort. Soldiers began cutting pine trees from nearby forests and hauling them to the construction site by wagon. Men used whip-saws to square logs by hand until a portable mule-driven sawmill could be obtained in November. Major Garnett hired a number of civilian laborers from The Dalles to help make bricks and construct chimneys and fireplaces.[17]

Camp Kittitas on the Yakima River disbanded in mid-September sending one hundred more soldiers to join Major Garnett at Fort Simcoe bringing the total number of men there to 218. Major Haller and Company I of the 4th Infantry Regiment left to establish a new post on the coast at Port Townsend helping to protect the region from raids by aggressive northern tribes arriving by canoe from the Russian territories.

Major Garnett departed for New York on November 19 to get married and prepare his wife Marianna for a journey west to join him at Fort Simcoe. Captain Dickinson Woodruff took command of the post in Garnett's absence. Soldiers slept in tents during the first weeks of winter while up to 14 inches of snow fell as work continued on the barracks. Falling temperatures caused ink to freeze in officers' pens. The men finally moved into solid buildings with fireplaces on December 14, 1856. Deep snow in the Simcoe Mountains prevented express riders and wagons from passing over the summit for the next couple of months. Local Indians with snowshoes carried mail over the mountains between Fort Simcoe and Fort Dalles until spring arrived.

Chapter 6 notes

1. Granville O. Haller Papers, 1839-1896, Diary 1856, microfilm, acc. # 3437-001, Special Collections, UW Libraries Seattle, WA.
2. George Wright to Capt. D.R. Jones Asst. Adjt. Genl. May 1, 1856, in William N. Bischoff, "The Yakima Campaign of 1856", *Mid-America* 31, reprint 20 (1949), 170-1.
3. Wright to Jones May 8, 1856 in Bischoff, 175-7.
4. Wright to Jones May 9, 11, 15, 1856 in Bischoff, 177-81.
5. Wright to Jones May 18, 1856 in Bischoff, 181-3.
6. Wright to Jones May 30, 1856 in Bischoff, 183-4.
7. James J. Archer Letters June 8, 1856, Relander Collection, typescript box 40-2, microfilm box 62-2, YVL.
8. Haller Diary 1856.
9. Col. Wright to R.R. Thompson, June 8, 1856 RBIA (RG 75) WS Misc. LR 1853-1861, NARA microfilm M5 Roll 23.
10. Wright to Jones, June 11, 1856 RAGO (RG 94) LR 1822-1860, NARA microfilm, M567 Roll 545.
11. Haller Diary June 10, 1856.
12. Wright to Jones June 25, 1856 in Bischoff, 190-1.
13. Archer Letters, July 4, 1856.
14. Colonel George Wright to Major W.W. Mackall July 25, 1856, "Reports from the Department of the Pacific No. 20", U.S. Senate 34th Congress, 3rd session 1856, SED No. 5, SS 876, 186-8.
15. Wright to Mackall July 18, 1856 No. 18 SED No. 5, 177-8.
16. Wright to Mackall August 3, 1856 in Bischoff, 207.
17. H. Dean Guie, *Bugles in the Valley Garnett's Fort Simcoe*, (Portland, OR: Oregon Historical Society, 1977), 43-7.

CHAPTER SEVEN

Volunteers Crossing the Cascades 1856

CITIZEN SOLDIERS AND THEIR CONTENTIOUS GOVERNORS

As Colonel Wright and some 500 soldiers marched through the Yakima Valley during the summer of 1856, Governor Stevens and the Washington Territory Volunteers organized an expedition of their own to take place east of the Cascade Mountains. Stevens had written to Wright earlier proposing that volunteers cooperate with regular troops in the Yakima Valley before proceeding to Walla Walla and taking action against tribes reported to be hostile there.[1] Wright declined under strict orders he received from General Wool's adjutant, "You will recollect that you have nothing to do with Volunteers or Governor Stevens. If you should find them or any citizens in your way, you will arrest, disarm and send them out of the Yakama Country."[2]

One of Stevens' top commanders in the field was 27-year-old Lieutenant Colonel Benjamin F. "Frank" Shaw. Shaw had arrived by wagon train in 1844 with his parents when he was just 15. He received his first taste of war as a member of his father's volunteer company responding to the Whitman Massacre in 1847. Shaw later settled in Olympia where he became proficient speaking Chinook jargon. Nisqually Indians called him "Quatlich", the redhead.[3] The governor selected Shaw to serve as interpreter during the Medicine Creek Treaty Council of 1854 and approved his election as commander of the Washington Territory Volunteers' Central and Southern Battalions during the war.

Shaw wrote to the governor on May 22, 1856 recommending an expedition be conducted to the east side of the Cascade Mountains because tribes on the west side had been beaten and the enemy on the east side "has never been checked."[4] He also declared that volunteers needed a fight before their enlistments ended. Stevens authorized two columns, one led by Shaw traveling over Naches Pass and another from Portland under Captain Francis M. P. Goff of Company K and Captain John A. Richards of Company N, made up of recruits from both Washington and Oregon. The governor believed military action was necessary because of information received from Nez Perce Indian Agent and volunteer lieutenant colonel William Craig in Lapwai that hostile tribes on the Walla Walla River, Snake River and Umatilla River were "determined to prosecute the war."[5] Reports also came from volunteer captain Henry Chase and captain/quartermaster/Indian Agent Albert Hugh Robie that "they are constantly being threatened with an attack from the Spokane, Palloose, Cayuses and Snakes."[6]

Camp Montgomery, located about six miles south of Fort Steilacoom, served as the volunteers' base of operations in western Washington. Shaw's right wing of the Second Regiment left Montgomery on June 12, 1856 heading east composed of four companies totaling 175 officers and men. An accompanying pack train consisted of 26 packers, 82 pack animals and 23 beef cattle. Six of the pack animals carried ammunition.[7] After five days on the trail they reached the summit of Naches Pass and discovered a number of snowshoes supposed to have been left by Qualchan's band of 50 or 60 that had returned from fighting in Puget Sound early in the spring. Qualchan's group had been larger coming back to the Yakima Valley than going over due to the addition of Nisqually allies seeking refuge from military pressure on the west side.

As volunteers neared the headwaters of the Naches River, Shaw's men found a prairie containing remnants of campfires made by Captain Maloney's troops the previous October. After following the Naches River two more days, they came to Edgar's Rock, named for guide John Edgar who had been married to a Yakama woman and traveled the route on his way to and from trading with Indians. Edgar died after being shot during a fight November 6, 1855, while accompanying volunteers south of Connell's Prairie.[8]

Shaw's expedition camped and rested on Wenas Creek on June 20 and remained until the 23. Volunteer scouts discovered Colonel Wright's soldiers camped a few miles away on the Yakima River in the Kittitas Valley, and Lieutenant Colonel Steptoe's troops on the lower Naches River. Shaw's express man, N. B. Coffee, visited with

Major Haller, and learned that Colonel Wright "had nothing particular to send to Col. Shaw."[9] On May 29 Wright had politely advised Shaw by correspondence that no volunteers were required despite sterner language Wright had received from his superiors. Volunteers broke camp and proceeded on their own following the Naches River to its mouth, then down the Yakima River toward the Columbia and Walla Walla Rivers.

At a camp between Ahtanum Creek and Toppenish Creek on June 26, Shaw placed Major Hamilton J. G. Maxon of the Southern Battalion under arrest after the officer of the day Lieutenant John A. Kemp reported that the major had ordered his men to fire their weapons contrary to orders. The 43-year-old major denied the accusation and refused to submit to arrest. A petition signed by seven men stated Maxon did not order the discharge of firearms to verify that guns were in working order after a previous night's rain. Maxon had told his men it was the officer of the day's duty to enforce the order and that "he would not do anything with us if we discharged our guns."[10] In protest, Maxon pulled his Clark County Mounted Rifles company from the colonel's ranks, and for the next several days marched a mile or two behind the rest of the command. The volunteers proceeded as two columns down the bank of the Yakima River then southeast down the bank of the Columbia River until reaching a point across from Fort Walla Walla. All waited for boats to be delivered by Captain Goff's men who were camped nearly forty miles away on the Umatilla River above Fort Henrietta.

Lieutenant Samuel Wilkes of Goff's company delivered boats to Shaw's men on the 4th of July. Volunteers celebrated the holiday by firing rounds from an old iron canon they had discovered hidden at Fort Walla Walla. Coincidentally Goff's men had found a canon abandoned in a well at Fort Henrietta and fired it in celebration also. Shaw's men spent July 5 boating across the Columbia River with their provisions and equipment while horses swam. After the main party crossed over, the boats were left behind for Major Maxon's company to make the crossing on its own.

Goff left more than half of his and Richards' command on the Umatilla River July 6 when he departed with 68 mounted soldiers to join 75 Oregon volunteers under Major Davis Layton and several Wasco scouts to pursue a party of 300 reported hostiles on the John

Day River in Oregon. For nine days the combined volunteer forces tracked the Indian party upstream until reaching the Burnt River on July 15. Lieutenant John Estis, Private Daniel Smith and Private N. J. Richards ascended a hill in advance of the others to look for hostiles. All three were ambushed and Estis and Smith fell dead while Richards escaped by running through trees after a bullet narrowly missed him and hit his rifle causing it to fire. A battle took place the rest of the day resulting in volunteers killing seven warriors, and dispersing the remainder.[11]

Meanwhile Shaw's command moved up the Walla Walla River July 7 to look for a camp site that contained ample grass for horses. The men passed the scene of battle fought by Oregon Volunteers the previous December. On July 8 they reached the abandoned Whitman Mission where they found "orchards laden with fruit with none to gather it – a sad picture."[12]

After staying a night near the former mission, the men moved farther up Mill Creek where they met William Craig and a group of 100 Nez Perce warriors. The Nez Perce gave the volunteers a rousing welcome singing and parading on horseback while displaying an American flag and firing salutes. Shaw's men returned the favor with loud cheers and salutes of their own. A large pack train arrived July 9 from The Dalles under the charge of Captain Robie with 50 loaded wagons and 75 pack horses laden with goods for peaceful Indians and supplies for volunteers. The remainder of Goff's men who had not gone with Major Layton into Oregon accompanied the pack train from Umatilla to Mill Creek. Maxon's men approached July 12 asking for food. Shaw refused. After the company submitted a letter agreeing to return to duty, Shaw allowed Maxon's men to re-join the battalion.[13]

Volunteers moved to a camp on Mill Creek approximately seven miles above the Nez Perce camp where Shaw ordered a corral built and headquarters established for upcoming operations. The officers rode over to the Nez Perce camp where Shaw "was pained to learn" from Spotted Eagle that the Cayuse and many Nez Perce no longer considered him a chief because he had aligned with the Washington Volunteers.[14] Spotted Eagle had been a courageous war chief during battles against Blackfeet in prior years, and he vowed to stay loyal to the Americans as his forefathers had done before him.

Colonel Shaw and Nez Perce guide Captain John figured that the Grand Ronde River Valley in Oregon southeast of Mill Creek likely held Cayuse and other allies gathering roots and fishing while keeping their distance from soldiers occupying the Walla Walla and Umatilla Valleys. Shaw wished to do damage to the tribes that had not yet exhibited peace toward the governor, and had not followed the examples of Howlish Wampoo of the Cayuse, Pierre of the Walla Walla, and many Nez Perce chiefs who had received protection, gifts, and provisions from the territorial government for their good behavior.

Shaw's men started for Grand Ronde on July 14 with 190 mounted soldiers plus 20 packers carrying 10 days of rations. They began at night to avoid detection from dust created by their horses' hooves on the dry summer soil. Nez Perce guide Captain John led the soldiers to the Walla Walla River where they made camp. Next day, the men ascended the Blue Mountains between the Walla Walla River and Pine Creek until they reached the headwaters of the Umatilla River where they camped again. On July 16 after traveling another 22 miles they crossed the main ridge of the Blue Mountains and descended into the valley of the Grand Ronde.

On the morning of July 17 Shaw's men spotted a dust cloud extending approximately three miles up and down the river bank indicating a large Indian village on the move. The soldiers pressed forward to within a half mile of the village while a large number of warriors came up singing and whooping to meet the volunteers. The leaders signaled for Captain John to come forward. One of the chiefs displayed a scalp dangling from a pole, and a number of warriors called out for others to shoot Captain John. Shaw called back his guide and gave the order for his men to charge.[15] Most of the warriors turned toward the banks of the river to draw soldiers away from their families, baggage and pack horses. But the volunteers rode straight for the pack train. "The chase commenced steadily and in order. Not a gun was fired for some distance," wrote Major George C. Blankenship. "They were expecting us to fight at a distance of a quarter of a mile, or thereabouts, which we had no notion of doing. As we took our course and moved forward, a large portion of the enemy who were in sight commenced moving in the same direction, as if to cut us off. For the first three miles they kept out of our reach, when we commenced gaining on them, and were in sight of a large portion of their stock and pack train. As we drew near, they began cutting their packs from the horses."[16]

While the soldiers closed in, the Indians "attempted to fight and individually did fight to the last, but all in vain", wrote Captain Walter W. DeLacy, topographer and adjutant who took part in the charge. "Many of their women even were unable to escape and were overtaken in the pursuit. None that were recognized were harmed, but were suffered to ride off free, which they gladly availed themselves of."[17]

Eyewitness Matthew P. Burns, surgeon, wrote, "Very few Indians were wounded as it was a hand to hand encounter, sometimes the Indians and our men beating each other's heads with their guns...I captured two squaws and a pack-horse; I brought the squaws into camp, and they told us that there were eight chiefs present...I counted fourteen dead Indians on one side of the Grand Ronde river, and nine on the other."[18]

Colonel Shaw learned from the captured Indian women that warriors that day came from Cayuse, Walla Walla, Umatilla, Tygh, John Day and Des Chutes tribes including chiefs; "Stock Whitley and Sim-mis-tas-tas, Des Chutes and Tyh; Chick-iah, Plyon, Wec-e-cai, Wat-ah-stuar-tih, Win-imi-swoot, Cayuses; Tah-kin, Cayuse, the son of Peu-peu-mox-mox, Walla Walla , and other chiefs of less note." He added, "The enemy was run on the gallop for 15 miles, and most of those who fell were shot with the revolver."[19]

Doctor Burns described the aftermath, "The prairie was literally covered with Indian food and clothing, ammunition, guns, pistols, axes, nets, and buffalo robes, with horses yet unpacked, also fine articles of Indian dress, both male and female, in a word their whole commissary was captured. The food consisted principally of camas, couse, dried beef, salmon, peas, corn, dried berries, some flour, coffee, sugar, and rice, with all their cooking utensils, consisting of brass kettles, pans, plates, knives, and in fact everything they had." Burns discovered "two scalps which had been taken from white men; one of a dark color with gray hairs in it, the other light hair, belonging to a young man. I think the scalp with the gray hair belonged to Capt. A. J. Hembree, as the hair was short and of the above color."[20]

The volunteers lost three killed after Major Maxon took 16 of his men across the river and disappeared while making a side charge on his own. Two of Maxon's group, James Irvine and William F. Tooley were found killed on July 17. The following day, William Holmes was killed while accompanying a search party looking for the lost detachment. Maxon had attempted to re-join the main party after dark, but when hearing cries coming from one of the female captives, he believed he was near an Indian camp and turned back to the trail leading to the headquarters on Mill Creek.

Shaw and his men chased the last of the Natives south toward Powder River before the colonel decided on July 19 to turn back toward the Emigrant Road, make camp and continue the search for Maxon. The procession moved back over the battlefield setting ablaze packs that had been left abandoned. They came to the site of the Indian village where 120 abandoned lodges still stood and burned them also. After searching the countryside on July 20, Shaw determined that no more of Maxon's men had been killed and that the major had most likely returned to the temporary headquarters.

A great military victory was declared by volunteers, the governor and newspaper editors, but others disagreed. Howlish Wampoo complained to Colonel Wright that some of Shaw's men failed to recognize non-combatants as Captain DeLacy had implied, and that old men, women and children had needlessly died.[21] Rather than subdue hostile factions, Shaw's aggression alienated even more. Word brought to The Dalles from the interior by one of the territory's noted express riders, William H. Pearson, declared, "The Nez Perce are rapidly becoming disaffected a majority of them are so at present. They are headed by the chiefs Looking Glass, Three Feathers, Red Bear, Eagle from the Light, The Man with the Rope in his mouth, and Red Wolf. Those mostly disaffected are known as the Buffalo People or, Upper Nez Perce."[22]

Stevens was convinced that tribes had become hostile because Colonel Wright had been too lenient while negotiating in the Yakima Valley by "talking and not fighting...and not reducing them to submission, thus giving safe conduct to murderers and assassins,(Leschi, Nelson and Kitsap) and not seizing them for summary and exemplary punishment."[23]

Shaw's volunteers returned to headquarters on Mill Creek July 23 and relieved Lieutenant Benjamin F. Ruth who had been left behind with 30 men to herd pack animals, stand guard at night and defend the compound. Major Maxon's company had arrived at headquarters but became restless to depart on July 26 with only 18 days left to serve on their enlistments. During a final act of insubordination, some of the major's men took a number of captured horses that had been branded and assigned to the quartermaster department. Shaw sent Lieutenant Thomas B. Wait with a detachment of men to recover the animals. Wait found the stock near the Walla Walla River ridden by men under the command of Lieutenant William S. Bennington. Wait requested that Bennington's men halt and give up the horses so they could be returned to headquarters, but Bennington and his men ignored the lieutenant and rode on. Undaunted, Wait's men pressed forward and forcefully extracted the others from their mounts except for one man, Jack McGuire, who drew a pistol and shot the horse that he claimed was his. Fourteen animals were eventually recovered and returned to Colonel Shaw.[24]

On July 31 Shaw moved camp five miles to a lower branch of Mill Creek where there was fresh grass for livestock. The next few days were spent constructing a corral and block house. On August 14 an express arrived from Governor Stevens stating he was on his way to Mill Creek to hold another council with local tribes. Colonel Craig was advised to invite all the Nez Perce including hostiles to attend.

Governor Stevens arrived August 23 with a small pack train carrying goods for the Indians. Two days later a pack train from The Dalles hauling additional supplies intended for Stevens' party lost 13 pack animals after being run off at night while camped at Butter Creek. The pack-master, Mr. Scott, sent an express to Colonel Shaw asking for additional animals and armed guards to continue. Shaw immediately sent replacement animals and 20 armed volunteers under the command of Lieutenant Albert Gates of Company N. The pack train was re-loaded and as it approached the Walla Walla Valley on August 28, the men were fired upon and attacked by approximately 100 warriors.

The volunteers circled the wagons and made breastworks out of packs while they returned fire. A barrel of bacon was set on fire to create smoke and alert soldiers at Shaw's camp eight miles away. The smoke wasn't noticed until just before nightfall when Captain Goff was sent with a detachment to investigate. Goff discovered the force of Indians to be too large, and returned to camp for reinforcements. Gates' and Scott's men had suffered without water since their last camp at Wild Horse Creek the previous day. Also low on ammunition, the men could no longer wait for rescuers, so they stole away at midnight in the dark on foot toward Shaw's camp leaving behind 41 animals and 33 packs of provisions all lost to the raiders.[25]

Stevens was very disappointed with his men for losing the pack train and supplies in such a manner. He issued fresh orders emphasizing a more proactive approach. The governor stressed "Bold and repeated charges upon the enemy, even when the disparity of numbers is great, will alone lead to results. In this way only can the superiority of our race be established. In all mere defensive contests with Indians, whether behind breastworks, or in the brush, an Indian is as good as a white man; few laurels can thus be won, and the result may be discreditable."[26]

Colonel Steptoe arrived from The Dalles September 5 with three companies of regular troops choosing a site on Mill Creek for a military post some seven miles away from Stevens' council grounds. Captain Robie and a pack train arrived safely two days later. The governor retained 69 volunteers under Captain Goff and Colonel Shaw plus a few civilian packers as he opened the 2nd Walla Walla Council on September 11, 1856. One of Governor Stevens' interpreters, Andrew D. Pambrun, noted that some of the tribesmen came in riding stolen pack mules and wearing clothes that had been intended for the volunteers.[27]

After two days of Stevens and the Natives exchanging accusations over the other sides' hostilities, Stevens sent a message to Colonel Steptoe asking for a company of regular soldiers for protection. Steptoe advised that the council participants move to the vicinity of the soldiers' camp instead. The governor made the move and attempted three more days of council. One contentious problem came from the Columbia Sinkiuse' (also called Isle des Pierres) chief Quiltenock who was dissatisfied about not being represented at the 1855 treaty council. Stevens tried to explain (unconvincingly) that Quiltenock's people fell under the jurisdiction of the Yakama Nation and Chief Kamiakin's authority.[28]

By September 18 there was enough dissension even William Craig was told he was no longer welcome in Nez Perce country. Stevens decided to close the proceedings and depart for The Dalles. Before leaving, Chief Owhi and Stock Whitley called upon Doctor Burns to ask for medicine.

Stevens and the volunteers left Walla Walla on September 19 and at 1:00 p.m. came under attack approximately three miles from Colonel Steptoe's camp.[29] An estimated 400 braves charged at the rear guard as the column moved down the road. Volunteers returned fire and proceeded another mile before circling the wagons near a stream and sending the Nez Perce away so they would not be mistaken for hostiles. After trading shots for a time, Colonel Shaw mounted a detachment of 25 men and led them headlong into the attackers while blazing away with revolvers. The bold charge held off the warriors until Lieutenant Davidson arrived that night with 70 U.S. Army regulars. All returned to Steptoe's post after losing one volunteer dead and killing five warriors.[30] Stevens identified hostile representatives from Yakama, Palouse, Cayuse, Walla Walla, Umatilla and Nez Perce tribes. Matthew Burns also identified Rock Island (Columbia Sinkiuse), Tygh and Des Chutes participants.

The area around Steptoe's post was devoid of grass after tribes had set the countryside ablaze during the previous several days. Steptoe and Stevens decided to construct a blockhouse together and store supplies leaving behind one company of soldiers and a howitzer to guard it while the remaining troops accompanied Governor Stevens and his men out of the valley. Colonel Steptoe planned to graze his hungry livestock along the Umatilla River, then proceed to The Dalles and purchase several wagon loads of oats to transport back to Walla Walla for the winter.

After the Grand Ronde fight and before Stevens' second council, a band of 250 Tygh Indians with 600 horses turned themselves in at Fort Dalles and surrendered their arms.[31] Although based in Oregon, some Tygh had fought at Walla Walla and been pursued by Washington Volunteers into Oregon during the war. They joined most of the Yakama, a number of Columbia River bands and all the west side tribes who had placed themselves under the supervision of Indian agents and the military. Colonel Wright spent 16 days in the Walla Walla Valley during the construction of Fort Walla Walla meeting with local chiefs and gauging their mood for or against peace. He found most favorable to peace. Kamiakin and Young Chief of the Cayuse, however, did not meet with Wright and were considered hostile. Kamiakin's influence continued to stretch across the territory, causing Wright to station a detachment and build a blockhouse as far westward as White Salmon, "simply to gratify the Indians, and quiet their fears of that ubiquitous individual Kamiakin."[32] Also, Chief Owhi and Qualchan had left the Yakima Valley to reside with their Columbia Sinkiuse and Spokane in-laws outside the influence of Indian agents and army officers. The Spokane, Colville, and Coeur d'Alene tribes north of Fort Walla Walla remained without a treaty and had told Governor Stevens they would remain peaceful as long as soldiers did not cross the Snake River into their territory.[33] The volunteers disbanded. Colonel Steptoe maintained a boundary of sorts at Fort Walla Walla. No settlers were allowed in Indian Country, the region east of the Cascade Mountains designated as ceded in the treaties but not yet ratified by Congress. The Army did allow Hudson's Bay Company employees to remain there, and miners were free to travel to the Colville mines.[34]

A month after the failed 2nd Walla Walla council, Leschi's Nisqually brother, Quiemuth was slain November 19 under mysterious circumstances in Governor Stevens' Olympia office at 3 o'clock in the morning while Stevens rested in another room. Quiemuth had agreed to surrender peacefully and was accompanied to Olympia by James Longmire, Van Ogle, George Brail, Oska a Frenchman, and John Edgar's Yakama widow, Betsy. The party arrived in the middle of the night at Stevens' office attached to the governor's residence. Stevens told guards to wait with Quiemuth while another party could be raised to take the Nisqually chief to Fort Steilacoom. Before that could happen Quiemuth was shot and wounded while sleeping on the office floor by someone firing in the darkness. The injured chief rose to his feet and tried to escape out the doorway, but was then stabbed to death.[35]

A number of people believed that Quiemuth was the one who had killed James McAllister at the beginning of hostilities in October. A son-in-law of McAllister, James Burton, was present among the crowd that had gathered outside Stevens' office door the night of Quiemuth's death, and newspapers "supposed" that son-in-law Burton did the killing, but a coroner's jury took no action to prosecute a suspect.[36]

Chapter 7 notes

1. State of Washington Office of the Adjutant General, *The Official History of the Washington National Guard* volume 2 Washington Territorial Militia in the Indian Wars of 1855-56, (Tacoma, WA: Camp Murray, 1961), 82.

2. W.W. Mackall to Colonel George Wright, July 3, 1856, RAGO (RG 94) LR 1822-1860, NARA microfilm M567 Roll 545.

3. Benjamin F. Shaw Papers MSS 412, Oregon Historical Society, Portland, OR.

4. B.F. Shaw to I.I. Stevens, May 22, 1856, WOAG 85-6.

5. Stevens to Wright, May 8, 1856, WOAG, 82.

6. A.H. Robie to I.I. Stevnes, May 30, 1856, RBIA (RG 75) WS Letters from employees assigned to the Col. R. or so. Distr. and Yakima Agency 1854-1861, NARA microfilm M5 Roll 17.

7. Captain Walter Washington DeLacy, Diary, June 12 to August 29, 1856, WOAG, 104.

8. Elwood Evans, ed. *History of the Pacific Northwest: Oregon and Washington* 2 vols. (Portland, OR: North Pacific History Company, 1889), 1:544.

9. DeLacy Diary, WOAG, 106.

10. H.H.G. Maxon to Benjamin F. Shaw, June 26, 1856, and Charles Dustin to Benjamin F. Shaw, June 28, 1856, Papers of the Washington Territorial Volunteers Indian War Correspondence 1855-1857, Series V, Colonel B.F. Shaw (Southern Battalion) Correspondence-Incoming Washington State Archives, Olympia.

11. Capt. F.M.P. Goff to Lt. Col. Benjamin F. Shaw, July 26, 1856, Volunteers Papers, WSA.

12. DeLacy Diary, WOAG, 109.

13. Company Washington Mounted Rifles to Benjamin F. Shaw, July 12, 1856, Volunteers Papers, WSA.

14. Shaw to Stevens, July 12, 1856, U.S. House of Representatives 34th Congress 3rd session 1856'57, Ex. Doc. No. 76, Indian Affairs on the Pacific, 13 volumes, vol. 9, 176-7.

15. (Olympia, WA) *Pioneer and Democrat*, August 8, 1856, B.F. Shaw to James Tilton, July 24, 1856.

16. *Pioneer and Democrat*, August 8, 1856, Major George C. Blankenship to J.W. Wiley, July 24, 1856.

17. DeLacy Diary, WOAG, 111.

18. Weekly (Portland) *Oregonian*, August 2, 1856, Matthew P. Burns, "Particulars of the Battle of the Grand Ronde".

19. Shaw in *Pioneer and Democrat*, August 8, 1856.

20. Burns in *Weekly Oregonian*, August 2, 1856.

21. Wright to Mackall, October 31, 1856 RAGO (RG 94) LR 1822-1860, NARA microfilm, M567 Roll 545.

22. *Weekly Oregonian*, August 2, 1856, Dalles Correspondent to Thomas J. Dryer; DeLacy Diary, WOAG, 114.

23. Isaac I. Stevens to Jefferson Davis, October 22, 1856, WOAG, 122.

24. Lt. Thomas B. Wait to Lt. Col. B.F. Shaw, July (27), 1856, Volunteers Papers, WSA.

25. *Pioneer and Democrat*, September 12, 1856, John Dunn, Express man to J. W. Wiley-Editor.

26. General Orders No. 6, September 4, 1856, WOAG, 116-7.

27. Andrew D. Pambrun, *Sixty Years on the Frontier in the Pacific Northwest*. (Fairfield, WA: Ye Galleon Press, 1978), 102.

28. Kent D. Richards, *Isaac I. Stevens Young Man in a Hurry*, (Pullman, WA: WSU Press, 1993), 305.

29. Stevens to Davis, October 22, 1856, WOAG, 120.

30. *Weekly Oregonian*, October 4, 1856, Matthew P. Burns to J.J. Dryer, September

23, 1856.
31. Wright to Mackall, August 24, 1856, NARA M567 Roll 545.
32. Wright to Stevens, December 9, 1856, RBIA (RG 75) WS Misc. LR 1853-1861, NARA microfilm M5 Roll 23.
33. Spokane Garry and Schlat-eal, December 2, 1855 in James Doty, Edward J. Kowrach, ed. *Journal of Operations of Governor Isaac Ingalls Stevens of Washington Territory in 1855*, (Fairfield, WA: Ye Galleon Press, 1878), 45-55.
34. Edward J. Steptoe, Copy of Order, August 20, 1856, WOAG, 118.
35. David Longmire, "First Immigrants to Cross the Cascades", *The Washington Historical Quarterly* 8, (January 1917): 27; Van Ogle, "Van Ogle's Memory of Pioneer Days", *The Washington Historical Quarterly* 13, (October 1922): 279-81.
36. *Weekly Oregonian*, November 29, 1856, "Quiemeth, a Nisqually Chief, Killed at Olympia".

Standoff and Transition 1857

A LULL IN THE ACTION WHILE PERSONNEL CHANGES

Late in December, 1856, deep snows at the remote post of Fort Simcoe prevented the army's horses and cattle from grazing near barracks and houses where soldiers resided. Four civilian herders accompanied by six soldiers drove the stock approximately 20 miles south to lower elevations where the animals could forage on natural grasses. At the same time Chief Kamiakin's fugitive brothers Skloom and Showaway had set up winter camp near White Bluffs on the Columbia River, and kept a wary eye on operations at Fort Simcoe.

Two days after Christmas, Skloom and 14 warriors crept up to the army's herd in the middle of the night and stole 50 cattle and 20 horses while unsuspecting guards slept beneath their blankets inside tents. In the morning, chief herder Frederick White went looking for the animals and was captured himself and taken to a temporary camp on the Yakima River. Skloom had long had an interest in reading and writing, and forced White to write a letter addressed to the commander at Fort Simcoe. The chief complained that Indians who cooperated with the military at Fort Simcoe were two-faced and did not deserve free handouts. Skloom declared that "The Chiefs, who have the power and right to sell the lands...will then take provisions, clothing, and money from you for our lands but we do not wish any of our people to have them for nothing." The chief expressed a desire to meet officials in council, "to make a good and straight peace, & treaty", and that "All the trouble we have had has been brought about by the bad talk of Stevens at the grand talk at Walla Walla."[1]

White wrote again on December 31, after being transported to Skloom's and Showaway's winter camp at White Bluffs. The chiefs continued to protest that the government was giving away thousands of dollars in flour, meat and sugar to Indians who did not have authority to take payments for land or the right to sell Kamiakin's wild horses for profit. "If we do not make peace now, it shall be war for life time. We'll swear then never & never to give up our arms as long as one of us lives. Not only Kamaiakin and his men, but all the Indians will take up arms against the Americans. We know well the Americans are a good many, but we are not afraid. We much rather die than live like dogs."[2] White added a post script asking that an answer be sent to the Indians as soon as possible. And if the herder did not survive, to please pay a debt of $102 owed to a Mr. Lucas.

Acting post commander, Captain Dickinson Woodruff, filling in for Major Garnett while he traveled back east, quickly replied to Skloom and assured him that Colonel Wright would be willing to accommodate the chiefs by holding a peace council. Woodruff also asked that Fred White be kept safe and returned to the post unharmed. White wrote three more letters written in his native German language that were translated by a man named Caso at Fort Simcoe. One of the letters contained details about the men who killed Indian Agent A. J. Bolon prior to the battle at Toppenish Creek. "Their names, Mitchell, (Showawash son), Wattashin, Nanginim, (an old man)… Woppy, Sukei, and Stuchen."[3] The names matched those provided earlier by Wasco Chief Kaskala to Major Haller, and neither list included Qualchan's name. Although a number of civilians assumed Qualchan was involved with Bolon's murder, the army had known for some time that Owhi's son was not part of that incident. The chiefs said they considered Bolon to be their friend and were angry about the agent's regrettable death.

Other letters written by Fred White represented the chiefs' feelings about the causes of war. "Then came Gov. Stevens & said I am the Boston Chief. I was sent by the Americans to buy your land, if you will sell with a good will. If you will not sell with a good will, I'll come with my soldiers & fight for it."[4] And when Skloom learned that Captain Woodruff had told other Indians that the army would drive the chief into the mountains if he did not exhibit good behavior, Skloom replied, "Does he think to scare us as Governor Stevens did?"[5]

White received a number of personal items from Fort Simcoe while in captivity, and he asked for additional tobacco, soap, a razor and some paper. In February, Skloom moved White to the Palouse

River. The herder was released and arrived safely at The Dalles on the first of March 1857.[6] Skloom returned the stolen cattle and horses to the army in April without further incident.[7]

Hostilities subsided during 1857, but war remained unfinished in eastern Washington while the army occupied the posts at Fort Simcoe and Fort Walla Walla. Soldiers kept settlers out of ceded Indian country while waiting for Congress to ratify treaties. During the lull between battles, citizens and newspaper editors remained aware that war had not ended, and hostile chiefs still remained at large. The *Weekly Oregonian* published a lively parody imagining what it would be like if Kamiakin had taken over the whole country. "President Kamiakin's Inaguration...Secretary of State-Teias, Secretary of War-Looking Glass, Secretary of Navy-Leschi, Attorney General-Owhi... Colonel Qualshun, a son of the venerable Attorney General...Chief Justice Lawyer, Lt. General Skloom...Chaplain of the Senate the Rev. Mr. Pandosy...Brig. Gen Towatox...Commodore Kitsap", all with the purported goal to achieve "utter extinction of the White Race within fifty years."[8] Extermination of a competing culture was an idea favored and discussed by a few extremists on all sides of the conflict. The editorial mood in Washington and Oregon revealed some of those views.

Fort Simcoe teemed with activity on May 15 when Major Garnett returned with his bride, Marianna, and joined four other military wives and more than 300 men at work finishing the post and constructing permanent quarters for officers and their families.[9] Garnett insisted upon high standards of quality. After the quartermaster department in San Francisco denied the major's order for paint and reduced the allowance for lime to make plaster, Garnett wrote a letter directly to the adjutant general of the army in Washington D.C. asking for help to "preserve those habits of neatness and cleanliness common among the class of people in civil life from whom the officers of our army are supposed to come." And, "to see that the small portion of the army entrusted to my care and command be provided for in a manner becoming our government and people."[10] Major and Mrs. Garnett had a son, Arthur Nelson, born at the post in February 1858.

In the Walla Walla Valley, Lieutenant Colonel Steptoe's troops spent the winter of 1856-57 in temporary quarters on Mill Creek, "housed in our log huts, roofed with sod and dirt."[11] As the men hunkered down for the winter, General Wool wrote to Washington D.C. and asked to be relieved of his command and reassigned to the Eastern Department in Albany, New York. His request was approved and Wool was replaced on the west coast by General Newman S. Clarke. In the spring, Steptoe looked for and found a more desirable location up a hill west of Mill Creek, and began permanent construction of the army's Fort Walla Walla buildings.

Puget Sound residents focused on trying to get their lives back to normal. A war debt of approximately $1.6 million had been accumulated to pay for operations conducted by Washington's volunteers. Scrip had been issued rather than cash payments to merchants and citizens for horses, equipment, forage, guns, ammunition, clothing, subsistence and pay for the volunteers. In order to get reimbursed, the U.S. Congress would have to agree that the expenses had been legitimate to protect the lives of citizens. Oregon accumulated costs valued at more than $4.5 million.

Residents of the territories needed to have effective representation in Washington D.C. to counter arguments from General Wool and his supporters that the volunteers' efforts were unnecessary. Civilians also wished to have the treaties ratified so that settlement could proceed in the ceded areas. Stevens decided to run for the office of territorial delegate to Congress. The governor's second job — superintending Indian affairs — had ended March 18 with the appointment of James W. Nesmith as superintendent for both Washington and Oregon Territories. Nesmith had been colonel and field commander of the Oregon Mounted Volunteers during the campaign into Yakama country and Two Buttes in November 1855.

Democrat Isaac I. Stevens campaigned for delegate to Congress against Republican Alexander S. Abernathy. The former Whig had support from many anti-martial law voters, but even some of them realized that the best qualities to convince Congress to approve the war debt might be Stevens' fiery determination, previous political experience and effective speaking skills. Stevens won the election in July with 65 percent of approximately 1500 votes cast.

Delegate Stevens arrived in Washington D.C. about the same time a report came from Californian J. Ross Browne, a special agent of the Treasury Department assigned to examine the causes of war in Oregon and Washington. Congress needed assistance from a third party to try and determine whether General Wool's view or the territorial governors' views were most legitimate. Browne made his report after touring the region for approximately six months. The agent's findings largely supported the governors' actions to mobilize the volunteers needed for the defense of territorial citizens. But Stevens and Oregon delegate Joe Lane faced an uphill battle lobbying Congress for nearly two years before having to settle for about half the amount they originally had applied for.[12]

As the year 1857 ended, hostile chiefs and warriors remained at large east of the Cascade Mountains. Qualchan and his brothers stayed close to their Columbia-Sinkiuse in-laws, Quiltenock and Moses. Qualchan also stayed linked to the Spokane tribe through his wife, Whistalks, a daughter of Chief Polatkin. Yakama chief Kamiakin, a Palouse by birth on his father's side, kept his family isolated from soldiers in Palouse country while rumors circulated that the army planned to cross the Snake River and wipe out northern tribes. The previously neutral Coeur d'Alene tribe faced recruitment overtures from the "blood-thirsty" Palouse and Kamiakin, all said to be advocating war against Americans.[13]

The killing of Isaac N. Ebey on August 11, 1857 at his home on Whidbey Island by northern (Alaska region) Indians was unrelated to the war with tribes in Washington Territory. The episode began in November 1856 when a group of about 150 tribesmen from the vicinity of Russian settlements around Sitka arrived in large seaworthy canoes at Puget Sound. The northern Indians began harassing and raiding white and native residents near Steilacoom. Commander Samuel Swartwout of the U.S. steamer *Massachusetts* pursued the raiders about 45 miles north where they had made camp at Port Gamble.

Through an interpreter on November 21 Swartwout tried to persuade the chiefs to allow their canoes to be towed behind the *Massachusetts* to Victoria, Vancouver Island where they would be released and allowed to proceed to their homes as long as they promised not to return to Puget Sound. The chiefs refused and threatened to fight the ship's crew. The commander attempted two more diplomatic overtures without success. Swartwout reported, "It was not until after every argument had failed to convince them of the folly of any further resistance, and they had taken positions behind logs and trees, with their guns pointed toward our party on the beach in a hostile manner, that the order was given to fire."[14]

The navy employed a field piece and howitzer that raked round shot and grape into the woods ahead of 30 armed sailors and marines who charged the encampment, burned dwellings and destroyed canoes. The following day the chiefs agreed to board the *Massachusetts* and be transported to Victoria after suffering 27 killed and 21 wounded. The navy lost one sailor killed.

The following August members of a northern tribe arrived at Whidbey Island seeking a white chief to slay in revenge for the defeat at Port Gamble (Ebey held the title of Adjutant General of the Washington Territory Militia). The attackers shot Ebey, removed his head and took it with them up the coast north of Sitka, above the 58th parallel. Two years later Hudson's Bay Company chief trader Dodd aboard the ship *Labouchre* successfully negotiated the recovery of Ebey's scalp and returned it to the family.[15] The army had established posts at Port Townsend and at Bellingham Bay in 1856 to protect settlers and local Indians against northern tribes, but efforts were not enough to save Ebey.

Chapter 8 notes

1. Fred White Letters, "Skilloom to the Officer in Command", December (28), 1856 Near the Yakima River, RAGO (RG 94) LR from Department of the Pacific, 1857 File W9, Relander Collection, typescript 45-12, YVL (original Wright to Mackall, February 6, 1857 missing from NARA - 2003).

2. "Skilloom & Showawash to the Government", December 31, 1856, Relander, 45-12.

3. "Fred White to the Government", January 1, 1857, Relander, 45-12.

4. Fred White letter, January 12, 1857, Relander, 45-12.

5. ibid

6. A.H. Robie to I.I. Stevens, March 2, 1857, RBIA (RG 75) WS Letters from employees assigned to the Col. R. or so. Distr. and Yakima Agency 1854-1861, microfilm NARA M5 Roll 17.

7. James J. Archer Letters, April 17, 1857, typescript Relander Collection, box 40-2, YVL.

8. Weekly (Portland) *Oregonian*, May 30, 1857.

9. H. Dean Guie, *Bugles in the Valley Garnett's Fort Simcoe*, (Portland, OR: Oregon Historical Society, 1977), 72-80.

10. R.S. Garnett to Col. S. Cooper, November 4, 1857, typescript, Relander Collection, 42-13, YVL.

11. Lewis McMorris in Robert A. Bennett, *We'll All Go Home in the Spring Personal Accounts and Adventures as Told by the Pioneers of the West*, (Walla Walla, WA: Pioneer Press Books, 1984), 121.

12. Kent D. Richard, *Isaac I. Stevens Young Man in a Hurry*, (Pullman, WA: WSU Press, 1993), 342.

13. Joset to Congiato June 27, 1858, U.S. Senate 35th Congress 2nd session 1859, SED No. 32 Topographical Memoir of Colonel Wright's Campaign, 43-7.

14. Samuel Swartwout to Lt. Col. Silas Casey, November 23, 1856, House of Representatives 34th Congress 3rd session 1856-'57, Ex. Doc. No. 76, Indian Affairs on the Pacific, in thirteen volumes, vol. 9, 247.

15. Evans, 1:512.

CHAPTER NINE

Leschi's Trials and Execution 1856 - 58

OUTCOMES THAT JOLTED THE TERRITORY

Sarah McAllister's father James was one of the first Puget Sound fatalities during the territory's war. He and Michael Connell died in an ambush near White River on October 27, 1855 while looking for Leschi to ask him about reports that the Nisqually leader was planning to go to war.

The McAllister family had arrived at Puget Sound in 1845 with the first group of settlers to make their homes there. Sarah recollected Leschi's early hospitality and her happy childhood growing up with neighboring Nisqually people eating the same foods and speaking the Native language.[1]At the beginning of the year 1855, the Medicine Creek Treaty negotiated a month earlier had changed attitudes and conditions around Puget Sound. Many settlers had arrived taking up farms and homesteads while the terms of the treaty greatly reduced the amount of land reserved for Nisqually people compared to what they were accustomed to using. When news of Kamiakin's triumph over the soldiers at Toppenish Creek reached Native people on the west side in October, hope surged in the hearts of many that perhaps the intruders could be expelled forever.

The Yakama and Nisqually tribes had been closely linked for generations. Leschi had been born to a Nisqually father and a Yakama mother related to Chief Owhi. Fort Nisqually recorded visits from Yakama people as early as 1835 verifying coming and going regularly across the Cascade Mountains to trade at the Hudson's Bay Company post. Leschi and other Puget Sound chiefs inspired by Kamiakin's early victory reacted by attacking settlers and soldiers west of the Cascade Mountains. After some initial success with the help of Qualchan's Yakama warriors, the tide changed when regular army reinforcements from California, combined with determined local volunteers and artillery from the warship *Decatur,* effectively suppressed the tribal uprising in Puget Sound. Leschi, his brother Quiemuth along with Chiefs Nelson and Kitsap fled east over the Cascade Mountains to the Yakima Valley where they met Colonel George Wright and convinced the army officer that the Puget Sound chiefs wanted to quit the war and become peaceful.

Governor Stevens, however, refused to allow amnesty. He condemned the chiefs to death before they were brought to trial. "In reference to Leschi, Nelson, Kitsap and Quiemuth from the Sound... no arrangement be made which shall save their necks from the Executioner."[2]

The four chiefs returned to Puget Sound where Leschi was apprehended November 13, 1856 by two of his own tribesmen for a reward of 50 blankets offered from the commissary of the Washington Volunteers. Quiemuth turned himself in November 19 and was slain by an unidentified assailant on the floor of Governor Stevens' office. Kitsap and Nelson went to trial two and a half years later in 1859 after Governor Stevens had moved to Washington D.C. Those chiefs were acquitted and released.[3]

Leschi received a speedy trial four days after his capture in Judge Chenoweth's U.S. District Court held at Steilacoom on November 17, 1856. Attorney Frank Clark defended Leschi against the charge of murdering Colonel Abraham Benton Moses, a Pierce County militia officer killed October 31, 1855 during an ambush in a swamp near White River. Antonio B. Rabbeson provided key eyewitness testimony claiming that he observed Leschi firing the fatal shot that killed Moses. A second militia officer, Lieutenant Colonel Joseph Miles, also died during the same ambush but his assailant had not been identified. Judge Chenoweth instructed jurors that if they determined that death had occurred during an act of war, the civil court had no jurisdiction. Two jurors, William M. Kincaid and Ezra Meeker, believed the act had occurred during war, and held out for acquittal.[4] The judge dismissed the jury, and Leschi was retained in custody to await a new trial.

Leschi's second trial commenced March 18, 1857 in district court at Olympia, Judge Lander presiding. A.B. Rabbeson again gave testimony identifying Leschi as the shooter that killed Moses. Testifying for the defense, Andrew J. Bradley, an express messenger in the party that accompanied Moses on the day of the attack, stated that he did not see Leschi at the scene. Others, not with Moses on the day he died, gave favorable testimony about Leschi's previously reliable conduct and good character. But the jury unanimously found the defendant guilty and sentenced him to death.[5]

Leschi's defenders appealed to the Washington Territory Supreme Court. They were over-ruled and the execution set for January 22, 1858. A committee composed of Leschi's supporters including Dr. William Tolmie, Chief Factor of the Hudson's Bay Company at Nisqually, and Lieutenant Colonel Silas Casey, U.S. Army commander at Fort Steilacoom, requested a pardon from Governor Fayette McMullen, but the request was denied.

On the day set for execution a last minute maneuver from officers at Fort Steilacoom appointed Lieutenant McKibben a special deputy U.S. marshall authorized by U.S. Commissioner J. M. Batchelder, a sutler at the military post. A warrant was issued for the arrest of Sheriff Isaac Hays for the unlikely offense of selling whiskey to Indians. Some said that the sheriff submitted willingly. The tactic delayed Leschi's execution but enraged a local committee of citizens who immediately adopted a resolution protesting "a most unnatural and unreasonable sympathy for the Indian, who was known to have engaged in the fiendish massacre of helpless women and children on White River in the fall of 1855…"[6] Of course, Leschi never stood trial for the White River massacre, but nevertheless the incident became the reason why many Olympia citizens wanted him hanged. The committee also wanted the military officers responsible for delaying the execution to be removed from the territory and dismissed from the army.

The territorial legislature, which happened to be in session at the time, promptly passed an act requiring the territorial Supreme Court to hold a special session and make a ruling on the status of Leschi's case. The prisoner was re-sentenced to hang on Friday February 19 to be carried out by a new acting sheriff, William Mitchell. The site chosen to erect the gallows was located a mile east of Fort Steilacoom, near the north end of the lake in a natural amphitheater large enough to hold a substantial number of spectators. At 11:35 a.m. on the day scheduled, Leschi climbed the steps of the scaffold with his arms bound behind his back. He turned to the crowd, bowed his head, prayed out loud, and met his fate.[7]

Few settlers knew Leschi better than veteran Indian fighter Benjamin F. Shaw who had been interpreter at the Medicine Creek Council and at both of Leschi's trials. Shaw was credited with providing a transcript of Leschi's words after being sentenced, "I have supposed that the killing of armed men in wartime was not murder; if it was, the soldiers who killed Indians were guilty of murder, too…I deny that I had any part in killing Miles and Moses. I heard that a company of soldiers were coming out of Steilacoom, and determined to lay in ambush for it; but did not expect to catch anyone coming from the other way. I did not see Miles or Moses before or after they were dead, but was told by the Indians that they had been killed. As God sees me, this is the truth."[8]

Shaw joined a number of others skeptical of Rabbeson's incriminating testimony. They believed that it was not possible for a witness to recognize Leschi "among thirty or forty painted Indians all firing at them from the cover of bushes that surrounded the swamp they were in."[9]

Nearly 150 years later a modern Washington legislature asked a state supreme court justice to conduct a non-binding "Historical Court of Justice" and reconsider the charges against the Nisqually leader. A seven-member court unanimously exonerated Leschi by determining that he should never have been charged with the crime because he acted as a lawful combatant during a time of war.[10]

Leschi's Yakama relatives in eastern Washington took the news hard about the execution in 1858. Colonel Wright, the white-haired chief, had let Leschi go finding no reason to punish him. But the white men's courts in Puget Sound acted differently. The circumstances compounded ill feelings already festering among Owhi's and Kamiakin's people that had been caused by Indians around Fort Simcoe cooperating with the army and selling hundreds of the chiefs' horses for profit. Lieutenant Colonel Casey learned from Nelson and Kitsap that Owhi's son "was trying to get a war party against the whites and they would be killed – Leschi's death caused much excitement amongst those Indians."[11]

Chapter 9 notes

1. Sarah McAllister Hartman, "Early Reminiscences of a Nisqually Pioneer", *Told by the Pioneers* vol. 1 (Olympia, WA: Washington Secretary of State, 1937), 167-8.
2. State of Washington Office of the Adjutant General, *The Official History of the Washington National Guard* volume 2 Washington Territorial Militia in the Indian Wars of 1855-56, (Tacoma, WA: Camp Murray, 1961), 96.
3. Clinton A. Snowden, *History of Washington* 4 vols. (New York: The Century History Company, 1909), 4:13; Elwood Evans ed. *History of the Pacific Northwest: Oregon and Washington* 2 vols. (Portland, OR: North Pacific History Company, 1889), 1:509.
4. Ezra Meeker, *Pioneer Reminiscences of Puget Sound The Tragedy of Leschi,* (Seattle, WA: Lowman & Hanford, 1905), 420.
5. (Olympia, WA) *Pioneer and Democrat,* March 27, 1857.
6. Snowden, 4:10.
7. *Pioneer and Democrat*, February 26, 1858.
8. Snowden, 4:12.
9. Benjamin F. Shaw papers, Geo. H. Hines interview September 25, 1902, MSS 412, Oregon Historical Society, Portland, OR.
10. Yakima (WA) *Herald-Republic*, December 11, 2004.
11. Silas Casey to Major W.W. Mackall, June 16, 1858, RAGO (RG 94) LR 1822-1860, NARA microfilm M567 Roll 577.

CHAPTER TEN

The Spokane Campaign 1858

THE ARMY'S SOLUTION BY FORCE

S oon after Leschi's execution, new acts of violence broke out east of the Cascade Mountains following a year-long period of relative quiet.

An attack upon Lieutenant Colonel Edward Steptoe's soldiers by Spokane, Coeur d'Alene, Yakama, and Palouse warriors on May 17, 1858 came about due to a number of circumstances. Spokane chiefs had earlier informed Governor Stevens in December of 1855 that soldiers should not encroach upon land north of the Snake River in order for those tribes to remain peaceful.[1] Stevens may not have shared that conversation with Colonel Steptoe, and likely too, the army did not know the extent that Kamiakin and Palouse Chief Tilcoax had been actively recruiting Coeur d'Alene men to take up arms against Americans.[2]

U.S. Army Captain Woodruff's company had already gone north of the Snake River to escort a boundary survey along the 49th parallel, and with reports about Lieutenant John Mullan's party leaving Fort Dalles to survey a road through Spokane territory, it looked to the tribe as though the military might be invading without a warning. Steptoe and 157 soldiers left Walla Walla for Colville expecting to hunt down five Palouse renegades who had attacked two French Canadian miners earlier on the Tucannon River.[3] Troops also sought another group of six raiders that had stolen cattle belonging to the army.[4] In addition, Steptoe wished to calm nervous miners in the Colville area who had requested a military presence due to unspecified hostile threats from local tribes.

The soldiers were equipped to engage a few fugitives, and intimidate others with a pair of howitzers, but troops were not prepared for a battle against the combined forces of the Spokane and Coeur d'Alene nations plus their allies. Indeed, Steptoe anticipated that Spokane tribesmen would be willing to provide canoes to cross the Spokane River on the soldiers' way north. Two companies of troops carried outdated short range muskets. Only a few rounds of ammunition had been issued each man and no sabers for the dragoons. Colonel Steptoe rode along leisurely attired in civilian clothes, "and confidently carrying in his hand a small riding whip."[5]

Also not well known, Steptoe had been ill during the winter and may not have recovered by the time the expedition left in spring. The popular West Point graduate suffered spells of palsy late in 1857, and wrote home from Fort Walla Walla to his father, Dr. William Steptoe, on April 5, 1858. "I have suffered unusually this winter from colds – catarrh – indeed can scarcely say I have been well one day since Christmas." To his sister, Nannie, he confided, "This past winter has been especially grievous to me – sick, isolated – brooding painfully over the past and almost hopelessly on the future, I have grown ten years older in one, apparently."[6] Steptoe took sick leave in 1859 for three years while suffering continual ailments, and resigned his commission due to poor health in 1861. He died in 1865 at age forty-nine.[7]

The battle known as Steptoe's Defeat took place not long after the colonel wrote home that he had not been well for months. He and his troops on their way to Colville became surrounded near the present town of Rosalia by a force of warriors eight times greater than the soldiers. Two West Point graduates died during the battle, 32-year-old Captain Oliver Hazard Perry Taylor and 23-year-old Lieutenant William Gaston.[8] Privates Alfred Barnes, Charles H. Harnish and James Crozet also died fighting.[9]

At dusk on May 17, 1858, warriors fell back leaving soldiers stranded on a hilltop nearly out of ammunition. After consulting other officers, Steptoe ordered a nighttime retreat into darkness with campfires left burning and a few mules milling around to make the site appear occupied. The colonel had to abandon and bury two howitzers in the field to lighten the load and make the 85-mile escape to the Snake River. Friendly Nez Perce guides led the men overland to Alpowa where still more Nez Perce with Chief Timothy assisted the fatigued survivors across the river. Two wounded men, Sergeant

William C. Williams and Private Victor Charles De Moy, were in too much pain to proceed and pleaded to be left behind with provisions along the trail where they eventually died.[10] Williams' death was reported to have been hastened by a Palouse man who happened by, and was hanged for the act on September 25 by Colonel Wright's order.[11] The army lost a total of seven soldiers plus three friendly Nez Perce killed. Eyewitness Lieutenant David McMurtry Gregg counted 15 enemy warriors dead.[12]

Chief Kamiakin's connection to the battle was confirmed by Father Pierre De Smet after speaking with the chief months afterwards. "Kamiakin made an open avowal of all he had done in his wars against the Government of the country, particularly in the attack on Colonel Steptoe, and in the war with Colonel Wright."[13] Kamiakin trusted black robe missionaries such as De Smet, but not many other non-Natives. One of the chief's contemporaries, Yallup, once explained a common view held that Father Casimir Chirouse, for example, "was not a white man; he was a Frenchman."[14] Owhi's son, Lo-Kout, brother of Qualchan, also verified Kamiakin's presence at the Steptoe battle during a later speech attended by author A. J. Splawn.[15]

Immediately after the Steptoe battle the army called up more troops from throughout western United States, and assembled an imposing strike force to retaliate against the warring tribes. Under General Newman S. Clarke the role of the army changed from protector to conqueror.

While the army increased its supplies of arms, ammunition and personnel, hostile factions from inland tribes continued to make assaults on civilians. On June 20, Qualchan and his ally Columbia Sinkiuse Chief Quiltenock led an attack upon 76 miners from California at the mouth of the Wenatchee River. One miner was killed during the fight, one accidently shot himself dead, two drowned crossing a stream, one died of fright and one died of "pluresy" after retreating to Fort Simcoe.[16] Native casualties included Quiltenock killed, and Qualchan wounded by a bullet to the abdomen.

The following month, Okanogan and other warriors attacked a separate group of 25 miners at McLoughlin Canyon near the Okanogan River. At least one miner was killed, and the remainder proceeded north to the gold fields in British territory.[17]

At Fort Colvile, victorious Spokane and Couer D'Alene men danced and celebrated their triumph over the Steptoe expedition.[18] General Clarke sent a message to the tribes offering terms of unconditional surrender, but the peace chiefs did not want to give up their fellow tribe members to hangmen, and the war chiefs believed that they could beat the soldiers again.

Meanwhile, troop strength swelled at Fort Dalles and Fort Walla Walla. Between June 21 and July 7 Captain Erasmus D. Keyes held intense target practices at Fort Dalles every day including Sundays with four companies of Third Artillery soldiers issued new long range rifles.[19] Keyes' troops marched to Fort Walla Walla July 19 where they joined four more companies of the First Dragoons, and two of the Ninth Infantry. Along the way near Wild Horse Creek on July 24th, troops came across a white man "brutally butchered by the Walla-Walla Indians, and to whose body was given sepulture by a detachment of dragoons under Lieutenant Pender."[20] The perpetrators would later be found and hanged during the end of Wright's campaign. After reaching Fort Walla Walla, soldiers kept up light infantry drill tactics twice per day.[21] On August 7, Keyes left Fort Walla Walla with one company of dragoons and six companies of artillery, two mountain howitzers and 30,000 rations. They marched to the junction of the Tucannon and Snake Rivers where soldiers constructed a temporary supply depot they named Fort Taylor in honor of one of the officers killed at the Steptoe battle in May. The location would be used to support Colonel Wright's full force when it became ready to take the field.

About the same time, Major Robert S. Garnett organized a separate campaign at Fort Simcoe preparing a sweep through the Yakima and Wenatchee Valleys continuing up the Okanogan River. Garnett specifically targeted Owhi, Qualchan, Skloom and 25 others identified as being responsible for attacks on miners earlier in the year. Garnett figured there might be more suspects, but Indian informants named only those considered most guilty. The major's objective was "to capture and hang them."[22]

Four companies departed August 11, comprised of nine officers, 280 enlisted men and 50 packers and herders.[23] The expedition began pleasantly enough with Captain Archer writing home that he had caught a mess of trout up to 14 inches long while camped on Cowiche Creek. The mood changed at 3:00 a.m. August 15, when Lieutenant Jesse K.

Allen with 15 mounted men surprised Katihotes' party of 21 men and 50 women and children camped near the mouth of Teanaway River in the Kittitas Valley.[24] The incident turned bloody in the darkness when soldiers opened fire, killing two tribal men, and Lieutenant Allen was accidently shot and killed by his own men. Three men in the Indian camp were identified as murderers of miners, and they were shot on orders by Major Garnett.

Major Garnett sent another expedition of 60 men under Lieutenant George Crook to pursue additional suspects into the upper reaches of the Wenatchee River on August 21. Through the cooperation of Chief Skinar-wan, five miner attackers were identified and executed by firing squad.[25] Indian informants reported six more suspects hiding in the mountains west of the upper Wenatchee River. Garnett sent an additional party of 60 men under a captain and a lieutenant to find them. A three day search through thick forest and heavy underbrush proved fruitless. The men returned to Garnett's camp without finding the fugitives.

Indian informants advised Major Garnett that the remaining nine suspects were with Owhi, Qualchan and Moses opposite Hudson's Bay Company Fort Okanogan north of the Columbia River. Skloom had gone to join Kamiakin on the Spokane River.[26] The command continued up the Okanogan River for some 40 miles where on September 9, Private Liebe of Company C lagged behind the main party and was killed by a warrior named Klopoken.[27] Garnett's command returned to Fort Simcoe without further incident on September 23 only to learn that Major Garnett's wife, Marianna, and infant son, Arthur, had both died of bilious fever while the major was away. Garnett left the post in mid- October accompanying the bodies of his family back east for burial.

An oral version of Garnett's campaign persisted in the Wenatchee region for decades claiming that Captain Frazer and some other soldiers murdered a village of Wenatchee Indians somewhere near Raging Creek and White River during the summer of 1858.[28] Captain John W. Frazer had left the command to accompany the body of his co-commander of Company C, Lieutenant Allen, killed on August 15, whose remains were taken back to Fort Simcoe. After Crook's party returned from Skinar-wan's camp, Garnett's report published in congressional records stated that he sent "Captain Hager (sic) and

Lieutenant (Elisha E.) Camp, 9th infantry, to hunt up these remaining men."[29] However, Captain Frazer had returned to the command after delivering Allen's body to the fort, and the daily itinerary reports kept at the National Archives confirmed that Frazer did in fact accompany Lieutenant Camp on the mission to hunt up the remaining fugitives.[30] Garnett's handwriting transcribed into the printed congressional record was mistakenly typeset as "Hager" instead of Frazer. And Captain Anthony Heger, the surgeon assigned to Fort Simcoe, had remained back at the post caring for Garnett's wife and baby, and was not in the field with the rest of the command. Assistant Surgeon Charles C. Kerney accompanied the troops in the field.[31]

The army reported no contact or shots fired during the second mission led by Frazer and Camp. The army's version along with author A. J. Splawn's describe the occupants of a village managing to elude the army and successfully make its escape. Typically, regular army officers reported forthrightly when reporting their actions and mistakes (such as the error that killed Lieutenant Allen). West Point-trained United States officers like Frazer, class of 1849, were not known to have fired upon women or children during military operations in Washington Territory. On the other hand, less disciplined citizen volunteers were found to have been responsible for deaths of non-combatants at other incidents, as at the Cascades, Nisqually Valley and Grand Ronde in 1856, for example. Some versions of the Wenatchee oral history also claimed that four soldiers died there in 1858, but no army lives were lost other than Allen at the Yakima River and Liebe on the Okanogan.

No written or physical evidence existed that a village massacre took place. However, a few lingering questions remained about the incident. Later in life, Frazer served as a general in the Confederate Army, married, had a daughter and lived to the age of 79.

Colonel Wright's full command assembled at Fort Taylor on the Snake River August 25. It took two days for 570 soldiers, 400 mules, 300 horses and 100 civilian packers to cross the river. Another 65 men stayed behind to protect supplies at Fort Taylor. Thirty of Spotted Eagle's Nez Perce scouts outfitted with secondhand military uniforms accompanied the soldiers under the supervision of Lieutenant John Mullan. The scouts took charge of coaxing hundreds of animals to swim across the Snake River. The Nez Perce possessed a knack for swimming horses and mules that soldiers lacked.[32] Eyewitness George F. B. Dandy explained the technique: "By slipping off their backs, seizing and holding on by the ends of their tails, swimming alongside and splashing water on their faces, when necessary to keep their heads upstream towards the point of landing."[33] Canvas covered flat boats ferried personnel and baggage over to the opposite shore where mules were re-packed. There were enough provisions to last Wright's men 38 days. The colonel planned to finish the war, establish peace, and return to Fort Walla Walla by the first week of October.

During the four days' march in the direction of the Spokane River, hostiles set fire to the prairie grass all around the military and fired random shots at the rear guard. There were no casualties from gunfire, but two soldiers of the Third Artillery, Private Mark Adams and Private John Holland, died after eating wild parsnips growing along a lakeshore.[34] Wright prepared for hardships and expected that his soldiers might suffer from the effects of fires set to the surrounding countryside. "Should they burn all the grass in my rear, we can live on our animals, and if they die, we can take our provisions on our backs and march."[35]

At Four Lakes, a thousand warriors awaited Wright's arrival. As soldiers approached the mass of painted and plumed warriors, a chorus of threatening war whoops filled the air and tested the nerves of young army recruits facing battle for the first time. At 9:00 a.m. on September 1, Wright placed a strong guard around the pack train and sent mounted troops charging up an adjacent hill to drive warriors down to the valley floor. The two sides faced off as soldiers opened fire at 600 yards with new long range rifles that greatly surprised warriors who had last seen Steptoe's old muskets miss their marks at much closer range.

When warriors took cover in the woods they were blasted by shells from howitzers. Some seeking to escape were charged by mounted dragoons and cut down by shots from revolvers and slashes from sabers. But most Indian ponies were fresh and well-fed, allowing them to outrun the dragoons' worn mounts that had become weary from days traveling over grassless plains charred by fires. By 2:00 p.m. the soldiers had swept the opposition from the field without losing a man. Wright reported 18 to 20 of the enemy dead.[36]

The army rested until September 5, then resumed its march toward Spokane River where the opposition was last seen. Within three miles they found another group of warriors facing soldiers with renewed vigor. The braves immediately set fire to fields of dry grass surrounding the soldiers. The blaze rose up quickly in the wind and rushed dangerously close to the command. Wright ordered a bold charge into the fire and watched his troops as they "dashed gallantly through the roaring flames".[37]

The army pressed ahead and the battle known as Spokane Plains became a running fight that alternated from woods to rocky prairies over a course of 14 miles lasting seven hours. Again, Wright did not lose a man. The enemy was thoroughly routed. The colonel's report identified four chiefs and warriors killed, although the toll may have been higher from uncounted bodies carried away from the scene. Nez Perce scouts and guide Cutmouth John collected scalps from fallen warriors and celebrated by dancing and singing around their campfires at night.[38]

Most of Wright's enemy had fled and relatively few had been slain. The colonel needed to stamp a lasting impression on the survivors and remove any remaining armed resistance once and for all. He intended to complete the mission and establish a permanent peace while supplies lasted.

Wright began by calling nearby chiefs into council and explaining the terms of surrender. The colonel met with Spokane Garry and Chief Polatkin on the Spokane River two miles above the falls on September 7. Wright explained that his presence there was quite different from the previous Yakima campaign in 1856. "I did not come into this country to make peace; I came here to fight...You must come to me with your arms, with your women and children, and everything you have and lay them at my feet; you must put your faith in me and trust to my mercy."[39] If the tribes refused, Wright declared, they would be exterminated.

The following day, soldiers discovered Indians fleeing toward the mountains driving a large herd of horses. Dragoons and foot soldiers pursued and captured 800 horses believed to belong to hostile Chief Tilcoax of the Palouse. On the same day, the colonel held the first of several investigations involving prisoners suspected of murders. One

Palouse man accused of participating in killing two French Canadian miners in April was found guilty and hanged.

Wright's men inflicted more punishment September 9 when they destroyed and burned lodges and storehouses filled with winter food supplies. The colonel sent a messenger to the Coeur d'Alene tribe via Father Joset at the Catholic mission promising that no life would be taken for acts committed during the war. But Wright reserved the right to punish those who had killed civilians and stolen from the government.

Wright faced a dilemma about what to do with the 800 captured horses. Many were wild and could not be safely contained with 700 tame animals kept by the army. The colonel was determined not to let captured horses fall back into the hands of hostile chiefs. After consulting with other officers, it was decided reluctantly to send a strong message by shooting most of the horses and keeping a few of the best for the army's and Nez Perce's use.

After the horses were slaughtered, the command took five days from September 11 to 15 to march from Spokane River to the Coeur d'Alene Mission. The thickly forested trail required single-file travel stretching hundreds of men and animals over a distance of some eight miles. Mountain howitzers that had been pulled on wheels thus far had to be taken apart and packed onto the backs of mules. A number of infantrymen collapsed from heat exhaustion after struggling under the weight of heavy packs. Officers gave up their mounts to the fallen, and marched alongside enlisted men.

Father Joset persuaded the tribe to hold a council with Wright, and most of the Coeur d'Alene people waited in dread knowing that soldiers had cut a swath of destruction by shooting warriors with long range rifles, slaughtering horses, and destroying store houses full of winter food supplies. Wright wrote to his commanders, "The chastisement which these Indians have received has been severe but well merited, and absolutely necessary to impress them with our power."[40]

Wright held a treaty council with Coeur d'Alene chiefs and headmen where the colonel spared their lives as long as they agreed to remain peaceful and return horses, mules and camp equipment taken from Colonel Steptoe. To assure their good behavior, Wright selected a chief, four warriors and their families to be held as temporary hostages at Fort Walla Walla.

Father Joset vigorously assisted peace efforts between soldiers and tribes. The priest's admirable character was particularly noted by Captain Erasmus Keyes. The captain was impressed that a "cultivated gentleman" would spend more than fourteen years in the wilderness ministering to Native people while perfectly satisfied with his position in life. Father Joset's positive attitude and dedication inspired Keyes to become Catholic after he returned home from the war.[41]

Wright and the soldiers left the Coeur d'Alene Mission on September 18 taking a route south into traditional Spokane and Palouse country. After marching four days, camp was made on the Ned-Whauld River, later known as Latah, or Hangman Creek. The colonel held a council with Spokane chiefs and headmen on September 23 when he made a peace treaty agreement similar to that with the Coeur d'Alene. Wright also required one Spokane chief and four men with their families to be taken as hostages to Fort Walla Walla to insure good conduct from the remainder of the tribe.

In the evening, Yakama Chief Owhi came in and presented himself. The colonel placed Owhi under guard intending to hold him prisoner at Wright's headquarters at Fort Dalles, or with higher command at Presidio, California.[42] The colonel treated the Yakama Chief differently than Coeur d'Alene and Spokane chiefs because Wright had previously held a council with Owhi in 1856 after which the chief broke a verbal agreement to surrender peacefully. Instead, Owhi, Qualchan and the chief's other warrior sons had left the Yakima Valley and joined resistors northeast of the Columbia River where Kamiakin and Skloom had also gone.

The following morning, September 24, Qualchan came into Wright's camp, and the colonel had the warrior immediately seized and hanged.[43] Wright, Qualchan and Owhi had previously met together at camp on the Naches River in 1856. All had acknowledged previous acts of war including Qualchan's participation in battles and stealthy nighttime raids that had taken numerous horses and mules from the army. But instead of burying the hatchet and returning stolen goods, Qualchan branched away from the majority of Yakamas that remained peaceful with Owhi's older brother, Chief Teias. Qualchan the warrior went on to lead attacks against Governor Stevens and volunteers at the second Walla Walla Council. He helped attack miners at the Wenatchee River, and joined the fight against Colonel Steptoe. Those acts combined with Qualchan's ambushing miners at the beginning of the war in 1855, leading attacks on Puget Sound settlements, and participating in war parties throughout the territory caused Wright to carry out the execution. The colonel knew Qualchan was not among the group that had killed A. J. Bolon. The names of the Indian agent's murderers had previously been provided to the army via Major Haller's Wasco informants and letters sent to Wright from Frederick White while he was detained by Chief Skloom. Wright judged Qualchan not on Bolon's murder (some civilians believed the warrior had slain the agent) but as a killer of miners and civilians during multiple attacks on both sides of the Cascade Mountains. Those acts set him apart from Coeur d'Alene and Spokane warriors who Wright had excused because their aggression had been limited to military combat with soldiers.

After the hanging, Major W. N. Grier and three troops of dragoons set off to visit the Steptoe battlefield located 12 miles south of the camp on Latah Creek. The bodies of Captain Taylor and Lieutenant Gaston were recovered along with two howitzers that had been buried prior to Steptoe's retreat.[44]

On the evening of September 25, a number of Palouse came into Wright's camp seeking peace after deciding not to follow Kamiakin's family into exile east of the Bitterroot Mountains. The colonel seized 15 of the men and held an investigation examining testimony from scouts and tribesmen familiar with the conduct of the suspects. One man was confirmed to have killed Sergeant Williams after he lagged behind Steptoe's troops returning to Fort Walla Walla. Five others were found to have been excessively hostile, and all six were hanged. The remaining nine were placed in irons.

After four more days on the trail, camp was made on the Palouse River where a council was held with approximately 100 more Palouse tribe members. Chief Slow-i-archy, whose band resided at the mouth of the Palouse River, had always been friendly, but a number of others had been hostile. First, Wright demanded the murderers of the two miners killed in April. One suspect was identified and hanged immediately. The second had already been hanged on the Spokane River on September 8. Witnesses identified three more hostiles who were not Palouse, but Walla Walla and Yakama. The colonel hanged those men without identifying their specific violations in his written report.[45] Wright also designated a Palouse chief, four warriors and their families be taken as hostages as he had done with the Spokane and Coeur D'Alene. He left a severe warning, that if he ever had to return on a hostile mission to their country, he would spare none of them.

Declaring the war ended, Wright sent his troops including 31 hostages to the Snake River to cross over and return to Fort Walla Walla. On October 3, Lieutenant Michael R. Morgan, a West Point graduate, was placed in charge of guarding Chief Owhi. Morgan and Owhi each rode a horse while four armed foot soldiers accompanied them while crossing the Tucannon River over a fallen log. When Morgan and the chief were temporarily out of sight, Owhi suddenly turned and whipped the lieutenant across the face, then galloped his pony across the stream attempting to escape. Morgan recovered from the blow and immediately charged after Owhi fearing that his military career would be ended if he let the chief get away. The lieutenant drew close to Owhi, pulled out a revolver and fired six shots, three of them striking the chief and his mount. Other soldiers quickly arrived to find Morgan holding an empty revolver next to the wounded Owhi. The lieutenant gave the order to finish the job, and the chief was shot from his horse by Sergeant Edward Ball and Private Behn. Nez Perce scouts gathered up Owhi's belongings except for a fancy saddle that was retained by Lieutenant Morgan. The chief lingered wounded for several hours before expiring at sunset.[46]

Owhi's death marked a solemn end for a conflicted chief who appeared sincere about wanting to end a devastating war, but he remained committed to following his warrior sons down a path of armed resistance.[47] Faced with the prospect of being sent to California as a prisoner, and fresh from witnessing the execution of his beloved son, Owhi may have taken a dangerous risk that others would not blame him for.

Back at Fort Walla Walla, Wright held yet another council with Cayuse and Walla Walla tribesmen on October 8. Some of the chiefs had advised the colonel that a number of Walla Walla men had joined the hostiles actively robbing, stealing, and fighting at the Steptoe battle. Approximately forty warriors admitted being part of the campaign at Four Lakes. Wright singled out one warrior known as Wild Cat who had been trusted by Colonel Steptoe to deliver a letter to the post at Walla Walla during the battle in May. Instead, Wild Cat did not deliver the letter, but told local warriors about the defeat in progress, and urged others to attack the few soldiers that remained at the fort. Wright wrote, "All these facts were proven and I hung him forthwith."[48] Two more Walla Walla men were charged with killing a white man on the Touchet River. They pleaded guilty and were hanged. Another Walla Walla man blamed for killing a white man at Wild Horse Creek also was hanged. Wright received assurances from the Cayuse, along with Nez Perce chiefs Lawyer and Looking Glass, that a lasting peace would now prevail. The colonel adjourned the council and departed for Fort Dalles after leaving orders at Fort Walla Walla: "The hostages and prisoners, thirty-one men, women and children should be provided with the necessary camp equipage, and one ration per day for each adult, and half a ration for each child – I will in addition direct that they be clothed."[49]

Officially, the war was over, but the army continued to round up and execute the remaining attackers of Agent Bolon and civilian miners. At Fort Simcoe, Major Garnett sent out squads of Yakama men to apprehend the remaining fugitives. Bolon's murderer, Mosheel, was shot and killed while attempting to escape from capturers on October 9. A party of twelve Yakama men went to Priest Rapids to capture Mosheel's co-conspirators, "Stakun and Wahi-wahi-cla."[50] The two were brought back to Fort Simcoe and hanged. The last of Bolon's murderers, So-qiekt, shot and killed himself after the war.[51]

The remaining fugitives associated with attacking miners were reported to have been living in Wenatchee and Okanogan country. During the month of November, 1858, Captain James J. Archer at Fort Simcoe hired Yakama Chief Shooshoosken and his men to make two expeditions to locate Yakama and Wenatchee suspects. Four were found and executed, Teanany, Pimp-sto-lock, Klopoken and Tom-teat-quen (son of peace chief Teias).[52] The army's cooperative agent, Chief Shooshoosken, lived at a village located on Manastash Creek near its junction with the Yakima River in the Kittitas Valley.[53]

The army enforced strong discipline upon its own members, especially for crimes of desertion, a frequent temptation for young soldiers dreaming of potential riches to be had in the gold fields out west. A convicted deserter could expect to be sentenced to two years of hard labor with one leg clasped to a ball and chain after having his bare back lashed in front of the other troops, followed by two weeks in solitary confinement with bread and water. Appeals from Captain Archer to reduce sentences for some men to less than two years were denied by higher command.

By the spring of 1859, the military's retribution had ended, Congress ratified the treaty, and Fort Simcoe became the Yakama Agency Headquarters and children's training school under the charge of Indian Agent Richard H. Lansdale. The period of war at last was over.

Chapter 10 notes

1. James Doty, *Journal of Operations of Governor Isaac Ingalls Stevens of Washington Territory in 1855*, Edward J. Kowrach ed. (Fairfield, Washington: Ye Galleon Press, 1978), 48-50.
2. Robert Ignatius Burns, S. J., *The Jesuits and the Indian Wars of the Northwest*, (New Haven, CT: Yale University Press, 1966), 194.
3. R. H. Lansdale to J.W. Nesmith, April 21, 1858, RBIA (RG 75) WS, Letters from employees assigned to the Columbia River or Southern District and Yakima Agency, 1854-1861, NARA microfilm, M-5 Roll 17.
4. Lawrence Kip, *Indian War in the Pacific Northwest The Journal of Lieutenant Lawrence Kip*, (Lincoln, NE: University of Nebraska Press, 1999), 117.
5. Will J. Trimble, "A Soldier of the Oregon Frontier", *Oregon Historical Quarterly* 8 (March: 1907), 47.
6. Edward Jenner Steptoe Papers, accession No. 4908-1, UW Libraries Special Collections Seattle, WA.
7. B. F. Manring, *The Conquest of the Coeur D'Alenes, Spokanes and Palouses*, (Spokane, WA: John W. Graham, 1912, reprint Fairfield, WA; Ye Galleon Press, 1975), 271-3; Utah History Encyclopedia, University of Utah, www.media.utah.edu/ UHE/s/STEPTOE,EDWARD.html.
8. Manring, 275-9.
9. Edward Steptoe to Major W. W. Mackall, May 23, 1858, U.S. Senate, 35th Congress 2nd session, 1859, "Report and correspondence relating to the operations of the army in the department of Pacific", SED No. 1, SS 975, 348.
10. The (Spokane, WA) *Spokesman Review*, April 2, 1905, John O'Neil, "Palouse and Spokane Campaign of 1858".
11. Kip, 110-1.
12. U.S. Senate, 35th Congress, 2nd session, 1859, "Topographical Memoir of Colonel George Wright's Campaign", SED No. 32, SS 984, 67.
13. Pierre-Jean De Smet, Life, *Letters and Travels of Father Pierre-Jean De Smet* SJ, Hiram Martin Chittenden ed. (New York: Francis P. Harper, 1905), 968.
14. Northern Pacific R.R. Co. et al vs. St. Josephs Roman Catholic Mission, 1895, 128, Henry J. Snively Collection No. 3095, box 1, UW Libraries Special Collections, Seattle, WA.
15. Splawn, 129, 476.
16. James J. Archer Letters, July 1, 1858, Relander Collection, box 40-2, YVL.
17. R.S. Garnett to W.W. Mackall, August 30, 1858, SED No. 1, 380.
18. Burns, 252-5.

19. Erasmus D. Keyes, *Fifty Years' Observation of Men and Events*, (New York: Scribner, 1884) reprint, *Fighting Indians in Washington Territory*, (Fairfield, WA: Ye Galleon Press, 1988), 21.
20. SED No. 32, 10.
21. Kip, 31-2.
22. Garnett to Mackall, July 17, 1858, typescript, Relander Collection, box 42-13, YVL.
23. Archer Letters, August 11, 1858.
24. Garnett to Mackall, August 15, 1858, typescript, Relander Collection, box 42-12, YVL.
25. George Crook, *General George Crook-His Autobiography*, Martin F. Schmitt, ed. (Norman, OK: University of Oklahoma Press, 1946), 62-3.
26. Garnett to Mackall, August 30, 1858.
27. Cpt. James J. Archer to Cpt. Alfred Pleasanton, Jan. 1, 1859, FD 248, Fort Dalles Records 1850-1885, H. Russell Smith Foundation Western Historical Manuscripts, The Huntington Library, San Marino, CA.
28. JoAnn Roe, *Stevens Pass*, (Caldwell, ID: The Caxton Printers, 2002), 25; Robert H. Ruby and John A. Brown, *Indians of the Pacific Northwest*, (Norman, OK: University of Oklahoma Press, 1981), 161.
29. Garnett to Mackall, August 30, 1858.
30. Capt. H.M. Black and Col. Jos. K.F. Mansfield, 23 October 1858, "Itinerary of the march of Major Garnett", RAGO (RG 94) LR 1780-1917, NARA (Courtesy of Steve C. Plucker).
31. Fort Simcoe Post Returns, August, 1858, Records of the War Dept. Office of the Adjutant General 1856-1859, NARA microfilm (1953), Relander Collection, box 63-10, YVL.
32. Michael Kenney, *We'll All Go Home in the Spring Personal Accounts and Adventures as Told by the Pioneers of the West*, Robert Bennett, ed. (Walla Walla, WA: Pioneer Press Books, 1984), 127.
33. Garrett B. Hunt, *Indian Wars of the Inland Empire*, George F. B. Dandy, "Dandy's Reminiscences", Spokane, WA: Spokane Community College, 1958), 92.
34. Manring, 187; "Register of Deceased Soldiers", 1848-1861, August 30, 1858, (entry 97), RAGO (RG 94), NARA.
35. Wright to W.W. Mackall, August 14, 1858 in Manring, 181.
36. Wright to W.W. Mackall, Sept. 2, 1858, SED No. 1, 386-390.
37. Wright to Mackall, Sept. 6, 1858, SED No. 1, 390-3.
38. Bennett, 129; Kip, 60.
39. Wright to Mackall, Sept. 9, 1858, SED No. 1, 393-4.
40. Wright to Mackall, Sept. 15, 1858, SED No. 1, 396-7.
41. Keyes, 50.
42. Wright to Mackall, Oct. 6, 1858, NARA M567 Roll 577.
43. Wright to Mackall, Sept. 24, 1858, SED No. 1, 399.
44. Wright to Mackall, Sept. 25, 1858, SED No. 1, 401.
45. Wright to Mackall, Sept 30, 1858, SED No. 1, 401-3.
46. Hunt, 99-101; Wright to Mackall, Oct. 6, 1858, NARA M567 Roll 577.
47. Lesh-hi-hit (son of Owhi), October 29, 1911, narrative, McWhorter Papers, box 44, folder 428, Holland Library MASC, Washington State University, Pullman, WA.
48. Wright to Mackall, Oct. 9, 1858, NARA M567 Roll 577.
49. Wright to Mackall, Oct. 12, 1858, NARA M567 Roll 577.
50. Garnett to Mackall, Oct. 15, 1858, NARA M567 Roll 577.
51. L. V. McWhorter, *Tragedy of the Wahk-shum The Killing of Major Bolon*, (Fairfield, WA: Ye Galleon Press, 1968), 30-1.
52. James J. Archer to Cpt. Alfred Pleasanton, Jan. 1, 1959, Fort Dalles Papers; Mary Moses, *Mary Moses' Statement*, (Fairfield, WA: Ye Galleon Press, 1988), 17.
53. Splawn, 268.

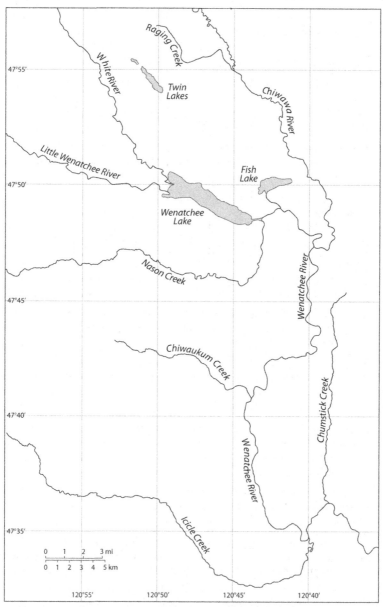

Upper Wenatchee Valley became a place of controversy regarding the location of the Wenatshapam fishery designated in the treaty of 1855, and scene of the U.S. Army's hunt for Native fugitives in 1858.

CHAPTER ELEVEN

Early Yakama Reservation Period 1859 - 1905

The Yakama Reservation officially began operations in 1859 after Congress ratified the treaty of 1855 that had been delayed more than three years by war. After peace was restored, the U.S. Army withdrew from Fort Simcoe and turned the buildings over to the Department of Interior under the jurisdiction of the commissioner of Indian Affairs.

The treaty ceded some 10.8 million acres to the United States, and established a reservation of approximately 1.37 million acres in exchange for $200,000 plus additional government support including schools, shops, mills and medical services for 20 years.[1] The reservation included large tracts of potential agricultural land plus substantial forests of harvestable timber, creeks, streams and wildlife.

Congress made its first funding appropriation for the reservation in 1860.[2] Agent Richard Lansdale served two years followed by Wesley B. Gosnell and Charles Hutchins for seven months, and Ashley Bancroft (father of historian Hubert H. Bancroft) from 1861 to mid-1864.[3] Chief Kamiakin and his family had fled east across the Bitterroot Mountains at the end of the war, and in 1860 they moved back as far as Lake Coeur d'Alene . Skloom returned to the reservation in poor health where he died February 1, 1861. No reprisals awaited Kamiakin; in fact, agents Lansdale and Bancroft tried to persuade the chief to move to the reservation and claim his annual salary and new house authorized by the terms of the treaty. Kamiakin refused ,preferring to establish his home off the reservation next to the Palouse River with his family in 1864. He later settled on the shores of Rock Lake, 20 miles southwest of the Steptoe battlefield where the chief and his family raised livestock and grew gardens independent from government financial support until Kamiakin's death in 1877.

James Wilbur took over the helm of the Yakama Agency in 1864 beginning a multi-year tenure characterized by hard work, discipline and reliance upon the Methodist faith.

For 25 years not many white men lived on the reservation except those employed by the Indian Agency. Ben E. Snipes, a white man, ranged cattle on and off the reservation near the mouth of Satus Creek. He made his permanent home at The Dalles, Oregon, and hired crews of Yakama horsemen to drive herds north and sell cattle to miners operating claims in British Columbia and Montana. Snipes paid lease fees to the Yakama Agency for grazing part of his cattle on tribal land.[4] Another stockman, Charlie Newell, raised mainly horses and operated from a ranch near Goldendale, Washington, also outside of the reservation. Newell leased grazing land from the agency beginning in 1879 while raising herds of thousands of horses.[5]

During the 1870s, Jock Morgan started a dairy ranch at Big Springs, about two miles south of the future town of Toppenish. The ranch was located inside the reservation along a public road that served as a stage coach line and mail route between The Dalles, Goldendale, Fort Simcoe and Yakima City. Indian Agent James Wilbur entrusted Morgan, a white man, to live on the ranch, and provide milk and butter products to stage passengers, the Yakama Agency and residents of The Dalles.[6]

Only a few white employees worked at agency headquarters at Fort Simcoe, and by 1875, Indian employees made up two thirds of the work force. At the same time, a census revealed that fewer than 60 percent of the population belonging to the 14 Confederated Tribes and Bands resided within the reservation boundaries. Article 2 of the treaty stated that tribes were "to remove to, and settle upon, the same, within one year after the ratification of this treaty."[7] The portion of the population that stayed on the reservation received annuities (useful goods) that were distributed over a period of more than 20 years until the purchase price of ceded lands was paid in full. Annuity goods for the year 1878 included 275 blankets, 1,910 yards of wool, flannel, and cotton cloth, 15 dozen shawls and scarves, 240 blouses, overalls, jumpers and shirts, 180 pairs of boots and shoes, and large quantities of coffee, sugar, rice, soap, dishes, hardware, tools, washboards, tubs and cooking stoves.[8] The cost of goods for annuities ordered for 1884 – 1885 amounted to $5,490.97.[9] Schools, shops, mills and medical services also operated under supervision of the reservation's agent.

Agent Wilbur relied heavily upon Bibles and plows as instruments for supplementing government financial aid and helping bring Native people to levels of independence and prosperity during a 17-year period from 1864 to 1882. More than 50 new houses and 43 barns were built by 1868.[10] After Wilbur served five years, he was suspended for a year in 1870 by Washington superintendent colonel Samuel Ross. His replacement, Lieutenant James M. Smith, served one year during a temporary change in policy when agency superintendents across the country were replaced by military personnel.[11]

Lieutenant Smith reported some faults he found with Wilbur's administration, alleging that the agent favored Methodists by issuing more materials and supplies to them than he did to Catholics and others.[12] But Smith's administration experienced problems of its own including losing the bulk of the cattle herd, mismanaging the school, and seeing a number of families abandon their farms during Wilbur's absence.

Agent Wilbur returned to his post on January 1, 1871.[13] Productivity increased, and in 1876 reservation residents raised 16,000 horses and 3,000 cattle. Head Chief Joe Stwire, also known as White Swan, elected in 1868, supervised a crew cutting and hauling logs to the tribal saw mill where another crew cut logs into lumber and fence posts. A team of carpenters, two white men and five Native men, constructed new houses each year complete with brick fireplaces.[14] Agent Wilbur reported in 1880 the Indians owned 100 plows, 75 wagons, 25 sewing machines, and built 12 new houses considered "first class in any country...and neatly painted."[15]

A new Methodist church large enough to seat 700 was "each Sunday filled with a well dressed, and well behaved congregation."[16] Wilbur's final report in 1882 declared that 42,000 bushels of wheat had been harvested plus 8,500 bushels of barley and oats. School enrollment reached 120 pupils, and more were turned away due to lack of building space. Many families willingly sent children to boarding school at Fort Simcoe during winter because students received free room and board, shelter and clothing along with education. Children rejoined their families in summer and fall for farming, fishing and working in hop harvests. Newly built irrigation ditches helped increase agricultural production and an all-Indian police force maintained law and order keeping whiskey sales to a minimum. Wilbur noted, however, that incessant gambling ruined some families by keeping them in constant poverty.[17]

More than 20 years after the treaty's ratification, an estimated 1,700 tribal members had homes on the reservation and operated farms, or at minimum grew gardens and raised livestock to provide varying levels of self-sufficiency. Many residents continued to rely on fishing at various times of the year, particularly when drought reduced the amount of crops, or severe winter reduced the number of livestock. At the same time there were more than 1,200 Natives subject to the treaty, still living off the reservation. They mostly followed traditional seasonal rounds and lived independently at old campsites.[18] Some were Yakama, but many were Palouse, Columbia Sinkiuse, Wenatchee, Wanapum, and bands along the Columbia River who saw themselves separate from the Yakama.[19]

Another 100 houses had been built on the reservation by the time it became known in 1884 that the Northern Pacific Railway planned to lay tracks across the reservation to reach Yakima City.[20] At this time nearly one half of the population still lived outside the reservation boundaries.[21] In response, the U.S. military came up with a proposed solution encouraging individual tribal members to file claims off the reservation under authority of the Indian Homestead Act of 1875. Generals O. O. Howard and Nelson A. Miles endorsed the idea and sent Major J. W. MacMurray to meet with tribal members and assist them with maps and filing procedures. The army's efforts were challenged by Indian Agent R. H. Milroy who objected to the military interfering with Indian policy. He believed that Indians should move to the reservation in compliance with the terms of the treaty. Ultimately, about 100 claims were taken off the reservation.[22] Many turned down the opportunity, being more interested in traditional relationships with the land rather accepting American rules of written deeds and boundaries.

Northern Pacific Railway construction crews began hauling timber and grading roadbeds on the reservation in October 1884. The track was completed on December 11, the day the first report came in complaining of livestock killed by a locomotive.[23] The railroad routinely paid stock owners for the loss of animals struck by trains. Article 3 of the 1855 treaty authorized roads for the convenience of the public, and Congress empowered the railroad in 1864 to lay track westward to Puget Sound. Subsequent acts by Congress approved the railroad's plans to lay tracks and build depots within the reservation's boundaries.[24]

The Fort Simcoe Council of 1885 formally relinquished the necessary property from the tribe and set a purchase price. The steps mirrored those taken at the Walla Walla Treaty Council of 1855. A commissioner, Robert S. Gardner, met with representatives of the tribes and bands. Also present were U.S. Indian agent R. H. Milroy, witness James McNaughton, and official interpreter Andrew Riddle. The documents were signed by 18 chiefs and head men.[25]

For a while the tribe gained more than the $5,309 in cash for the land. Apart from a written agreement, railway negotiators had verbally promised free passage to Yakamas wishing to travel by train between Toppenish, Wallula and Ellensburg. For a time, local Indians rode for free, but after a change in railroad administration, the program came to an end.[26]

The arrival of the railroad changed the face and nature of activities on the reservation dramatically. Soon, white employees began residing at new depots and occupying section houses located on land relinquished by the tribe. Farmers and settlers living outside the boundaries took advantage of the opportunity to ship goods to and from depots located at Toppenish and Simcoe (Wapato). The reservation soon became busy with non-Indian business; however, no store or non-railroad related business could operate without a license from the Indian Agency.

The Dawes Act (Allotment Act) of 1887 changed the nature of land ownership for tribal members. The concept of establishing allotments for individual Indians was written into article 6 of the 1855 treaty. "The President may, from time to time, at his discretion, cause the whole or such portions of such reservation as he may think proper, to be surveyed into lots, and assign the same to such individuals or families of the said confederated tribes and bands of Indians as are willing to avail themselves of the privilege, and will locate on the same as a permanent home..."[27] After Congress approved the law, it resulted in dividing Yakama reservation land into allotments of

80 acres assigned to each man, woman and child with at least one-quarter Indian blood. The remaining unallotted lands continued to be part of the reservation and could not be sold without consent of the tribes. News of impending allotments inspired some non-Indians to look for ways to get onto the reservation. The Yakama agent in 1889 complained of white men marrying Native women for the purpose of establishing homes on reservation land. Agent Thomas Priestly recommended that a rule be implemented, "to prevent any more white men from residing on this reservation, whose only claim is that their wives are of Indian blood."[28] Agent Webster L. Stabler wrote in 1890, "The squaw-men, whites who marry half-caste or full-blood Indian women, are a constant menace to the welfare of the Indians, with a few honorable exceptions."[29]

During the years 1892 and 1893, agency reports stated 1,075 Indians "cheerfully" came forward to make their allotment claims.[30] But the new program was not without opposition. The year the Dawes Act passed in 1887, the Yakama agent believed only about one fourth of the reservation population was in favor. By the time allotments were surveyed and assigned five years later, only seven or eight families were reported to have opposed the plan. Most families claimed their shares and made sure eligible children also received their entitlements. The agent assigned allotments to the reluctant few who did not wish to select on their own.

Jay Lynch was appointed Indian agent by Republican President Benjamin Harrison's administration in 1891. During Harrison's term progress began to correct an oversight regarding the Wenatshapam fishery. The place had not been surveyed or marked as it should have been according to article 10 of the 1855 treaty. Chief Kamiakin had personally negotiated the inclusion of the Wenatshapam Fishery, a six-square-mile piece of land on the "forks" of the Wenatchee River, on the last day of the treaty council June 9, 1855. Kamiakin announced early in the morning his intention to return home before the treaty was signed. Governor Stevens implored the chief to reconsider and agreed to the fishery deal as an inducement for Kamiakin to remain at the council grounds. The chief spoke for Pisquouse and Methow companions that accompanied him.[31] Article 10 stated that the fishery "shall be surveyed and marked out whenever the President may direct, and be subject to the same provisions and restrictions as other Indian reservations."[32] However, the president did not direct the survey until Harrison's administration 37 years after the council concluded.

In 1893, the administration under newly-elected President Grover Cleveland, a Democrat, removed Jay Lynch and replaced him with Lewis T. Erwin of Georgia, a personal friend of incoming Secretary of Interior Hoke Smith.[33] Erwin learned that months before his arrival, Lynch had discovered the exact location of the fishery as understood in 1855 was not clear in the memories of all those who survived in 1892. At a council held in 1878 between General O. O. Howard and Chief Moses, the chief said he knew nothing about a reservation "set apart years ago near the Wenatchee eight miles square..."[34] Consequently, a number of claims and improvements by white people had been made around Icicle Creek where it met the Wenatchee River, a place some believed to be the unnamed "forks" referred to in the treaty.

A report filed in 1889 based upon field investigations by Special Agent George Gordon found evidence of Indian fisheries up and down the Wenatchee River for some 20 miles. None of the places could be confirmed as the forks designated in the treaty.[35] Agent Lynch sought a suitable unclaimed site that would satisfy the intent of the treaty and not interfere with existing white development. Such a location was found at the forks of Chiwawa River and Wenatchee River near Lake Wenatchee approximately 15 miles upstream from Icicle.

When the survey team arrived in 1893, Irwin was the newly-appointed agent. Jay Lynch had previously sketched out a site that included part of Lake Wenatchee plus 10 miles of the Wenatchee River including two forks, one at Chiwawa River and the other at Chiwaukum Creek. Agent Irwin soon realized that the south and west boundaries conflicted with the route of railroad tracks being laid at the same time surveyors were in the field staking out the fishery. Railroad expansion trumped other projects during those days, and instructions from the interior secretary and President Harrison allowed the fishery boundaries to be adjusted in the field by the surveyor if need be and "not to interfere with the vested rights of any settlers or other parties that might be located theron."[36] Irwin ordered the survey stakes moved north and easterly away from the new tracks.

The 36-year-old agent had arrived from Georgia just a few days earlier and found himself plunged into a remote and unfamiliar forest trying to resolve unexpected problems more than 100 miles from agency headquarters. The finished site included part of Lake Wenatchee, all of Fish Lake, about four miles of the Wenatchee River, and some of the Chiwawa River. But the final location left out both of the intended forks envisioned by Lynch.[37] Agent Erwin soon heard complaints from 120 or so local Wenatchee that the latest site was not suitable as a fishery because it remained snowbound for too many months of the year and the area produced few fish. Nevertheless, the survey was approved, and the Wenatchee people became stuck with a fishery at a place many of them did not need or want.

To try and resolve the problem, the Department of Interior called a special council of confederated tribes and bands to meet and consider selling the surveyed fishery to the government. Also planned was an option to use the funds, if the tribes approved, to construct an irrigation canal to enhance agricultural production that would benefit the majority of the population residing on the Yakama Reservation.

A council was held at Fort Simcoe beginning December 18, 1893. Erwin had dispatched Chief of Police Peter Klickitat on December 6 to urge all Wenatchee males over the age of 18 to attend the "very important" general council meeting.[38] Representing the Wenatchee was their spokesman, 32-year-old John Hamilk (later spelled Hermilt and Harmelt) and two or three others who slogged their way through snow and icy conditions to attend.[39] For three days discussions took place between the government's two commissioners and a roomful of tribal representatives similar to the format used at the Walla Walla Council 38 years previous. While examining the pros and cons of selling the fishery, Special Agent John Lane stated, "...if you decide not to sell, the Government will not compel you to do so."[40] Agent Erwin spoke forthrightly regarding the altered survey boundaries: "I can say to you truthfully today that I don't think that fishery is properly located."[41]

Tribal testimony at first indicated an unwillingness to sell. But on the second and third days, tribal elders began talking about a purchase price after commissioners assured them the Wenatchee would be entitled to allotments and continue to keep their current homes along the Wenatchee River near the forks of the Icicle on land not yet claimed by whites. They also had fishing privileges at traditional fishing sites in common with whites. John Hamilk of the Wenatchee stated, "I am well satisfied between you two. These two old men (Chief Joe Stwire and Captain Eneas) are talking about selling that land and also talking about money. Whatever they ask for that land that is my same price... we would like to have our places allotted together."[42]

The delegation negotiated a price of $20,000.[43] The council adjourned until January 8, 1894 taking time to draw up papers and receive approval by telegraph from Washington D.C. John Hamilk and his companions departed for home to avoid further inclement weather. The Wenatchee representatives left the formal signing to those remaining on the reservation. The final agreement stated, "the Indians known as the Wenatshapam Indians, residing on the Wenatchee River, State of Washington, shall have land allotted to them in severalty, in the vicinity of where they now reside, or elsewhere, as they may select, in accordance with Article 4, of the General Allotment law."[44] The document contained the names and signatures of 246 tribal members representing a majority of adult males residing on the reservation.

Congress ratified the agreement but afterwards there were accusations that officials intentionally fumbled the matter to benefit non-Indians, and deny some Wenatchee residents their expected allotments.[45] John Hamilk protested that the Wenatchee band should have received the entire cash payment instead of a pro-rata portion divided among all 2,258 men, women and children falling under the authority of the Yakama Treaty (less than $10 each).[46] Erwin made a number of attempts in 1895 to assist the Wenatchee by encouraging them to select allotments on land unclaimed by whites. But the agent faced rejection and lack of cooperation because of dissatisfaction over the method of disbursing cash payment.[47] Hamilk did manage to remain living at his home in the Wenatchee River Valley for many years until his death in 1937 at age 76.

A general council meeting of tribal members held March 13, 1895 unanimously agreed to spend proceeds from the sale of the Wenatshapam fishery for irrigation improvements on the Yakama Reservation. Agent Erwin reported, "They recognize the fact they are receiving a twofold benefit. First, they will get the money for performing the work, and when the work is finished, they will have an improvement that will not only be a blessing to them, but to their children and their children's children."[48] The commissioner of Indian Affairs in Washington D.C. authorized more than $3,000 per month to pay Indian labor to extend canals and laterals expanding the irrigation system 29 additional miles including head gates.[49]

While the federal government supported advancement of agriculture, the Office of Indian Affairs kept tight rein over the rest of the budgets of 56 agents nationwide. For example, Erwin was denied travel expenses from Fort Simcoe to Yakima to purchase supplies because the commissioner preferred that business be conducted through the mail.[50] Prior approval from the commissioner of Indian Affairs was required to spend as little as $7 for leather to repair children's shoes, and inventory lists identified property down to the last whisk broom. Erwin received admonishments for purchasing logs without prior approval from Washington D.C., and for nominating a white woman instead of a Native for the position of assistant seamstress.[51] Other complaints included not moving fast enough processing allotments for Wenatchee Indians, and ordering too many blankets.[52] Erwin received approval from the commissioner to spend extra money on Christmas dinner for school children, but the use of agency funds for holiday presents was prohibited. A number of correction notices during Erwin's tenure received from the Treasury Department's auditor noted accounting discrepancies of up to $20,963.

The election of Republican President William McKinley led to Agent Erwin's resignation in 1897.[53] The 40-year-old Georgian moved his wife Mary and seven children to North Yakima and he left for Skagway, Alaska, to join the Klondike gold rush. Erwin closed out his final report by stating he would never have accepted the appointment as Indian agent had he known beforehand how difficult the job would be. Jay Lynch, 47, of Dayton, Washington, was chosen from over 40 applicants nationwide to return to his former post. Lynch would spend the next ten years striving to meet the needs of Native people by expanding agriculture and creating ways to generate cash income for them.

Allotment owners began earning income from reservation land beginning in 1898 when the Department of Interior allowed leases to non-Indian farmers. Agricultural leases created a cash source for individual Indians while opening the door for white farmers to reside legally inside reservation boundaries. In 1902, Congress granted Indian heirs the option of selling inherited allotments to outsiders if they so desired, and in 1905 Congress began to approve fee simple patents to individual allotment owners, many of whom elected to sell their property to non-Indians. The acts of Congress and decisions by individual tribal members resulted in checkerboard ownership patterns within the reservation boundaries. After the treaty obligation to provide federal financial support for twenty years had expired, Congress continued to fund educational services on the reservation for children, and encouraged opportunities for agricultural advancement for tribal adults. Fifty years after a historic treaty and the outbreak of war, a modern era began to take shape.

Chapter 11 notes

1. Charles J. Kappler, ed., Indian Affairs, Laws and Treaties, vol. 2(Washington D.C.: US Government Printing Office,1904), 700-1.
2. R.H. Lansdale, "Yakima Indian Agency, W.T.", Report of August 15, 1860. Report of the Commissioner of Indian Affairs, 1860, p 205-207, University of Washington Libraries Digital Collections.
3. A.A. Bancroft to C.H. Hale, May 15, 1864, RBIA (RG 75) WS, Letters from employees assigned to the Columbia River or southern district and Yakima Agency 1854-1861, NARA microfilm M5 Roll 17.
4. J.H. Fairchild, Acting Agent to Ben Snipes, June 27, 1881, RBIA (RG 75) General Correspondence 1873-1918, YK 90, NARA Seattle; Roscoe Sheller, Ben Snipes Northwest Cattle King, (Portland, OR: 1966), 155.
5. William D. Lyman, History of the Yakima Valley Washington, vol. 2 (S.J. Clarke, 1919), 89.
6. Dr. H.M. Johnson, A History of the City of Toppenish, 1927, (reprint Toppenish, WA: Toppenish Historical Museum Board, 1989), 4-5.
7. Kappler, 699.
8. "Annuity goods Required for the Yakama Indians at the Yakama Agency for 1878-79", RBIA (RG 75) WS LR 1824-81, NARA microfilm M234 Roll 918.
9. R.H. Milroy, "Estimate of Annuity Goods Required for the Yakama Indians 1884-1885", Yakima Indian Agency, Fort Simcoe, WA, records, MsSC 16, box 1/12, Washington State History Research Center, Tacoma, WA.
10. James H. Wilbur, Office Yakama Indian Agency, Report of June 30, 1868. Annual Report of the CIA for the Year 1868, p 100-102, UW Libraries Digital Collections.
11. James R. Masterson "The Records of the Washington Superintendency of Indian Affairs 1853-1874", Pacific Northwest Quarterly 37, (1946) 35.
12. James M. Smith, Office Yakama Indian Agency Report of August 31, 1870. Report of CIA to SI for the Year 1870, p 30-33, UW Libraries Digital Collections.
13. James H. Wilbur, Office Yakama Indian Agency Report of August 10, 1871. Report of CIA to SI for the Year 1871, p 282-285, UW Libraries Digital Collections.
14. James H. Wilbur, Office Yakama Indian Agency Report of September 1, 1876. Annual Report of CIA to SI for the Year 1876, p 144-146, UW Libraries Digital Collections.
15. James H. Wilbur, Office Yakama Indian Agency Report of August 20, 1880. Annual Report of CIA to SI for the Year 1880, p 167-168, UW Libraries Digital Collections.
16. ibid

17. James H. Wilbur, Yakama Agency Report of August 15, 1882. Annual Report of CIA to SI for the Year 1882, p 168-171, UW Libraries Digital Collections.
18. James H. Wilbur, Yakama Agency Report of August 15, 1881. Annual Report of CIA for the Year 1881, p 173-176, UW Libraries Digital Collections.
19. Andrew H. Fisher, *Shadow Tribe The Making of Columbia River Indian Identity*, (Seattle, WA: University of Washington Press, 2010), 68; Click Relander, *Drummers and Dreamers*, (Caldwell, ID: Caxton Press, 1956) 34, 122.
20. Timothy A. Byrnes to Hon. John Adkins Commissioner, Sept. 22, 1885, Yakima Indian Agency RBIA (RG 75) Press copies of letters sent to CIA, Box 11, 1882-1887, v. 3, YK 4, NARA, Seattle, 333-4.
21. R.H. Milroy, Yakama Agency Report of August 15, 1884. Annual Report of CIA to SI for the Year 1884, p 171-177, UW Libraries Digital Collections.
22. Fisher, 97.
23. Peter J. Lewty, *Across the Columbia Plain Railroad Expansion in the Interior Northwest, 1885-1893*, (Pullman, WA: WSU Press, 1995), 40; R.H. Milroy to Hiram Price Commissioner, December 15, 1884, RBIA (RG 75) Press Copies of Letters Sent to Commissioner of Indian Affairs 1882-1914, NARA, Seattle.
24. Northern Pacific Railroad Company, "Map of the Northern Pacific Railroad Through the Yakima Indian Reservation", October 11, 1884, Northern Pacific Railway Museum, Toppenish, WA.
25. Special Case 60, L.R. 1885-#1974, 11 E 3 Box 60, RBIA (RG 75) NARA, Washington D.C., pp c-6-c-12.
26. Johnson, 14, 18.
27. Kappler, 701.
28. Thomas Priestly, Report of Yakima Agency, August 16, 1889. Fifty-Eighth Annual Report of CIA to SI, 1889, p 290-295, UW Libraries Digital Collections.
29. Webster L. Stabler, Report of Yakima Agency, September 18, 1890. Report of CIA to SI for the Year 1890, p 231-234, UW Libraries Digital Collections.
30. Jay Lynch, Report of Yakima Agency, July 28, 1893. Report of CIA to SI for the Year 1893, p 337-340, UW Libraries Digital Collections; Jo N. Miles, "Toppenish A Washington Town that Grew Up on an Indian Reservation", COLUMBIA 28 (Spring 2014), Washington State Historical Society, 21-7.
31. James Doty, "Official Proceedings at the Council held at the Council Ground in the Walla Walla Valley", RBIA, Documents Relating to the Negotiation of Ratified and Unratified Treaties with Various Indian Tribes, 1801-1869, NARA microfilm T494 Roll 5, 3-2, 3-3.
32. Kappler, 701.
33. (Yakima, WA) *Yakima Herald,* Suzanne Erwin Bartholet, October 23, 1966.
34. Council at Priest Rapids, September 8, 1878, RBIA (RG 75) WS, LR 1824-81, NARA microfilm M234 Roll 918.
35. George W. Gordon, "The Wenatshapam Fishery & Reservation," To the Com. Of Indian Affairs, Washington D.C., February 6, 1889, RBIA (RG 75), copies of letters sent to CIA 1877-1921, Box #300 (entry 91), NARA Seattle; Jay Lynch to Commissioner, Oct. 24, (189)2, RBIA (RG 75) letters sent to CIA 1882-1914, Box 12, 1891-1893, NARA Seattle.
36. John W. Noble, Secretary to President Benj. Harrison, November 26, 1892, Yakima Indian Agency Records, 1936.79.1, T 141/2, p 5, Washington State History Research Center, Tacoma, WA.
37. Oliver B. Iverson, U.S. Deputy Surveyor, "Field Notes of the Survey of Wenatshapam Fishery Reserve", September 1, 1893, Vol. WA-R0103, Bureau of Land Management Information Access Center, Oregon, pp 8, 16.

38. L. T. Erwin to Peter Klickitat, Dec. 6, 1893, RBIA (RG 75), Letters sent to various parties 1886-1913, Box 26, vol. 6, NARA Seattle, 61.
39. Special Case 183, RBIA (RG 75) L. R. 1894 - #5058, 1/20/4 Box 184, NARA Washington D.C., 1-17.
40. Special Case 183, December 18, 1893, 7.
41. Special Case 183, December 18, 1893, 3.
42. Special Case 183, December 20, 1893, 36-7.
43. The amount increased to $69,000 after Indian Claims Commission, The Yakima Tribe Plaintiff vs. The United States, Docket No. 162, June 5, 1956, p 625, Oklahoma State University digital library.
44. Special Case 183, January 27, 1894, 4.
45. E. Richard Hart, "History of the Wenatchi Fishing Reservation", *Western Legal History* 13, (Summer/Fall 2000), 163-203; Richard Scheuerman, *The Wenatchee Valley and Its First Peoples*, (Walla Walla, WA: 2005), 115-128.
46. Louis Judge, "Wenatchee Indians Ask Justice", *The Washington Historical Quarterly* 16, (January, 1925), 20-8; Thos. P. Smith-Acting Commissioner to L.T. Erwin, May 22, 1896, RBIA (RG 75) Letters Rcvd from CIA 1894-1908, Box 1, NARA Seattle.
47. L. T. Erwin to J.J. Mathers, Jan. 18, 1895 and Judge Jas. H. Chase, March 12, 1895, and Louis J. Judge, March 28, 1895, RBIA (RG 75) Letters sent to various parties, 1886-1913, vol. 7, NARA Seattle, 32, 94,108.
48. L.T. Erwin, Report of Yakima Agency, August 25, 1896. Annual Report of CIA to SI for the Year 1896, p 317-321, UW Libraries Digital Collections.
49. L.T. Erwin, Report of Yakima Agency, August 31, 1897, RBIA (RG 75) Press copies of letters sent to Commissioner of Indian Affairs 1882-1914, NARA Seattle.
50. W.A. Jones, Commissioner, to L.T. Erwin, August 11, 1897, RBIA (RG 75) Letters rcvd from CIA 1894-1908, box 2, NARA Seattle.
51. Frank Armstrong, Acting Commissioner to L.T. Erwin, October 2 and November 14, 1894, RBIA (RG 75) Letters rcvd from CIA 1894-1908, box 1, NARA Seattle.
52. D. M. Browning, Commissioner to L. T. Erwin, January 8 and December 3, 1894, July 2, November 23 and December 17, 1895, RBIA (RG 75) letters rcvd from CIA 1894-1908, box 1, NARA Seattle.
53. Samuel Blackwell to L. T. Erwin, January 22 and September 28, 1896 and January 27, 1897, RBIA (RG 75) letters rcvd from CIA 1894-1908, box 1, NARA Seattle.

APPENDIX A

Native members of Washington Territory Volunteers
Muster Roll containing 81 names of Snoqualmie, Snohomish and
Scanamish Indians in 1856:

Captain Pat Kanim
John Taylor
Ass-How-is
Los-why
Ha Ha Call
Sow-How-is
Coc-nay-me-tal
No Qua Sal
Quat-a-napkin
Pa-Pa-Shat
Clem Skanion
Cha-go-ouse
Moos-Moos
Yap-ta
Sma-ka-nim
Lac-loose
Squah-am
Ca-touse
La-Hous
Telloch-Scot
Lad-es-Skin
Hal-lum
Lach-wha-ben
Wha-lud-Hud
Shet-tons
Quick
Cay-use
We-at-kan-ack
Sta-mal-ach
Skly-ip-kum
Lcia-achim
Stay-Shalt
Jackson
Has Sin

Zac-wa-Hut
Ell-Pas-Con
La-la-coomb
Coga-Saul
Led-ca-muse
Ca-yu-mese
Zoyult Canim
Te-pas
Cat-ai
Quilliam
Spurt-Can-im
Yi-a-lap
Cai-ous-cui
Tac-no-num
Swal-ka
Pems
Zed-tah-on
Yat-ta Coose
Sull-Canim
Stat-a-her
Cat-tu quin
Ta-ta Qual
Sco-ku-ler
Muc-la-ler
Wa-ta-Con
Tuc-Kanim
Mu-Pat Canim
Sal-tah
Qui-all-gud
Mu-Le-Lan-im
Qual-tak-up
Che-nac-gud
Mu-Yac-a-Mil-lai
Yapet-Sah

Muc-il-lai
Mu-Chib-bo-lit-zer
Sci-us-kum
Qua-lash-con
Lad-at
La-La-lap-cum
Squah Canim
Hut-the-Canim
Clat-Scoot
To-wai-tose
Son-in-well
Swy-oak
Mack-el[1]

Roster of 70 Nez Perce Mounted Volunteers, 1st Regiment Washington Territory Volunteers - December 15, 1855 to January 20, 1856:

War Chief Spotted Eagle*
Looking Glass
U-oo-li
Silas
Joseph
Tue-ee-takus
Seven-days-whiiping
Lone Bird
Wees-tass-kut
How-lish-wun
Three Feathers
Wah-wee-mash-wattus*
Boy
Real Grizzly
Red Eagle*
Him-in-ill-pilp
Red Crow
Tow-ish-pells
Lodge
Ou-tashen
Young-tow-hist
Hat-tun-bun
Wet-yalome-went

Fish-tone
Koos-hoots-u
James
Ess-schoh-tum
Ip-ni-pal-pun
Wetter-a-hi-pun
We-ass-kuss
Naph-for
Nats-en-pow
Peep-home-kin*
U-shay-ky-ik
Pall-a-hen
Will-lee-apum
Broken Arm
Has-hen-ka-kin
Sloop-toop-min
Bears Claw
Nosep-ta-kelso
Duck
Hump Back
Wanes-at-wates
Ack-ack-ton-hun
Koo-wanche
Nay-ap-an-ack
Wee-at-say-kun-att

The Old Bear
Billey
Red Bird
Hote-Hose
Talking Tobacco
Talla-home-mish
How-lish-toh-ky-ee-tut
Wahp-shee-li
Att-matt-sone-poo-un
Timothy*
George*
Ay-mop-ti-um-ipputs
Ume-u-il-pilp*
Tu-ki-en-lik-it
Tee-pahee-lis-kut
Al-wee-see-is-kum
Jason
Jessie*
U-me-ah
Captain John
Moh-see-chah[2]

*Also on roster of Company M 2nd Regiment Washington Territory Volunteers.

Roster of 42 Nez Perce serving under Captain Henri M. Chase Company M 2nd Regiment Washington Territory Volunteers from March 11 to July 12, 1856 – Walla Walla County.

Chief Spotted Eagle*
Samuel
Ko-ko-wy-e-he-nicht
Kulo-whike
Wat-i-wat-i-wohike
Weas-kishen
Tsun-is-tle-poos

Timothy*
Pip-hom-kun*
Pouen-in-il-pilps
Hiram
Tain-lik-ish
We-shin-me-shus-tim-tim

Ta-kah-mish
Sim-i-pello
Wat-yat-mus-wat-so-kown
Ip-ma-tam-owe-yet-wa
Ko-ko-il-pilp
Takin-kulst

APPENDIX A

Whe-tsme-ta-kal-si	Jesse*	In-ma-tu-wlaso
Tamsh-tle-wat	Quish-keesh	Hote-hose
Wow-inesh-ash-	Wap-tash	Wo-wo-kea-il-pilp
watish*	George*	Pierre
Nick-eas-tsultlem	Til-til-kos-tsut	Tlil-kun-kine
Waptash-tamana	In-skulta	Umea-il-pilp*
In-ma-tune-pun	Wash-ku-na-tu-	Red Eagle*[3]
Im-otus-tin-tin-im	tamosut	
Ea-kake-tam-otsut	Wat-yat-mus-waset	

* Also on the roster of 1st Regiment Nez Perce Mounted Volunteers.

Note: Three "friendly" Nez Perce (names unknown) died while accompanying Colonel Edward Steptoe at the battle that took place near present-day Rosalia on May 17, 1858.[4]

Chief Spotted Eagle also led 30 Nez Perce under U.S. Army Colonel George Wright, Ninth Infantry, and Lieutenant John Mullan during the battles at Four Lakes and Spokane Plains in September of 1858.[5]

Appendix A notes

1. "Muster Roll of Friendly Indians of Snohomish and Scanamish Tribes, under the chiefs, Pat Kanim and John Taylor, regiment of Washington Territory Volunteers" Biennial Report of the Adjutant General of the State of Washington for the Years 1891 and 1892", appendix schedule B, Olympia, Wash., 1893, 173-4 WSL.
2. "Nez Perce Mounted Volunteers, 1st Regt. Wash. Terr. Vols.", State of Washington Office of the Adjutant General, *The Official History of the Washington National Guard volume 2 Washington Territorial Militia in the Indian Wars of 1855-56*, (Tacoma, WA: Camp Murray, 1961), 129.
3. WOAG, 141.
4. Lieutenant David McMurtry Gregg, U.S. Senate, 35th Congress, 2nd Session 1859, "Topographical Memoir of Colonel George Wright's Campaign", SED No. 32 SS 984, 67.
5. Alvin M. Josephy, *The Nez Perce Indians and the Opening of the Northwest*, (Boston: Houghton Mifflin Company, 1997), 382.

APPENDIX B

Allied Cultural Groups (Cayuses, Walla Wallas, Oregon Volunteers and French settlers) in the Walla Walla Valley December 1855 – February 1856

List of "good" Cayuses and Walla Wallas identified by Narcisse Raymond December 9, 1855, three days before being aided by Company K of the Oregon Mounted Volunteers.

Cayuses

1st Lodge
Josue Howlishwonpo
Jacob Rarus
Dominique Shawaway
Stanislas
August Yeyawparle

2nd Lodge
Bazile Sheshnemken
Daniel – his son
Felesien his 2nd son

3rd Lodge
Ettienn Lovalkatumunare
Nicholas

4th Lodge
Edward Catalpos
Felix Towishshaloot

5th Lodge
Tintinmetzey
Victor Pinahantotase

Walla Wallas

1st Lodge
Pierre Mowatit
Ahyoumahken
We ah kah lucks
Leon Mowatit
Pierre Ahyanmahken

2nd Lodge
Samipahlo
Pahtitsham
Ah So
Jack
Pena

3rd Lodge
Sis-cawyou
Lu Poche
Tah mo

4th Lodge
Exselsier Shemunahshet
Sharclaymet

List of those accused by the Chuslikahyuh Indians
   Omscaqua
   Simion Muattowash
   Peter Coninsh
   Nicholas Ka et Kaysuot

The above are in our camp. More____are expected to join us[1]

Company K 1st Regiment Oregon Mounted Volunteers

Captain Narcisse Cornoyer
First lieutenant
Antoine Revais
Thomas J. Small
Alfred Kazey
Hugh Campbell
Issidore Beauchamp
Armatte Arquoit
Michael Bono
Michael Chasty

Thomas Collins
George Fuster
Isaac Gervais
John B. Gervais
Thos. Humphreyville
William Louis
Joseph Lucier
Michael Lucier
Vera McDonald
Louis Montour

Francis O'Slant
Regis Picard
Dominque Pichette
Charles Petite
Francis Quenelle
Charles Revais
Elexis Villerais
_____ Virette
Augustine De Lore
Joseph Despord[2]

Walla Walla Mounted Militia 1st Regiment Washington Territory Volunteers including French settlers from the Walla Walla Valley January 11 to February 10, 1856.

Captain Sidney S. Ford
Thomas Brunchall
Donald McKay
Green McAfferty
Joseph Barnaby
France Martin
L.T. Andrews
Edward Beauchemin
Pierre Newatil
Narcisse Raymond

Frank Chartier
Joseph Pairer
William McBean
Lewis Danney
Antoine Placie
William Scott
Baptiste Ignace
Pascal Pacquette
Batiste Piquette
Joseph LaRocque

John Pacquette
Charles Baker
Amabel LaCourse
Michel Thibault
Oliver Brisbais
Toussaint Morrisette
Lewis Tellier
Etienne Burnaess
John McBean[3]

Appendix B notes
1. WS, Misc. Letters Rcvd. 1853-1861, NARA M5 Roll 23.
2. Frances Fuller Victor, *The Early Indian Wars of Oregon*, (Salem, Oregon: Frank C. Baker State Printer, 1894), 555-6.
3. WOAG, 130.

APPENDIX C
WAR MEMORIAL AND RECORD OF FATALITIES
IN WASHINGTION TERRITORY, 1855 - 1858

Name   Date of Death   Affiliation   Location

1. Henry Mattice, September 1855, Gold Miner, East of Snoqualmie Pass
2. Cummings, September 1855, Gold Miner, East of Snoqualmie Pass
3. Fanjoy, September 1855, Gold Miner, East of Snoqualmie Pass
4. Huffman, September 1855, Gold Miner, East of Snoqualmie Pass
5. Jamison, September 1855, Gold Miner, East of Snoqualmie Pass
6. Walker, September 1855, Gold Miner, East of Snoqualmie Pass
7. Eaton, September 1855, Gold Miner, East of Snoqualmie Pass
8. Andrew J. Bolon, Sept. 23, 1855, Indian Agent, Klickitat Valley
9. Pvt. Herman, Oct. 6, 1855, U.S. Army, Toppenish Creek
10. Pah-chese, Oct. 6, 1855, Yakama, Toppenish Creek
11. Kah-sah-le-mah, Oct. 6, 1855, Yakama, Toppenish Creek
12. Four Indians, Oct. 7, 1855, Yakama and allies, Toppenish Creek
13. Pvt. Regan, Oct. 7, 1855, U.S. Army, Toppenish Creek
14. Sgt. James Mulholland, Oct. 8, 1855, U.S. Army, South of Eel Trail
15. Pvt. Charles Dreyer, Oct.8, 1855, U.S. Army, South of Eel Trail
16. Pvt. William Miller, Oct. 8, 1855, U.S. Army, South of Eel Trail
17. Lt. James McAllister, Oct. 27, 1855, Washington Volunteer, White River Crossing
18. Michael Connell, Oct. 27, 1855, Homesteader, White River Crossing
19. 7 unnamed warriors, Oct. 27, 1855, Nisqually/Puget Salish, White/ Green Rivers
20. Harvey H. Jones, Oct. 28, 1855, Homesteader, White River Valley
21. Eliza Jones, Oct. 28, 1855, Homesteader, White River Valley
22. Enos Cooper, Oct. 28, 1855, Settler/Hired Man, White River Valley
23. W. H. Brannan, Oct. 28, 1855, Homesteader, White River Valley
24. Elizabeth Brannan, Oct. 28, 1855, Homesteader, White River Valley
25. Infant Brannan, Oct. 28, 1855, Homesteader, White River Valley
26. George E. King, Oct. 28, 1855, Homesteader, White River Valley
27. Mary King, Oct. 28, 1855, Homesteader, White River Valley

28. Infant King, Oct. 28, 1855, Homesteader, White River Valley

29. Col. A. Benton Moses, Oct. 31, 1855, Washington Volunteers, White R. / Puyallup R.

30. Lt. Col. Joseph Miles, Oct. 31, 1855, Washington Volunteers, Connell's Prairie Swamp

31. Chief Umtuch, Oct. "late" 1855, Cowlitz/Klickitat, North of Vancouver

32. Pvt. Arthur Kay, Nov. 3, 1855, U.S. Army, Puyallup River

33. 30 unnamed warriors, Nov. 3, 1855, Nisqually/Puget Salish, White River

34. Pvt. John Edgar, Nov. 6, 1855, Washington Volunteers, So. of Connell's Prairie

35. Pvt. Joseph Moxeimer, Nov. 8, 1855, U.S. Army, Yakima River (drowned)

36. Pvt. Edward Crogan, Nov. 8, 1855, U.S. Army, Yakima River (drowned)

37. Tow-townah-hee, Nov. 10, 1855, Yakama, Two Buttes

38. Unnamed warrior, Nov. 10, 1855, Yakama, Two Buttes

39. Pvt. Elijah Price, Nov. 26, 1855, Washington Volunteers, Puyallup Valley

40. Pvt. William Andrews, Dec. 3, 1855, Oregon Volunteers, Fort Henrietta

41. Lt. William A. Slaughter, Dec. 4, 1855, U.S. Army, Forks White/Green River

42. Cpl. Ganett L. Barry , Dec. 4, 1855, U.S. Army, Forks White/Green R,

43. Cpl. Julian Clarendon, Dec. 4, 1855, Washington Volunteers, Forks White/Green R,

44. Pvt. John Cullum, Dec. 5, 1855, U.S. Army, Forks White/Green R,

45. Peo Peo Mox Mox, Dec. 7, 1855, Walla Walla chief, Walla Walla River

46. 4 unnamed hostages, Dec. 7, 1855, Walla Walla tribe, Walla Walla River

47. Lt. J. M. Burrows, Dec. 7, 1855, Oregon Volunteers, Walla Walla River

48. Cpt. Charles Bennett, Dec. 7, 1855, Oregon Volunteers, Walla Walla River

49. Pvt. Andrew Kelso, Dec. 7, 1855, Oregon Volunteers, Walla Walla River

50. Pvt. Simon Van Hagerman, Dec. 7, 1855, Oregon Volunteers, Walla Walla River

51. Pvt. Henry Crow, Dec. 7, 1855, Oregon Volunteers, Walla Walla River

52. 39 unnamed warriors, Dec. 7, 1855, Plateau Tribes, Walla Walla River

53. Pvt. Jesse Fleming, Dec. 10, 1855, Oregon Volunteers, Walla Walla River

54. Milton Holgate, Jan. 26, 1856, Settler, Seattle

55. Christian White, Jan. 26, 1856, Settler, Seattle

56. 4 unnamed warriors, Jan. – Feb. 1856, Yakama, Puget Sound

57. Kopt-chin-kin, Feb. 1856, Yakama chief, Puyallup River

58. 2 unnamed warriors, Feb. 8, 1856, Klickitat, Snoqualmie River

59. 9 unnamed warriors, Feb. 16, 1856, Nisqually, Leschi / Patkanim battle

60. 5 unnamed warriors, Feb. 16, 1856, Snoqualmie, Leschi / Patkanim battle

61. William Northcraft, Feb. 24, 1856, Teamster, Steilacoom

62. Kanaskat, Feb. 26, 1856, Klickitat chief, Puyallup River

63. Pvt. David Reitman, March 1, 1856, U.S. Army, Muckleshoot

64. William White, March 2, 1856, Homesteader, Olympia

65. Te-pe-al-an-at-ke-kek, March 7, 1856, Nez Perce, Walla Walla / Mill Creek

66. Unnamed warrior, March 10, 1856, Puget Salish, White River

67. 2 unnamed women, March 10, 1856, Nisqually/Coast Salish, White River

68. Chehalis John, March 10, 1856, Chehalis, Connell's Prairie

69. Unnamed warrior, March 12, 1856, Palouse, Lapwai

70. 4 unnamed warriors, March 12, 1856, Palouse, Snake River

71. 2 unnamed warriors, March 13, 1856, Yakama, Mouth of Yakima River

72. Montoui Bourbon, March 26, 1856, Settler, Columbia R. Cascades

73. B. W. Brown, March 26, 1856, Mill Foreman, Columbia R. Cascades

74. Mrs. Brown, March 26, 1856, wife/settler, Columbia R. Cascades

75. Henry Hager, March 26, 1856, settler, Columbia R. Cascades

76. Jacob Roush, March 26, 1856, carpenter, Columbia R. Cascades

77. Jimmy Watkins, March 26, 1856, carpenter, Columbia R. Cascades

78. George Watkins, March 26, 1856, settler, Columbia R. Cascades

79. Jacob White, March 26, 1856, mill sawyer, Columbia R. Cascades

80. Dick Turpin, March 26, 1856, cook, Columbia R. Cascades

81. Jake Kyle, March 26, 1856, German boy, Columbia R. Cascades

82. Norman Palmer, March 26, 1856, mill worker, Columbia R. Cascades

83. George Griswold, March 26, 1856, portage road operator, Columbia R. Cascades

84. Calderwood, March 26, 1856, mill worker, Columbia R. Cascades

85. James Sinclair, March 26, 1856, Hudson's Bay Co., Columbia R. Cascades

86. Pvt. Laurence Rooney, March 26, 1856, U.S. Army, Columbia R. Cascades R

87. Pvt. O. McManus, March 26, 1856, U.S. Army, Columbia R. Cascades

88. Unnamed warrior, March 26, 1856, Yakama/Klickitat, Cascades, Bradford Store

89. 2 unnamed warriors, March 26, 1856, Yakama/Klickitat, Cascades, Steamer *Mary*

90. Old Joanum, March 26, 1856, Cascade band, Middle Cascades

91. (1) unnamed soldier, March 26, 1856, U.S. Army, Columbia R. Cascades

92. Old Chenowith, March 29, 1856, Cascade chief, Columbia R. Cascades

93. Tecomeoc, March 29, 1856, Cascade band, Columbia R. Cascades

94. Captain Jo, March 29, 1856, Cascade band, Columbia R. Cascades

95. Toy, March 29, 1856, Cascade band, Columbia R. Cascades.

96. Sim Lasselas, March 29, 1856, Cascade band, Columbia R. Cascades

97. Four Fingered Johnny, March 29, 1856, Cascade band, Columbia R. Cascades.

98. Chenowith Jim, March 29, 1856, Cascade band, Columbia R, Cascades

99. Tumtah, March 29, 1856, Cascade band, Columbia R, Cascades

100. Old Skein, March 29, 1856, Cascade band, Columbia R, Cascades

101. Spencer's wife, March 30, 1856, Klickitat, Columbia R, Cascades

102. Spencer's father, March 30, 1856, Klickitat, Columbia R, Cascades

103. Spencer's child, March 30, 1856, Klickitat, Columbia R, Cascades

104. Scowites, March 30, 1856, Klickitat, Columbia R, Cascades

105. Daughter of Umtux, March 30, 1856, Klickitat/Cowlitz, Columbia R, Cascades

106. 7 unnamed warriors, March 30, 31, 1856, Nisqually, Nisqually/Mashel River

107. 3 women/children, March 30 (est.) 1856, Nisqually/Puget Salish, Near Mt. Rainier

108. Sky-skie, April 1, 1856, Nisqually, Mashel River

109. Unnamed warrior, April 1 (est.) 1856, Nisqually/Puget Salish, Camp Montgomery

110. Cpt. Absalom Hembree, April 10, 1856, Oregon Volunteers, Satus Creek

111. Unnamed warrior, April 10, 1856, Yakama, Satus Creek

112. Pah-ow-re, April 10, 1856, Yakama, Satus Creek

113. Shu-win-ne, April 10, 1856, Yakama, Satus Creek

114. Waken-shear, April 10, 1856, Yakama, Satus Creek

115. 2 unnamed warriors, April 12, 1856, Klickitat, Summit of Simcoe Mts.

116. Pvt. Lot Hollinger, April 20, 1856, Oregon Volunteers, Fort Henrietta

117. Qui-as-kut, April 1856, Puget Sound area, Olympia

118. Mowitch, May 17, 1856, Puget Sound area, Olympia

119. Sayshilloh (Bob), May 21, 1856, Nisqually, Fort Nisqually

120. Unnamed warrior, June 20, 1856, unknown tribe, The Dalles

121. Lt. John Estis, July 15, 1856, Washington Volunteers, John Day R. / Burnt R.,

122. Pvt. Daniel Smith, July 15, 1856, Washington Volunteers, John Day R. / Burnt R.

123. 7 unnamed warriors, July 15, 1856, Des Chutes/Tygh, John Day R. / Burnt R.

124. 23 unnamed warriors, July 17, 1856, Cayuse/Umatilla/W.W., Grand Ronde River

125. 3 women/child/elderly, July 17, 1856, Cayuse/Umatilla/W.W., Grand Ronde River

126. William F. Tooley, July 17, 1856, Washington Volunteers, Grand Ronde River

127. James Irvin, July 17, 1856, Washington Volunteers, Grand Ronde River

128. William Holmes, July 18, 1856, Washington Volunteers, Grand Ronde River

129. Elijah Hill, September 19, 1856, Washington Volunteers, Walla Walla Mill Creek

130. 5 unnamed warriors, September 19, 1856, Yakama and allies, Walla Walla Mill Creek

131. Quiemuth, Nov. 19, 1856, Nisqually, Olympia

132. Leschi, Feb. 19, 1858, Nisqually, Steilacoom

133. 2 French Canadians, April 8, 1858, Gold miners, Road to Colville

134. Jacques Nehlukteltshiye, May 17, 1858, Coeur d'Alene, Steptoe Battle

135. Zacharia Natatkem, May 17, 1858, Coeur d'Alene, Steptoe Battle

136. Victor Smena, May 17, 1858, Coeur d'Alene, Steptoe Battle

137. 12 unnamed warriors, May 17, 1858, Spokane/Coeur d'Alene, Steptoe Battle

138. Cpt. O. H. P. Taylor, May 17, 1858, U.S. Army, Steptoe Battle

139. Pvt. Alfred Barnes, May 17, 1858, U.S. Army, Steptoe Battle

140. Pvt. Victor C. DeMoy, May 17, 1858, U.S. Army, Steptoe Battle

141. Lt. William Gaston, May 17, 1858, U.S. Army, Steptoe Battle

142. Sgt. William C. Williams, May 17, 1858, U.S. Army, Steptoe Battle

143. Pvt. Charles H. Harnish, May 17, 1858, U.S. Army, Steptoe Battle

144. Pvt. James Crozet, May 17, 1858, U.S. Army, Steptoe Battle

145. 3 friendly Indians, May 17, 1858, Nez Perce, Steptoe Battle

146. Chief Quiltenock, June 20, 1858, Columbia Sinkiuse, Wenatchee River

147. 5 unnamed miners, June 20, 1858, Californians, Wenatchee River

148. Unnamed miner, July 1858, Civilian, McLoughlin Canyon

149. Unnamed white man, July 1858, Civilian, Wild Horse Creek

150. Lt. Jesse K. Allen, August 15, 1858, U.S. Army, Teanaway River

151. Schu-pascht, August 15, 1858, Yakama, Teanaway River

152. Too-we-no-pahl, August 15, 1858, Yakama, Teanaway River

153. Soo-pap-kin, August 15, 1858, Yakama, Teanaway River

154. Shut-tow-weh, August 15, 1858, Yakama, Teanaway River

155. Remaining warrior, August 15, 1858, Yakama, Teanaway River

156. Hign-shum, August 23, 1858, Wenatchee, Wenatchee River

157. Clum-stool, August 23, 1858, Wenatchee, Wenatchee River

158. Has-sa-lo, August 23, 1858, Wenatchee, Wenatchee River

159. Remaining warrior, August 23, 1858, Wenatchee, Wenatchee River

160. Medicine man, August 23, 1858, Wenatchee, Wenatchee River

161. 18 unnamed warriors, September 1, 1858, Spokane/Coeur d'Alene, Four Lakes

162. 4 chiefs and warriors, September 5, 1858, Spokane/Coeur d'Alene, Spokane Plains

163. Unnamed warrior, September 8, 1858, Spokane, Spokane Falls

164. Pvt. William Liebe , September 9, 1858, U.S. Army, Okanogan River

165. Qualchan, September 24, 1858, Yakama, Latah (Hangman) Creek

166. Unnamed emissary, September 24, 1858, Yakama, Klickitat Valley

167. 6 unnamed warriors, September 25, 1858, Palouse, Latah (Hangman) Creek

168. Unnamed warrior, September 30, 1858, Palouse, Palouse River Camp

169. 3 unnamed warriors, September 30, 1858, Walla Walla/Yakama, Palouse River Camp

170. Chief Owhi, Oct. 3, 1858, Yakama, Tucannon River

171. Wild Cat, Oct. 9, 1858, Walla Walla, Walla Walla Camp

172. 3 unnamed warriors, Oct. 9, 1858, Walla Walla, Walla Walla Camp

173. Mosheel, Oct. 9, 1858, Yakama, Satus Creek

174. Wah-pi-wah-pi-lah, Oct. 15, 1858, Yakama, Fort Simcoe

175. Stah-kin, Oct. 15, 1858, Yakama, Fort Simcoe

176. Teanany, Nov. 1858, Yakama, Yakima Valley
177. Tompteatquen, Nov. 1858, Yakama, Wenatchee/Okanogan
178. Pimp-sto-lock, Nov. 1858, Wenatchee/Okanogan, Wenatchee/
    Okanogan
179. Klopoken, Nov. 1858, Wenatchee/Okanogan, Wenatchee/Okanogan

The number of deaths include executions and hostile actions during the Washington Territory War of 1855-1858. (Figures indicate the minimum or lower field reports where actual bodies were counted in most cases).

"Yet if we cut ourselves the blood will be red – and so with the Whites it is the same." Chief Spokane Garry, Dec. 5, 1855.

Tribal chiefs and warriors, 259
United States civilians, 45
United States Army , 24
Tribal women, children, elders, 13*
Washington Territory Volunteers, 12
Oregon Mounted Volunteers, 9
Snoqualmie Tribe allies, 5
Nez Perce Tribe allies, 3
TOTAL, 370

* Presumed to be lower than actual number due to eyewitnesses rarely
    reporting specific counts of slain women, children, and elderly.

Appendix C notes

1. – 7. Elwood Evans, ed. *History of the Pacific Northwest: Oregon and Washington* 2 vols. (Portland, OR: North Pacific History Company, 1889), 1:493; (Olympia, WA) *Pioneer and Democrat*, September 28, 1855.

8. Lucullus Virgil McWhorter, *Tragedy of the Wahk-Shum: The Death of Andrew J. Bolon Indian Agent to the Yakima Nation, in Mid-September, 1855*, (Fairfield, WA: Ye Galleon Press, 1968).

9. Granville O. Haller, Diary October 7, 1855, microfilm, acc. 3437-001, Granville O. Haller Papers, UW Libraries Special Collections, Seattle, WA.

10. - 11. "Smat-Lowit's Story of the Yakima War: 1855", January, 1912, Louis Mann, interpreter, L.V. McWhorter Papers, cage 55, box 45, folder 434, MASC, WSU, Pullman, WA.

12. – 13. G.O. Haller to Lieut. Henry C. Hodges, 4th Inf. AG to Head Qrs. Of Dist. Fort Dalles, O.T., "Report of the Operations of the Troops of the Yakima Expedition Oct. 16, 1855", typescript, box 42-11, Relander Collection, YVL.

14. Granville O. Haller, "The Indian War of 1855-6 in Washington and Oregon", typescript ca. 1894, part 4, 4-4, box 2 acc. 3437-001, Granville O. Haller Papers, UW Libraries Special Collections, Seattle, WA.

15. – 16. "Register of Deceased Soldiers, 1848-1861" (entry 97), Records of the Adjutant General's Office (RG 94), NARA.

17. – 18. (Olympia, WA) *Pioneer and Democrat*, November 9, 1855, J.W. Wiley, Wm. Cock and E. Evans.

19. *Weekly* (Portland) *Oregonian*, November 10, 1855, Major Tidd's report.

20. – 22. *Pioneer and Democrat*, November 16, 1855, C.C. Hewitt's letter; Stan Flewelling, "The Treaty Wars Sesquicentennial", *The White River Journal*, (October 2005).

23. – 27. Werner Lenggenhager, Historical Markers and Monuments of the State of Washington, vol. 1, "IN Indians of the State of Washington", (Seattle, WA: Seattle Public Library, 1965), 18.

28. Arthur A. Denny, *Pioneer Days on Puget Sound*, (Fairfield, WA: Ye Galleon Press, 1979), 74.

29. *Pioneer and Democrat*, November 9, 1855, obituary.

30. *Pioneer and Democrat*, March 27, 1856, trial testimony.

31. Charles Miles, ed. Building a State: Washington 1889-1939, (Tacoma, WA: Washington State Historical Society, 1940), 512-14.

32. "Register of Deceased Soldiers", NARA.

33. William P. Bonney, *History of Pierce County Washington*, vol. 1, (Chicago, IL: Pioneer Historical Publishing Company, 1927), 183.

34. Evans, 1:544.

35. – 36. NARA, "Register of Deceased Soldiers".

37. Monument on State Hwy 97 south of Union Gap erected by the "Yakimas and Friends" Nov 9, 1917.

38. *Weekly Oregonian*, November 24, 1855, A.J. Price, "Journal".

39. Bonney, 189.

40. J.W. Reese, "OMV's Fort Henrietta: On Winter Duty, 1855-56", *Oregon Historical Quarterly* 66 (Mar-Dec 1965):148.

41. Erasmus D. Keyes, *Fifty Years' Observation of Men and Events* (New York: Scribner, 1884) reprint, *Fighting Indians in Washington Territory*, (Fairfield, WA:

Ye Galleon Press, 1988), 8-10.

42. – 44. John A. Hemphill, West Pointers and Early Washington, (Seattle, WA: West Point Society of Puget Sound, 1992), 129.

45. James K. Kelly to George L. Curry, January 15, 1856, House of Representatives 34th Congress 3rd session 1856-'57, Ex. Doc. No. 76, Indian Affairs on the Pacific, in thirteen volumes, vol. 9, 198-201.

46. – 51. Weekly Oregonian, January 5, 1856, Lt. Col. James Kelly to Adjutant Farrar, December 14, 1855.

52. – 53. Weekly Oregonian, December 15, 1855, Lt. Col. James Kelly to Adjutant Farrar, December 8, 1855.

54. – 55. Pioneer and Democrat, February 1, 1856, Letter from W.N. Bell.

56. Haller Diary, June 10, 1856 (Interview with Owhi).

57. "Smat-Lowit's Story".

58. Evans, 1:577.

59. – 60. James Gilchrist Swan, The Northwest Coast or Three Years' Residence in Washington Territory, (New York: Harper & Brothers, 1857) reprint, (Seattle, WA: University of Washington Press, 1992), 396.

61. Bonney, 200.

62. Keyes, 8-10.

63. NARA, "Register of Deceased Soldiers".

64. Bonney, 200.

65. T. R. Cornelius to W. H. Farrar, March 6, 1856, HED 76, 215.

66. Bonney, 202.

67. Urban E. Hicks, Yakima and Clickitat Indian Wars, 1855 and 1856, (Portland, OR: Himes the Printer, 1886), 11.

68. G. Hayes to I. Stevens, March 10, 1856, State of Washington Office of the Adjutant General, The Official History of the Washington National Guard volume 2 Washington Territorial Militia in the Indian Wars of 1855-56, (Tacoma, WA: Camp Murray, 1961).

69. H. M. Chase to James Tilton, July 31, 1856, WOAG, 101.

70. T. Cornelius to G. Curry, April 2, 1856, NARA microfilm 1954, Relander Collection, box 63-5, YVL.

71. Thomas Cornelius to Florentine Cornelius, April 3, 1856, Cornelius Correspondence and Records 1856-1864, NWC-043, Spokane Public Library, Spokane, WA.

72. – 90. J.H. Herman, Lawrence W. Coe, Robert Williams, "The Cascade Massacre Told by Three Different Eye-Witnesses", Oregon Native Son (February, 1900): 495-505.

91. Philip H. Sheridan, Personal Memoirs of P. H. Sheridan vol. 1, (New York: Jenkins & McCowan, 1888), 55.

92. – 100. Herman, Coe, Williams, 495-505.

101. – 105. H. Field, Local Indian Agent, Vancouver, W.T. May 12, 1856, RBIA (RG 75) WS, Letters from employees assigned to the Col. R. or so. Distr. and Yakima Agency, 1854-1861, microfilm, NARA M5 Roll 17.

106. Pioneer and Democrat, April 11, 1856, A.J. Kane.

107. Hicks, 16.

108. Evans, 1:579-80.

109. Hicks, 16.

110. – 111. (Portland) *Oregon Weekly Times,* A.V. Wilson.

112. – 114. A.J. Splawn, *KA-MI-AKIN The Last Hero of the Yakimas,* (1917) reprint (Caldwell, ID: The Caxton Printers, 1980), 75.

115. William N. Bischoff, ed., *We Were Not Summer Soldiers: The Indian War Diary of Plympton J. Kelly, 1855-1856,* (Tacoma, WA: Washington State Historical society, 1976), 97.

116. James K. Kelly, MS 28, Memory Book 1856, Oregon Historical Society, Portland, OR.

117. Thomas Phelps, *Reminiscences of Seattle, Washington Territory and of the U.S. Sloop-of-War Decatur during the Indian War of 1855-1856,* (Fairfield, WA: Ye Galleon Press, 1970), 42.

118. Brad Asher, *Beyond the Reservation: Indians, Settlers and the Law in Washington Territory, 1853-1889,* (Norman, OK: University of Oklahoma Press, 1999), 112.

119. Ezra Meeker, *Pioneer Reminiscences of Puget Sound the Tragedy of Leschi,* (Seattle, WA: Lowman & Hanford, 1905), 367.

120. Victor Monroe, Judge, WOAG, 93.

121. *Weekly Oregonian,* August 2, 1856, B.F. Dowell.

122. *Weekly Oregonian,* August 2, 1856, Matthew Burns.

123. Capt. F.M.P. Goff to Lt. Col. Benjamin F. Shaw, July 26, 1856, Papers of the Washington Territorial Volunteers Indian War Correspondence 1855-1857, Series V, Colonel B.F. Shaw (Southern Battalion) Correspondence-Incoming, WSA.

124. *Weekly Oregonian,* August 2, 1856, Matthew P. Burns, "Particulars of the Battle of the Grand Ronde".

125. Wright to Mackall, October 31, 1856, RAGO (RG 94) LR 1822-1860, NARA microfilm, M567 Roll 545.

126. *Weekly Oregonian,* August 2, 1856.

127. – 128. WOAG, 101,135.

129. – 130. *Weekly Oregonian,* October 4, 1856, Report of Matthew Burns.

131. Van Ogle, "Van Ogle's Memory of Pioneer Days", The Washington Historical Quarterly 13, (October 1922): 279-81.

132. *Pioneer and Democrat,* February 26, 1858.

133. A.P. Dennison to J.W. Nesmith, April 24, 1858, RBIA (RG 75) OS, LR January 1-December 30, 1858, microfilm NARA M2 Roll 16.

134. – 136. Robert Ignatius Burns, *The Jesuits and the Indian Wars of the Northwest,* (New Haven, CT: Yale University Press, 1966), 221; B.F. Manring, *The Conquest of the Coeur D'Alenes, Spokanes and Palouses,* (Spokane, WA: John W. Graham, 1912) reprint (Fairfield, WA: Ye Galleon Press, 1975), 152.

137. U.S. Senate, 35th Congress, 2nd session, 1859, "Topographical Memoir of Colonel George Wright's Campaign", SED No. 32, SS 984, 67.

138. – 144. Edward Steptoe to W. W. Mackall, May 23, 1858, SED No. 32, 60-2.

145. SED No. 32, 67.

146. R. H. Lansdale to J. W. Nesmith, June 30, 1858, RBIA (RG 75) WS NARA M5 Roll 17.

147. James J. Archer Letters, July 1, 1858, Relander Collection, box 40-2, YVL.

148. U.S. Senate, 35th Congress 2nd session, 1859, "Report and correspondence

relating to the operations of the army in the department of Pacific", SED No. 1, SS 975, 380.

149. SED No. 32, 10.

150. Archer, August 30, 1858.

151. – 154. Splawn, 102.

155. Garnett to Mackall, August 30, 1858.

156. – 158. Splawn, 104.

159. – 160. George Crook, *General George Crook – His Autobiography*, ed. Martin F. Schmitt, (Norman, OK: University of Oklahoma Press, 1946), 60-4.

161. Wright to Mackall, September 2, 1858, SED No. 1, 386-90.

162. Wright to Mackall, September 6, 1858, SED No. 1, 390-3.

163. Wright to Mackall, September 9, 1858, SED No. 1, 393-4.

164. Capt. H. M. Black and Col. Jos. K. F. Mansfield, 23 October 1858, "Itinerary of the march of Major Garnett", RAGO (RG 94) LR 1780-1917, NARA.

165. Wright to Mackall, September 24, 1858, SED No. 1, 399.

166. Robert Garnett to W.W. Mackall, October 15, 1858, RAGO (RG 94) LR 1822-1860, microfilm, NARA M567 Roll 577.

167. – 169. Wright to Mackall, September 30, 1858, SED No. 1, 401-3.

170. Wright to Mackall, October 6, 1858, NARA M567 Roll 577.

171. – 172. Wright to Mackall, October 9, 1858, NARA M567 Roll 577.

173. Garnett to Mackall, October 15, 1858, NARA M567 Roll 577.

174. – 175. McWhorter, 30-1.

176. – 179. Cpt. James J. Archer to Cpt. Alfred Pleasanton, Jan. 1, 1859, FD 248, Fort Dalles Records 1850-1885, H. Russell Smith Foundation Western Historical Manuscripts, The Huntington Library, San Marino.

ABBREVIATIONS

ACAS   Archives of the Catholic Archdiocese of Seattle
CIA   Commissioner of Indian Affairs – Washington D.C.
HED   (U.S.) House (of Representatives) Executive Document
LR   Letters Received
LS   Letters Sent
MASC   Manuscripts, Archives, Special Collections
NARA   National Archives and Records Administration
OHS   Oregon Historical Society
OS   Oregon Superintendency 1848-1873
RAGO   Records of the Adjutant General's Office
RBIA   Records of the Bureau of Indian Affairs
RG   Record Group
SED   (U.S.) Senate Executive Document
SI   Secretary of Interior-Washington D.C.
UW   University of Washington
WOAG   (State of) Washington Office of the Adjutant General
WS   Washington Superintendency 1853-1874
WSA   Washington State Archives - Olympia
WSL   Washington State Library
WSU   Washington State University
WW   Walla Walla
YVL   Yakima Valley Libraries

BIBLIOGRAPHY

Andrew, Clarence L. "Warfield's Story of Peo Peo Mox Mox." *The Washington Historical Quarterly* 25 (July 1934): 182-184.

Archer, James J. (1817-1864) – Letters 1856-58, typescripts box 40-2, microfilm box 62-1. Relander Collection, YVL.

Asher, Brad. *Beyond the Reservation: Indians, Settlers and the Law in Washington Territory, 1853-1880.* Norman: University of Oklahoma Press, 1999.

Ballou, Robert. *Early Klickitat Valley Days.* Goldendale, WA: *Goldendale Sentinel*, 1938.

Bancroft, Hubert Howe. *History of the Pacific States of North America Vol. XXVI Washington, Idaho and Montana, 1845-1889.* San Francisco: The History Company, 1890.

_____. *The Native Races of the Pacific States of North America, Vol. 1, Wild Tribes.* New York: D. Appleton and Company, 1874.

Beal, Thomas B. "Pioneer Reminiscences." *The Washington Historical Quarterly* 7 (April 1917): 83-90.

Beavert, Virginia. *The Way It Was (Anaku Iwacha) Yakima Indian Legends.* Yakima, WA: The Consortium of Johnson O'Malley Committees of Region IV State of Washington, Franklin Press, 1974.

Bennett, Robert A. – ed., *We'll All Go Home in the Spring Personal Accounts and Adventures as Told by the Pioneers of the West.* Walla Walla, Washington: Pioneer Press Books, 1984.

Bischoff, William Norbert S.J. "The Yakima Campaign of 1856." *Mid-America* reprint 20 (1949): 163-208.

_____, ed. *We Were Not Summer Soldiers: The Indian War Diary of Plympton J. Kelly, 1855-1856.* Tacoma: Washington State Historical Society, 1976.

_____. "The Yakima Indian War, 1855-1856, a Problem in Research." *Pacific Northwest Quarterly* 41 (1950): 162-169.

_____. Microfilm Collection, Gonzaga University Cowles Rare Book Library Special Collections Foley Center, Spokane, WA.

Blanchet, Francis Norbert. *Historical Sketches of the Catholic Church in Oregon.* Fairfield, Washington: Ye Galleon Press, 1983.

Bonney, William P. *History of Pierce County Washington*. Vol. 1, Chicago: Pioneer Historical Publishing Company, 1927.

_____ "Monument to Captain Hembree." *The Washington Historical Quarterly* 11 (July 1920): 178-182.

Boyd, Robert. *People of The Dalles The Indians of Wascopam Mission*. Lincoln: University of Nebraska Press, 1996.

_____ . *The Coming of the Spirit of Pestilence Introduced Infectious Diseases and Population Decline among Northwest Coast Indians, 1774-1874*. Seattle: University of Washington Press, 1999.

Boyden (Knudsen), T.G. *Warrior of the Mist*. Fairfield, WA: Ye Galleon Press, 1996.

Brouillet, J.B.A. *Authentic Account of the Murder of Dr. Whitman and Other Missionaries by the Cayuse Indians of Oregon in 1847*. Portland: S.J. McCormick, 1869.

Brown, William Compton. *The Indian Side of the Story: Being a Concourse of Presentations Historical and Biographical in Character Relating to the Indian Wars*. Spokane: C.W. Hill Printing Co., 1961.

Browne, Lina Fergusson, ed. *J. Ross Browne; his letters, journals and writings*. Albuquerque: University of New Mexico Press, 1969.

Buerge, David M. "The Unspoiled Northwest Some of the best paintings of the area's earliest artists." *COLUMBIA* 1 (Summer 1987) 21-28.

Bunnell, Clarence Orvel. *Legends of the Klickitats*. Portland: Binfords & Mort Publishers, 1935.

Burnham, Howard J. "Government Grants and Patents in Vancouver, Washington." *Oregon Historical Quarterly* 48 (June 1947): 9.

Burns, Robert Ignatius S. J. *The Jesuits and the Indian Wars of the Northwest*. New Haven: Yale University Press, 1966.

_____ . "Pere Joset's Account of the Indian War of 1858." *Pacific Northwest Quarterly* 38 (October 1947): 285-314.

Butler, David F. *United States Firearms the First Century 1776-1875*. New York: Winchester Press, 1971.

Carriere, Gaston. "The Yakima War an Episode in the History of the Oregon Missions." *Vie Oblate Life* 34 (1975): 149-173.

Chamberlain, Martin N. "Love Hennie Writing Home about Pioneer Life on the Columbia, 1853-1854." *COLUMBIA* 17, (Winter 2003-4): 11-16.

Chance, David H. *People of the Falls*. Colville, WA: Kettle Falls Historical Center, 1985.

Coan, C. F. "The Adoption of the Reservation Policy in Pacific Northwest, 1835-1855." *Oregon Historical Quarterly* 23 (March 1922): 24.

Coe, Lawrence W., J.H. Herman and Robert Williams, "The Cascade Massacre Told by Three Different Eye-Witnesses." *Oregon Native Son and Historical Magazine* (February 1900): 495-505.

Cornelius, Thomas R. 1827-1899. Correspondence and Records 1856-1864, NWC-043. Spokane Public Library Downtown Northwest Room, Spokane, WA.

Cronin, Kay. *Cross in the Wilderness.* Vancouver, British Columbia: Mitchell Press, 1960.

Crook, George. *General George Crook-His Autobiography.* ed., Martin F. Schmitt, Norman: University of Oklahoma Press, 1946.

Curtis, Edward S. *The North American Indian,* Vol. 7, The Yakima. The Klickitat. Salishan Tribes of the interior. The Kutenai. ed. Frederick Webb Hodge, 1911, New York: Johnson Reprint Corporation, 1976.

Denny, Arthur Armstrong. *Pioneer Days on Puget Sound* (1890). Reprint Fairfield, Washington: Ye Galleon Press, 1979.

Denny, Emily Inez. *Blazing the Way True Stories, Songs and Sketches of Puget Sound and Other Pioneers.* Seattle: Rainier Printing Company, 1909.

DeSmet, Pierre-Jean, *Life, Letters and Travels of Father Pierre-Jean DeSmet S.J.* ed. Hiram Martin Chittenden, New York: Francis P. Harper, 1905.

Doty, James. *Journal of Operations of Governor Isaac Ingalls Stevens of Washington Territory in 1855.* Ed., Edward J. Kowrach, Fairfield, WA: Ye Galleon Press, 1979.

Drouin, Paul ed., *Les Oblats de Marie Immaculee en Oregon 1847-1860: Documents d'archives.* 3 vols. Ottawa: Archives Deschatelets, 1992.

Durieu, Pierre-Paul to Pascal Ricard, September 30, 1855. (Letters) Archives of the Catholic Archdiocese of Seattle.

Ebey, Winfield Scott. *The 1854 Diary of Winfield Scott Ebey.* ed., Susan Badger Doyle and Fred W. Dykes. Independence, Missouri: Oregon-California Trails Association, 1997.

Eells, D.D. *Marcus Whitman Pathfinder and Patriot.* Seattle: The Alice Harriman Company, 1909.

Ellison, Joseph. "The Covered Wagon Centennial." *The Washington Historical Quarterly* 21 (July 1930) 163-178.

Evans, Elwood, ed. *History of the Pacific Northwest: Oregon and Washington* 2 vols. Portland: North Pacific History Company, 1889.

Fisher, Andrew H. *Shadow Tribe the Making of Columbia River Indian Identity.* Seattle: University of Washington Press, 2010.

Flewelling, Stan. "One Pioneer Family's Story of War in the White River Valley." *White River Journal – A Newsletter of the White River Valley Museum* (April 1998).

Fort Dalles Papers 1850-1885. H. Russell Smith Foundation, Library for Western History, Huntington Library, San Marino, CA.

173

Fridlund, Paul. *Washington's Story The Conquest*. Puyallup, Washington: Paul Fridlund, 2003.

Gansevoort, Guert. "Seattle's First Taste of Battle, 1856." *Pacific Northwest Quarterly* 47 (Jan 1956): 1-8.

Gates, Charles M. ed. *Messages of the Governors of the Territory of Washington to the Legislative Assembly, 1854-1889*. Seattle: University of Washington Press, 1940.

Gilbert, Frank T. *Historic Sketches Walla Walla, Whitman, Columbia and Garfield Counties Washington Territory*. Portland: A.G. Walling, 1882.

Gosnell, W.B. "Documents-Indian War in Washington Territory-Special Agent W.B. Gosnell's Report in 1856." *The Washington Historical Quarterly* 17 (October 1926): 289-299.

Guie, H. Dean. *Bugles in the Valley Garnett's Fort Simcoe*. Portland: Oregon Historical Society, 1977.

Haller, Granville Owen. Diary 1855 and Diary 1856 microfilm. Acc. 3437-001, UW Libraries Special Collections, Seattle, WA.

_____. "Indian Fighting in Oregon and Washington" typescript. Pac MS B-60, Bancroft Collection of Western Americana, University of California, Berkeley.

_____. "The Indian War of 1855-6 in Washington and Oregon" typescript, part 4. Acc. 3437-001, UW Libraries Special Collections, Seattle, WA.

_____. "Journal of the Third Expedition into the Yakima Country Made in the Summer of 1856 in May" typescript. Box 55-15, Relander Collection, YVL.

_____. "Kamiarkin in History1855-1856" manuscript. MSS P-A, Bancroft Library, University of California, Berkeley.

_____. "Order No. 6 Winnass Expedition, Camp at Massacre Ground, Boise River July 18,1855" typescript. Box 55-14, Relander Collection, YVL.

_____. "Report of the Operations of the Troops of the Yakima Expedition Oct. 16, 1855" typescript. Box 42-11, Relander Collection, YVL.

Haller, Theodore N. "Life and Public Services of Colonel Granville O. Haller." *The Washington Historian* 1 (April 1900): 102-104.

Hart, E. Richard. "History of the Wenatchi Fishing Reservation." *Western Legal History* 13 (Summer/Fall 2000): 163-203.

Heath, Joseph Thomas. *Memoirs of Nisqually*. Fairfield, WA: Ye Galleon Press, 1979.

Hemphill, John A. *West Pointers and Early Washington*. Seattle: West Point Society of Puget Sound, 1992.

Hines, Donald M. *Celilo Tales*. Issaquah, Washington: Great Eagle Publishing, 1996.

_____. *The Forgotten Tribes*. Issaquah, WA: Great Eagle Publishing, 1997.

_____. *Ghost Voices Yakima Indian Myths, Legends, Humor and Hunting Stories*. Issaquah, WA: Great Eagle Publishing, 1992.

_____. *Magic in the Mountains the Yakima Shaman: Power & Practice*. Issaquah, WA: Great Eagle Publishing, 1993.

Holbrook, Francis X. and John Nikol. "The Navy in the Puget Sound War, 1855-1857." *Pacific Northwest Quarterly* 67 (Jan 1976): 10-20.

Howard, Oliver O. *My Life and Experiences among Our Hostile Indians*. Hartford: A.D. Worthington & Company, 1907.

Howay-Lewis-Meyers, "Angus McDonald: A Few Items of the West." *The Washington Historical Quarterly* 8 (July 1917): 188-229.

Hunn, Eugene S. *Nch I-Wana the Big River*. Seattle: University of Washington Press, 1997.

Hunt, Garrett B. *Indian Wars of the Inland Empire*. Spokane: Spokane Community College, 1958.

Hunter, George. *Reminiscences of an Old Timer*. San Francisco: H.S. Crocker and Company, 1887.

Johnson, H.M. Dr. *A History of the City of Toppenish*. (1927) Reprint, Toppenish, WA, Toppenish Historical Museum Board, 1989.

Josephy, Alvin M. *The Nez Perce Indians and the Opening of the Northwest*. Boston: Houghton Mifflin Company, 1997.

Judge, Louis. "Wenatchee Indians Ask Justice." *The Washington Historical Quarterly* 16 (January 1925): 20-28.

Kappler, Charles J. ed. *Indian Affairs, Laws and Treaties* 2 vols. Washington D.C.: U.S. Government Printing Office, 1904.

Karson, Jennifer- ed. *Wiyaxayxt*as days go by*wiyaakaa'awn Our History, Our Land, and Our People The Cayuse, Umatilla, and Walla Walla*. Pendleton, Oregon: Tamastslikt Cultural Institute, 2006.

Kelly, James K. 1819-1903 Memory Book 1856, MS 28, Oregon Historical Society, Portland, OR.

Keyes, Erasmus D. *Fifty Years' Observation of Men and Events*. (1884) Reprint. *Fighting Indians in Washington Territory*. Fairfield, WA: Ye Galleon Press, 1988.

Keyser, James D. *Indian Rock Art of the Columbia Plateau*. Seattle: University of Washington Press, 1992.

Kip, Lawrence. *Army Life on the Pacific A Journal*. (1859) Reprint Fairfield, Washington: Ye Galleon Press, 1986.

_____. *Indian War in the Pacific Northwest – The Journal of Lieutenant Lawrence Kip*. Lincoln: University of Nebraska Press, 1999.

Knuth, Priscilla. *Picturesque Frontier The Army's Fort Dalles*. Portland: Oregon Historical Society, 1968.

Kowrach, Edward J. *Mie. Charles Pandosy, O.M.I. Missionary of the Northwest*. Fairfield, Washington: Ye Galleon Press, 1992.

Lansdale, Richard Hyatt 1810-1897 Journals 1854-1858. WA MSS 292 Yale Collection of Western Americana, Beinecke Rare Book and Manuscript Library, New Haven, CT.

Lenggenhager, Werner. *Historical Markers and Monuments of the State of Washington.* Seattle: Seattle Public Library, 1965.

Lent, Geneva D. *West of the Mountains James Sinclair and the Hudson's Bay Company.* Seattle: University of Washington Press, 1963

Lewis, William S. *The Case of Spokane Garry* (1917) Reprint - Fairfield, WA: Ye Galleon Press, 1987.

_____. "The First Militia Companies in Eastern Washington." *The Washington Historical Quarterly* 11 (October 1920): 243-249.

Lewty, Peter J. *Across the Columbia Plain Railroad Expansion in the Interior Northwest, 1885-1893*. Pullman, WA: Washington State University Press, 1995.

Longmire, James. "Narrative of James Longmire a Pioneer of 1853", *Told by the Pioneers.* Vol. 1, U.S. Works Progress Administration, Olympia: Washington Secretary of State, 1937.

Lyman, W.D. *History of the Yakima Valley Washington.* Chicago: S.J. Clarke, 1919.

Manring, B.F. *The Conquest of the Coeur D'Alenes, Spokanes and Palouses*. Spokane: John W. Graham, 1912 and reprint Fairfield, Washington: Ye Galleon Press, 1975.

Masterson, James R. "The Records of the Washington Superintendency of Indian Affairs, 1853-1974." *Pacific Northwest Quarterly* 37 (1946): 31-57.

McClellan, George B. – Diary 1853, George Brinton McClellan Papers, Library of Congress Manuscripts Division, Washington D.C.

McConaghy, Lorraine. *Warship Under Sail The USS Decatur in the Pacific West.* Seattle: University of Washington Press, 2009.

McDermott, Paul D. and Ronald E. Grim. "The Artistic Views of Gustavus Sohon Images of Colonel George Wright's Campaign of 1858." *COLUMBIA* 16 (Summer 2002): 16-22.

McKay, William Cameron 1824-1893. Papers (microfilm) Pendleton Public Library, Pendleton, OR.

_____. Papers MSS 413, 1855-1894 Oregon Historical Society, Portland, OR.

McWhorter, Lucullus Virgil. *Tragedy of the Wahk-shum The Death of Andrew J. Bolon Yakima Indian Agent.* Fairfield, WA: Ye Galleon Press, 1968; and Issaquah, WA: Great Eagle Publishing, 1994.

_____Papers – Cage 55, Holland and Terrell Library, MASC, Washington State University, Pullman, WA.

Meany, Edmond S. "Chief Patkanim." *The Washington Historical Quarterly* 15 (July 1924): 187-198.

Meeker, Ezra. *Pioneer Reminiscences of Puget Sound the Tragedy of Leschi.* Seattle: Lowman & Hanford, 1905.

Meinig, Donald W. *The Great Columbia Plain.* Seattle: University of Washington Press, 1995.

Mercer, K.B. "Yakima War Diary 1855-1856", WA MSS 339, Yale Collection of Western Americana, Beinecke Rare Book and Manuscript Library, New Haven, CT.

Merk, Frederick. *The Oregon Question.* Cambridge: Harvard University Press, 1967.

Miles, Charles and O.B. Sperlin eds. *Building a State 1889-1939.* Tacoma, WA: Washington State Historical Society, 1940.

Miles, Jo N. "Kamiakin's Impact on Early Washington Territory." *Pacific Northwest Quarterly* 99 (Fall 2008): 159-172.

_____. "The Life and Death of A.J. Bolon, 1826-1855." *Pacific Northwest Quarterly* 97 (Winter 2005/2006): 31-38.

_____. "Toppenish A Washington Town that Grew Up on an Indian Reservation." *COLUMBIA* 28 Washington State Historical Society, (Spring 2014): 21-7.

Moses, Mary. *Mary Moses' Statement.* Fairfield, WA: Ye Galleon Press, 1988.

Munnick, Harriet D. and A.R. Munnick. *Catholic Church Records of the Pacific Northwest Missions of St. Ann and St. Rose of the Cayouse 1847-1872.* Portland: Binford & Mort Publishing, 1989.

Nalty, Bernard C. and Truman R. Strobridge, "The Defense of Seattle, 1856." *Pacific Northwest Quarterly* 55 (July 1964): 105-110.

National Archives and Records Administration – microfilms

M-2 Roll 5 (RG 75) RBIA OS, LS LR Superintendent Joel Palmer 1854-55.

M-2 Roll 7 (RG 75) RBIA OS, Reports of Supt. Palmer and subordinates.

M-2 Roll 16 (RG 75) RBIA OS, LR January 1-December 30, 1858.

M-5 Roll 17 (RG 75) RBIA WS, LR from employees assigned to the Col. R. or so. Distr. and Yakima Agency 1854-1861.

M-5 Roll 20 (RG 75) RBIA WS LR from employees of central or middle district 1854-1874.

M5 Roll 23 (RG 75) RBIA WS, LR August 22, 1853-April 9, 1861.

M-567 Roll 545 (RG 94) RAGO LR 1822-1860, (1856).

M-567 Roll 577 (RG 94) RAGO LR 1822-1860, (1858).

1953 (RG 98) Dept. of the Pacific, Selected LR 1856-58, Relander Collection box 63-11, YVL.

1954 (RG 94) RAGO LR 1854-58, Relander Collection box 63-5, YVL.

National Archives and Records Administration – Washington D.C.

   Capt. H.M. Black and Col. Jos. K.F. Mansfield, 23 October 1858, "Itinerary of the March of Major Garnett" RAGO (RG 94) LR 1780-1917.

   Register of Deceased Soldiers 1848-1861, entry 97 (RG 94).

   Yakama Indian Country Maps 1855, 1856. (RG 77) Office of the Chief of Engineers. Fortifications Map file, Department of the Pacific Booklet.

Nicandri, David L. *Northwest Chiefs – Gustav Sohon's Views of the 1855 Stevens Treaty Councils.* Tacoma: Washington State Historical Society, 1986.

Oliphant, J. Orin – ed., "Journals of the Indian War of 1855-1856." *The Washington Historical Quarterly* 15 (January 1924): 11-31.

Overmeyer, Philip Henry. "George B. McClellan and the Pacific Northwest." *Pacific Northwest Quarterly* 32 (1941): 3-60.

Pambrun, Andrew Dominique 1821-1895. "Reminiscences", Athens, Oregon (microfilm). Pendleton Public Library, Pendleton, OR.

_____. *Sixty Years on the Frontier in the Pacific Northwest.* Fairfield, Washington: Ye Galleon Press, 1978.

Pandosy, Charles and Chief Kamiakin, "Write to the soldiers" October 6, 1855 typescript box 55-19, Relander Collection, YVL.

_____. to Toussaint Mesplie, April 1853 (Letters) Archives of the Catholic Archdiocese of Seattle.

Parker, Samuel. *Journal of an Exploring Tour Beyond the Rocky Mountains...1835, '36 and '37.* (1838), Reprint - Minneapolis: Ross & Haines, 1967.

Phelps, Thomas. *Reminiscences of Seattle, Washington Territory and of the U.S. Sloop-of-War Decatur during the Indian War of 1855-1856.* Fairfield, Washington: Ye Galleon Press, 1970.

Prosch, Thomas W. "The Indian War in Washington Territory." *Oregon Historical Quarterly* 16 (March 1915).

Prosch, Charles. *Reminiscences of Washington Territory.* Reprint, Fairfield, WA: Ye Galleon Press, 1969.

Pucci, Joseph J. ed. *The Yakima Valley Catholic Centennial: 1847-1947.* Moxee, WA: Holy Rosary Church, 1947.

Rau, Weldon Willis. "Frontier Conflict a Pioneer Family's Perspective on Events in the Puyallup Valley during 1855-56." *COLUMBIA* 7 (Spring 1993):8-14.

Ray, Verne F. "Native Villages and Groupings of the Columbia Basin." *Pacific Northwest Quarterly* 27 (April 1936): 99-152.

Reese, J. W. "OMV's Fort Henrietta: On Winter Duty, 1855-56." *Oregon Historical Quarterly* 66 (1965): 133-160.

Relander, Click. *Drummers and Dreamers.* Caldwell Idaho: The Caxton Printers, 1956.

_____ ed. *Strangers on the Land.* Yakima, Washington: Franklin Press, 1962.

_____ ed. *The Yakima Treaty Centennial 1855-1955.* Yakima: The Republic Press, 1955.

Richards, Kent D. *Isaac I. Stevens Young Man in a Hurry.* Pullman: Washington State University Press, 1993.

Rock, Francis John. *J. Ross Browne: a biography. Washington D.C.:* Catholic University of America, 1929.

Roe, JoAnn. *Stevens Pass The Story of Railroading and Recreation in the North Cascades.* Caldwell, Idaho: The Caxton Printers, 2002.

Ruby, Robert H. and John A. Brown. *The Cayuse Indians Imperial Tribesmen of Old Oregon.* Norman: University of Oklahoma Press, 1972.

_____. *Guide to the Indian Tribes of the Pacific Northwest.* Norman: University of Oklahoma Press, 1986.

_____. *Half Sun on the Columbia-A Biography of Chief Moses.* Norman: University of Oklahoma Press, 1965, 1995.

_____ . *Indians of the Pacific Northwest.* norman: University of Oklahoma Press, 1981.

Sale, A.H. "Indian War Recollections*" Oregon Native Son and Historical Magazine.* Portland, (December 1899): 387-391 and (February 1900): 491-494.

Santee, J. F. "The Slaying of Pio Pio Mox Mox." *The Washington Historical Quarterly* 25 (April 1934): 128-132.

Scheuerman, Richard. *The Wenatchee Valley and its First Peoples.* Walla Walla: Color Press, 2005.

_____and Michael O. Finley. *Finding Chief Kamiakin The Life and Legacy of a Northwest Patriot.* Pullman: Washington State University Press, 2008.

Schlicke, Carl P. *General George Wright: Guardian of the Pacific Coast.* Norman: University of Oklahoma Press, 1988.

Schuster, Helen H. *The Yakimas.* Bloomington: Indiana University Press, 1982.

_____. *The Yakima.* New York: Chelsea House Publishers, 1990.

Sebring, F.M. "The Indian Raid on the Cascades in March, 1856." *The Washington Historical Quarterly* 19 (April 1928): 99-107.

Shaw, Benjamin F. 1829-1908, Papers MSS 412, Oregon Historical Society, Portland, OR.

Sheridan, Philip H. *Personal Memoirs of P.H. Sheridan.* Vol. 1, New York: Jenkins & McCowan, 1888.

Snively, Henry J. Collection, acc. 3095, UW Libraries Special Collections, Seattle, WA.

Snowden, Clinton A. *History of Washington.* 3 volumes, New York: The Century History Company, 1909.

Splawn, A.J. *KA-MI-AKIN The Last Hero of the Yakimas.* (1917)Reprint Caldwell, Idaho: The Caxton Printers, 1980.

Steptoe, Edward Jenner. Papers, acc. 4908, UW Libraries Special Collections, Seattle, WA.

Stern, Theodore. *Chiefs & Chief Traders Indian Relations at Fort Nez Perces, 1818-1855.* vol. 1 Corvallis: Oregon State University Press, 1993.

_____. *Chiefs & Change in the Oregon Country.* Vol. 2 Corvallis: Oregon State University Press, 1996.

Stevens, Hazard. Collection AX 42, University of Oregon Special Collections, Eugene, OR.

_____. *The Life of Isaac Ingalls Stevens.* Boston: Houghton, Mifflin and Company, 1901.

Stevens, Isaac Ingalls, *Speech of the Hon. Isaac I. Stevens Delegate from Washington Territory on the Washington & Oregon War Claims.* House of Representatives of the United States, May 31, 1858, Fairfield, WA: Ye Galleon Press, 1970.

Stevens, Isaac Ingalls. *A True Copy of the Record of the Official Proceedings at the Council in the Walla Walla Valley, 1855.* Darrell Scott, ed. Fairfield, WA: Ye Galleon Press, 1996.

Stillwell, William D. 1824-1921 MSS 1514 Military Collection, "Account of fight April 10, 1856." Oregon Historical Society, Portland, OR.

Sturtevant, William C., ed. *Handbook of North American Indians Volume 12 Plateau.* Washington D.C.: Smithsonian Institution, 1998.

Swan, James Gilchrist. *The Northwest Coast or Three Years' Residence in Washington Territory.* (1857) Reprint Fairfield, WA: Ye Galleon Press, 1966; and Seattle: University of Washington Press, 1972.

Todd, Ronald – ed. "Letters of Governor Isaac I. Stevens 1857-1858." *Pacific Northwest Quarterly* 31 (1940): 403-459.

Tracy, Charles Abbot III. "Police Function In Portland, 1851-1874." Part 1, *Oregon Historical Quarterly* 80 (Spring 1979): 14.

Trafzer, Clifford E. *Yakima, Palouse, Cayuse, Umatilla, Walla Walla, and Wanapum Indians – An Historical Bibliography*. Metuchen, New Jersey: The Scarecrow Press, 1992.

_____ and Richard D. Scheuerman. *Renegade Tribe The Palouse Indians and the Invasion of the Inland Pacific Northwest*. Pullman: Washington State University Press, 1986.

U.S. Court of Claims 1835 - 1966 (RG123) Indian Depredation Case #2117 (RG 123) 16E3 326, box 170, National Archives and Records Administration, Washington D.C.

U.S. House of Representatives, 33rd Congress 2nd session, 1854. HED No. 91. *Report upon the Northern Pacific Railroad Exploration and Survey*.

_____. 34th Congress 1st session 1856, HED No. 93. *Indian Hostilities in Oregon and Washington*.

_____. 34th Congress 3rd session 1856-'57. HED No. 76. *Indian Affairs on the Pacific Washington and Oregon Territories*.

_____. 35th Congress 1st session 1858. HED No. 38. J. Ross Browne, *Indian War in Oregon and Washington Territories*.

_____. 35th Congress 2nd session 1858-'59. HED No. 114. Cpt. T.J. Cram, *Topographical Memoir of the Department of the Pacific*.

_____. 35th Congress 2nd session 1858-'59. HED No. 51. *Claims Growing Out of Indian Hostilities in Oregon and Washington*.

U.S. Ordnance Department, *The Ordnance Manual for the Use of the Officers of the United States Army*. Alfred Mordecai-ed. Washington D.C. (1850): digitalized by Google.

U.S. Senate, 34th Congress 3rd session, 1856. SED No. 5. *Reports from the Department of the Pacific*.

_____. 35th Congress 2nd session, 1859. SED No. 1. *Report and correspondence relating to the operations of the army in the department of the Pacific*.

_____. 35th Congress 2nd session, 1859. SED No. 32. Lt. John Mullan, *Topographical Memoir of Col. Wright's Campaign*.

Utley, Robert M. *Frontiersmen in Blue: The United States Army and the Indian 1848-1865*. Lincoln: University of Nebraska Press, 1981.

Victor, Frances Fuller. *The Early Indian Wars of Oregon*. Salem, Oregon: Frank C. Baker, 1894.

Washington Office of the Adjutant General. *The Official History of the Washington National Guard volume 2 Washington Territorial Militia in the Indian Wars of 1855-56*. Tacoma, WA: Camp Murray, 1961.

_____. *Biennial Report of the Adjutant General of the State of Washington for the Years 1891 and 1892*. Olympia, Washington: O.C. White, State Printer, 1893.

Washington Territorial Volunteers Indian War Correspondence 1855 - 1857, Washington State Archives, Olympia, WA.

Weibel, George S.J. "Fifty Years of a Peaceful Conquest." *Gonzaga* 5, (December 1913): 125-130.

White, Fred. Letters 1856-57, Records of the War Department, U.S. Army Commands G-9, typescript, box 45-12, Relander Collection, YVL.

Whiting, J.S. *Forts of the State of Washington a Record of Military and Semi-Military Establishments Designated as Forts from May 29, 1792 to November 15, 1951*. Seattle: J.S. Whiting, 1951.

Williams, Christina M. "The Daughter of Angus MacDonald." *Washington Historical Quarterly* 13, (April 1922): 107-117.

Wilkes, Charles, U.S.N. *Narrative of the United States Exploring Expedition During the Years 1838, 1839,1840,1841,1842*. Philadelphia: Lea & Blanchard, 1845.

Wilkinson, Charles. *Messages from Frank's Landing A Story of Salmon, Treaties and the Indian Way*. Seattle: University of Washington Press, 2000.

Winans, William P. Papers Cage 147, Holland and Terrell Library MASC, Washington State University, Pullman, WA.

Winthrop, Theodore. *The Canoe and the Saddle or Klalam and Klickatat*. Tacoma, WA: John H. Williams, 1913.

Newspapers

Catholic Sentinel, Portland	1871
Columbian, Olympia	1852
Daily National Intelligencer, Washington D.C.	1856
New York Herald	1856
Oregon Weekly Times, Portland	1856
Pioneer and Democrat, Olympia	1855, 1856, 1857, 1858
Puget Sound Courier, Steilacoom	1855, 1856
Spokesman-Review	1895, 1905
Walla Walla Union Bulletin	1945, 1947
The Washington Farmer, Yakima	1884
Weekly Oregonian, Portland	1855, 1856, 1857
Yakama Nation Review, Toppenish	1978, 2000

The Author

Photo by Mike Hiler

"Kamiakan" Butte, Yakima County

Jo N. Miles was born and raised in Richland, Washington. He studied at the University of Arizona earning a Bachelor of Science degree in Public Administration. After graduation, Miles completed active duty in the U.S. Army, and returned to Washington where he spent more than 30 years working in public administration including 17 years on the Yakama Reservation. He retired as municipal public works director in Toppenish, WA and spent subsequent years researching and writing about the early history of Washington Territory. Miles has published articles in *Pacific Northwest Quarterly* (Winter 2005/2006, and Fall 2008) and *COLUMBIA* Magazine (Spring 2014). He contributed to *Bluelight to Pucker Huddle: Discovering Klickitat County*, published by Friends of the Goldendale Community Library, 2005.

INDEX

185

For a free catalog of Caxton titles write to:

CAXTON PRESS
312 Main Street
Caldwell, Idaho 83605-3299

or

Visit our web site:

www.caxtonpress.com

Caxton Press is a division of THE CAXTON PRINTERS, Ltd.